Friends, Lovers,
and the
Big Terrible Thing

Friends, Lovers,
and the
Big Terrible Thing

A Memoir

MATTHEW PERRY

FLATIRON
BOOKS
NEW YORK

www.flatironbooks.com

Designed by Steven Seighman

All photographs provided courtesy of the author unless otherwise noted.

Library of Congress Cataloging-in-Publication Data

Names: Perry, Matthew, 1969– author.
Title: Friends, lovers, and the big terrible thing : a memoir / Matthew Perry.
Description: First U.S. edition. | New York, NY : Flatiron Books, 2022.
Identifiers: LCCN 2022028340 | ISBN 9781250866448 (hardcover) |
    ISBN 9781250879547 (international, sold outside the U.S., subject to rights
    availability) | ISBN 9781250866462 (ebook)
Subjects: LCSH: Perry, Matthew, 1969– | Friends (Television program) | Actors—
    United States—Biography. | Addicts—United States—Biography. | Substance
    abuse—United States. | LCGFT: Autobiographies.
Classification: LCC PN2287.P3955 A3 2022 | DDC 791.4502/8092 [B]—dc23/
    eng/20220805
LC record available at https://lccn.loc.gov/2022028340

Our books may be purchased in bulk for promotional, educational, or business use. Please contact your local bookseller or the Macmillan Corporate and Premium Sales Department at 1-800-221-7945, extension 5442, or by email at MacmillanSpecialMarkets@macmillan.com.

First U.S. Edition: 2022
First International Edition: 2022

20 19 18 17

For all of the sufferers out there.
You know who you are.

The best way out is always through.
—Robert Frost

You've just got to see me through another day.
—James Taylor

Contents

Foreword
by Lisa Kudrow

"How's Matthew Perry doing?"

Over the many years since I was first asked, it's been, at different times, the most asked question for me. I understand why so many people asked it: they love Matthew and they want him to be OK. Me too. But I always bristled at that question from the press, because I couldn't say what I wanted to say: "It's his story to tell and I'm not authorized to tell it really, am I!" I would have wanted to go on to say, "This is very intimate personal stuff and if you don't hear it from the actual person, it is, to my mind, gossip and I'm not gossiping about Matthew with you." Knowing that no response at all could do more damage, sometimes I would just say, "I think he's doing well." At least that doesn't amplify the spotlight and maybe he can have a fraction of privacy as he tries to deal with this disease. But truly, I wasn't exactly sure how Matthew was doing. As he'll tell you in this book, he was keeping it a secret. And it took some time for him to feel comfortable enough to tell us some of what he was going through. Over those years I didn't really try to intervene or confront him, because the little I knew about addiction was that his sobriety was out of my hands. And yet, I would have periods of wondering if I was wrong for not doing more, doing something. But I did come to understand that this disease relentlessly fed itself and was determined to keep going.

So, I just focused on Matthew, who could make me laugh so hard every day, and once a week, laugh so hard I cried and couldn't breathe. He was there, Matthew Perry, who is whip smart . . . charming, sweet, sensitive, very reasonable and rational. That guy, with everything he was battling, was still there. The same Matthew who, from the beginning, could lift us all up during a grueling night shoot for the opening titles inside that fountain. "Can't remember a time I wasn't in a fountain!" "What are we, wet?" "Can't remember a time I wasn't wet . . . I!" (Matthew is the reason we are all laughing in that fountain in the opening titles.)

After *Friends* I didn't see Matthew every day, and I couldn't even hazard a guess with regard to his well-being.

This book is the first time I'm hearing what living with and surviving his addiction really was. Matthew has told me some things, but not in this kind of detail. He's now letting us into Matthew's head and heart in honest and very exposed detail. And finally, no one needs to ask me or anyone else how Matthew's doing. He's letting you know himself.

He has survived impossible odds, but I had no idea how many times he almost didn't make it. I'm glad you're here, Matty. Good for you. I love you.

—Lisa

Friends, Lovers,
and the
Big Terrible Thing

Prologue

Hi, my name is Matthew, although you may know me by another name. My friends call me Matty.

And I should be dead.

If you like, you can consider what you're about to read to be a message from the beyond, my beyond.

It's Day Seven of the Pain. And by Pain, I don't mean a stubbed toe or "The Whole Ten Yards." I capitalize Pain because this was the worst Pain I've ever experienced—it was the Platonic Ideal of Pain, the exemplar. I've heard people claim that the worst pain is childbirth: well, this was the worst pain imaginable, but without the joy of a newborn in my arms at the end of it.

And it may have been Day Seven of Pain, but it was also Day Ten of No Movement. If you catch my drift. I hadn't taken a shit in ten days—there, there's the drift. Something was wrong, very wrong. This was not a dull, throbbing pain, like a headache; it wasn't even a piercing, stabbing pain, like the pancreatitis I'd had when I was thirty. This was a different kind of Pain. Like my body was going to burst. Like my insides were trying to force their way out. This was the no-fucking-around kind of Pain.

And the sounds. My God, the sounds. Ordinarily, I'm a pretty quiet, keep-to-myself kinda fella. But on this night, I was screaming at the top of my lungs. Some nights, when the wind is right and the cars are all parked up for the night, you can hear the horrific sounds of coyotes ripping apart something that is howling in the Hollywood Hills. At first it sounds like children laughing way, way off in the distance, until you realize it's not that—it's the foothills of death. But the worst part, of course, is when the howling stops, because you know whatever has been attacked is now dead. This is hell.

And yes, there is a hell. Don't let anyone tell you different. I've been there; it exists; end of discussion.

On this night the animal was me. I was still screaming, fighting tooth and nail for survival. Silence meant the end. Little did I know how close I was to the end.

At the time, I was living in a sober living house in Southern California. This was no surprise—I have lived half my life in one form or another of treatment center or sober living house. Which is fine when you are twenty-four years old, less fine when you are forty-two years old. Now I was forty-nine, still struggling to get this monkey off my back.

By this point, I knew more about drug addiction and alcoholism than any of the coaches and most of the doctors I encountered at these facilities. Unfortunately, such self-knowledge avails you nothing. If the golden ticket to sobriety involved hard work and learned information, this beast would be nothing but a faint unpleasant memory. To simply stay alive, I had turned myself into a professional patient. Let's not sugarcoat it. At forty-nine, I was still afraid to be alone. Left alone, my crazy brain (crazy only in this area by the way) would find some excuse to do the unthinkable: drink and drugs. In the face of decades of my life having been ruined by doing this, I'm terrified of doing it again. I have no fear of talking in front of twenty thousand people, but put me alone on my couch in front of a TV for the night and I get scared. And that fear is of my own mind; fear of my own thoughts; fear that my mind will urge me to turn to drugs, as it has so many times before. My mind is out to kill me, and I know it. I am constantly filled with a lurking loneliness, a yearning, clinging to the notion that something outside of me will fix me. But I had had all that the outside had to offer!

Julia Roberts is my girlfriend. *It doesn't matter, you have to drink.*

I just bought my dream house—it looks out across the whole city! *Can't enjoy that without a drug dealer.*

I'm making a million dollars a week—I win right? *Would you like to drink? Why yes, I would. Thank you very much.*

I'd had it all. But it was all a trick. Nothing was going to fix this. It would be years before I even grasped the notion of a solution. Please don't misunderstand me. All of those things—Julia and the dream house and $1 million a week—were wonderful, and I will be eternally grateful for all of them. I am one of the luckiest men on the planet. And boy did I have fun.

They just weren't the answer. If I had to do it all over again, would I still audition for *Friends*? You bet your ass I would. Would I drink again? You bet your ass I would. If I didn't have alcohol to soothe my nerves and help me have fun, I would have leaped off a tall building sometime in my twenties. My grandfather, the wonderful Alton L. Perry, grew up around an alcoholic father, and as a result, he never touched a drink in his life, all ninety-six long, wonderful years of it.

I am not my grandfather.

I don't write all this so anyone will feel sorry for me—I write these words because they are true. I write them because someone else may be confused by the fact that they know they should stop drinking—like me, they have all the information, and they understand the consequences—but they still can't stop drinking. You are not alone, my brothers and sisters. (In the dictionary under the word "addict," there should be a picture of me looking around, very confused.)

In the sober living house in Southern California, I had a view of West LA and two queen-size beds. The other bed was occupied by my assistant/best friend, Erin, a lesbian whose friendship I treasure because it brings me the joy of female companionship without the romantic tension that has seemed to ruin my friendships with straight women (not to mention, we can talk about hot women together). I'd met her two years earlier, at another rehab where she had been working at the time. I didn't get sober back then, but I saw how wonderful she was in every way and promptly stole her from that sober living rehab and made her my assistant, and she became my best friend. She, too, understood the nature of addiction and would come to know my struggles better than any doctor I'd ever seen.

Despite the comfort that Erin brought to the situation, I still spent many sleepless nights in Southern California. Sleep is a real issue for me, especially when I'm in one of these places. That said, I don't think I have ever slept for more than four hours straight in my entire life. It didn't help that we'd been watching nothing but prison documentaries—and I was coming off so much Xanax my brain had fried to the point where I was convinced that I was an actual prisoner and that this sober living place was an actual jail. I have a shrink whose mantra is "reality is an acquired taste"—well, I'd lost both my taste and smell of reality by that point; I had Covid of the understanding; I was completely delusional.

There was nothing delusional about the Pain, though; in fact, it hurt so much I'd stopped smoking, which if you knew how much I smoked, you'd think was a pretty sure sign that something very serious was wrong. One employee of the place, whose name badge might as well have read NURSE FUCKFACE, suggested taking an Epsom salts bath to alleviate the "discomfort." You wouldn't take a Band-Aid to a road traffic accident; you don't put someone in this much Pain in water filled with his own sauce. But reality is an acquired taste, remember, so I actually took the actual Epsom salts bath.

There I sat, naked, in Pain, howling like a dog being ripped to shreds by coyotes. Erin heard me—hell, people in San Diego heard me. She appeared at the bathroom door, and looking down upon my sad, naked form as I writhed in Pain, she said very simply, "Do you want to go to the hospital?"

If Erin thought it was hospital-bad, it was hospital-bad. Plus, she'd already noticed I wasn't smoking.

"That sounds like a pretty damn good idea to me," I said in between howls.

Somehow, Erin helped me out of the bath and dried me off. I started to put my clothes back on just as a counselor—alerted by the slaughter of a dog on the premises, presumably—appeared at the door.

"I'm taking him to the hospital," Erin said.

Catherine, the counselor, just so happened to be a beautiful blond woman to whom I had apparently proposed upon my arrival, so she probably wasn't my biggest fan. (Not kidding, I had been so out of it when we'd arrived that I'd asked her to marry me, and then promptly fell down a flight of stairs.)

"This is just drug-seeking behavior," Catherine said to Erin as I continued to dress. "He's going to ask for drugs at the hospital."

Well, this marriage is off, I thought.

By now, the howls had alerted others that there were probably canine entrails all over the bathroom floor, or someone was in real Pain. The head counselor, Charles—think: male model father, homeless mother—joined Catherine in the doorway, to help her block our expected exit.

Block our exit? What were we, twelve years old?

"He's our patient," Catherine said. "You don't have the right to take him."

"I know Matty," Erin insisted. "He isn't trying to get drugs."

Then Erin turned to me.

"Do you need to go to the hospital, Matty?" I nodded and screamed some more.

"I'm taking him," Erin said.

Somehow, we pushed past Catherine and Charles, out of the building, and into the parking lot. I say "somehow" not because Catherine and Charles made much of a fuss about stopping us, but because every time my feet touched the ground, the Pain became even more excruciating.

Up there in the sky, looking down on me with scorn, caring not for my agony, was a bright yellow ball.

What's that? I thought through paroxysms of agony. *Oh, the sun. Right* . . . I didn't get out much.

"We have a high-profile coming in with severe abdominal pain," Erin said into her phone as she unlocked the car. Cars are stupid, ordinary things until you're not allowed to drive them, at which point they become magical boxes of freedom and signs of a successful previous life. Erin lifted me into the passenger seat, and I lay back. My belly was twisting in agony.

Erin got into the driver's seat, turned to me, and said, "Do you want to get there fast, or do you want me to avoid the LA potholes?"

"Just get there, woman!" I managed to say.

By now Charles and Catherine had decided to up their efforts to thwart us and now stood in front of the car, blocking us. Charles's hands were lifted, his palms facing us, as if to say "No!", as though three thousand pounds of motor vehicle could be stopped with the force of his mitts.

To make matters worse, Erin couldn't start the car. The ignition works via *telling* the car to start out loud, because you know, I was on *Friends*. Catherine and the Palms didn't budge. Once she worked out how to start the damn thing, there was only one thing more to do: Erin revved the engine, put the car in drive, and slewed it up and onto a curb—the jolt of that action alone, ricocheting through my entire body, almost caused me to die right there. With two wheels up on the curb, she revved past Catherine and Charles, and out into the street. They just watched us drive away, though by this point I would have urged her to drive over them—not being able to stop screaming is a very scary state to be in.

If I were just doing this to get drugs, then I deserved an Oscar.

"Are you aiming for the speed bumps? I don't know if you've noticed, but I'm kind of struggling right now. Slow down," I begged her. We both had tears streaming down our faces.

"I have to go fast," Erin said, her brown, compassionate eyes looking over at me with concern and fear. "We have to get you there now."

It was right about here that I drifted out of consciousness. (A 10 on the pain scale is losing consciousness by the way.)

[Please note: for the next few paragraphs, this book will be a biography rather than a memoir because I was no longer there.]

The closest hospital to the sober house was Saint John's. Since Erin had had the foresight to call ahead and alert them that a VIP was en route, someone met us at the emergency valet. Not knowing at the time how crazy sick I was when she made the call, Erin had been concerned about my privacy. But the folks at the hospital could see something was seriously wrong and rushed me to a treatment room. There, I was heard to say, "Erin, why are there Ping-Pong balls on the couch?"

There was no couch, and there were no Ping-Pong balls—I was just completely delusional. (I wasn't aware that pain could make you delusional, but there ya go.) Then the Dilaudid (my personal favorite drug in the whole wide world) hit my brain, and I briefly regained consciousness.

I was told I needed surgery immediately, and suddenly, every nurse in California descended upon my room. One of them turned to Erin and said, "Get ready to run!" Erin was ready, and we all ran—well, *they* ran, I was merely wheeled at high speed to a procedure room. Erin was asked to leave mere seconds after I'd said to her "Please don't leave," then I closed my eyes, and they wouldn't open again for two weeks.

Yes, that's right: a coma, ladies and gentlemen! (And those motherfuckers back at the sober living had tried to block the car?)

The first thing that happened when I lapsed into a coma was that I aspirated into my breathing tube, vomiting ten days' worth of toxic shit directly into my lungs. My lungs didn't like that very much—enter instant pneumonia—and that is when my colon exploded. Let me repeat for those in the back: my colon exploded! I've been accused of being full of shit before, but this time I really was.

I'm glad I wasn't there for that.

It was almost certain at that point that I was going to die. Was I unlucky that my colon exploded? Or was I lucky that it happened in the one room in Southern California where they could do something about it? Either way, I now faced a seven-hour surgery, which at least gave all my loved ones ample time to race to the hospital. As they arrived they were each told, "Matthew has a two percent chance of making it through the night."

Everyone was so wrought with emotion that some crumbled to the ground right there in the hospital lobby. I will have to live out the rest of my days knowing that my mother and others heard those words.

With me in surgery for at least seven hours and convinced that the hospital would do everything they could, my family and friends went home for the night for some rest while my subconscious fought for my life amid the knives and tubes and blood.

Spoiler alert: I *did* make it through the night. But I wasn't out of the woods yet. My family and friends were told that the only thing that could keep me alive short-term was an ECMO machine (ECMO stands for Extracorporeal Membrane Oxygenation). The ECMO move is often called a Hail Mary—for a start, four patients that week at UCLA had been put on ECMO, and they all died.

Making things even tougher, Saint John's didn't have an ECMO machine. Cedars-Sinai was called—they took one look at my chart and apparently said, "Matthew Perry is not dying in our hospital."

Thanks, guys.

UCLA wasn't willing to take me, either—for the same reason? Who can say?—but at least they were willing to send an ECMO machine and a team. I was hooked up to it for several hours, and it seemed to work! I was then transferred to UCLA itself, in an ambulance filled with doctors and nurses. (There was no way I'd survive a fifteen-minute car ride, especially the way Erin drives.)

At UCLA I was taken to the heart and lung ICU unit; it would become my home for the next six weeks. I was still in a coma, but honestly, I probably loved it. I was lying down, all snuggled up, and they were pumping drugs into me—what's better than that?

I'm told that during my coma I was never left alone, not once—there was always a member of my family or a friend in the room with me. They held candlelight vigils; did prayer circles. Love was all around me.

Eventually, my eyes magically opened.

[Back to the memoir.]

The first thing I saw was my mother.

"What's going on?" I managed to croak. "Where the hell am I?"

The last thing I remembered was being in a car with Erin.

"Your colon exploded," Mom said.

With that information, I did what any comic actor might do: I rolled my eyes and went back to sleep.

I have been told that when someone is *really* sick a kind of disconnect happens—a "God only gives you what you can handle" kind of thing kicks in. As for me, well, in the weeks after I came out of my coma, I refused to let anyone tell me exactly what had happened. I was too afraid that it was my fault; that I had done this to myself. So instead of talking about it, I did the one thing I felt I *could* do—during the days in the hospital I threw myself into family, spending hours with my beautiful sisters, Emily, Maria, and Madeline, who were funny and caring and *there*. At night it was Erin; I was never alone once again.

Eventually, one day Maria—the hub of the Perry family (my mom is the hub of the Morrison side)—decided it was time for me to be told what had happened. There I was, attached to fifty wires like a robot, bedridden, as Maria filled me in. My very fears had been true: I had done this; this was my fault.

I cried—oh *boy* did I cry. Maria did her best to be wonderfully consoling, but there was no consoling this. I had all but killed myself. I had never been a partier—taking all of those drugs (and it was a *lot* of drugs) was just a futile attempt to feel better. Trust me to take trying to feel better to death's door. And yet here I was, still alive. *Why*? Why had I been spared?

Things got worse before they got better, though.

Every morning, it seemed, some doctor would come into my room and give me more bad news. If something could go wrong, it did. I already had a colostomy bag—at least I'd been told it was reversible, thank God—but now, apparently, there was a fistula, a hole in one of my intestines. Problem was, they couldn't find it. To help, I was given *another* bag that oozed out gross green stuff, but that new bag meant that I was not allowed to eat or drink anything until they found it. They searched daily for that fistula while I got thirstier and thirstier. I was literally begging for a Diet Coke and having dreams of being chased by a gigantic can of Diet Sprite. After a full month—a month!—they finally found the fistula in some tube behind my colon. I thought, *Hey fellas, if you are looking for a hole in my intestine, why not start looking behind the thing that FUCKING EXPLODED.* Now that they'd found the hole, they could start to fix it, and I could learn to walk again.

I knew I was on my way back when I realized that I was attracted to the therapist they assigned to me. True, I had a giant scar on my stomach, but I was never a guy who took his shirt off much anyway. I'm no Matthew McConaughey, and when I take a shower, I just make sure to keep my eyes closed.

As I've said, for the entire stay in those hospitals, I was never left alone—not once. So, there *is* light in the darkness. It's there—you just have to look hard enough for it.

After five very long months, I was released. I was told that within the year, everything inside me would heal enough so that I could have a second surgery to reverse the colostomy bag. But for now, we packed my overnight bags—five months of overnights—and we made the voyage home.

Also, I'm Batman.

1

The View

Nobody ever thinks that something really bad is going to happen to them. Until it does. And nobody comes back from a perforated bowel, aspiration pneumonia, and an ECMO machine. Until somebody did.

Me.

I'm writing this in a rented house overlooking the Pacific Ocean. (My real house is down the street being renovated—they say it will take six months, so I figure about a year.) A pair of red-tailed hawks is circling below me in the canyon that brings the Palisades down to the water. It's a gorgeous spring day in Los Angeles. This morning I've been busy hanging art on my walls (or rather, having them hung—I'm not so handy). I've really gotten into art in the last few years, and if you look close enough, you'll find the odd Banksy or two. I'm also working on the second draft of a screenplay. There's fresh Diet Coke in my glass, and a full pack of Marlboros in my pocket. Sometimes, these things are enough.

Sometimes.

I keep coming back to this singular, inescapable fact: I am *alive*. Given the odds, those three words are more miraculous than you might imagine; to me, they have an odd, shiny quality, like rocks brought back from a distant planet. No one can quite believe it. It is very odd to live in a world where if you died, it would shock people but surprise no one.

What those three words—*I am alive*—fill me with, above all else, is a sense of profound gratitude. When you've been as close to the celestial as I have, you don't really have a choice about gratitude: it sits on your living room table like a coffee-table book—you barely notice it, but it's there. Yet stalking that gratitude, buried deep somewhere in the faint-anise-distant-licorice of the Diet Coke, and filling my lungs like every drag of every cigarette, there's a nagging agony.

I can't help but ask myself the overwhelming question: Why? Why am I alive? I have a hint to the answer, but it is not fully formed yet. It's in the vicinity of helping people, I know that, but I don't know how. The best thing about me, bar none, is that if a fellow alcoholic comes up to me and asks me if I can help them stop drinking, I can say yes, and actually follow up and do it. I can help a desperate man get sober. The answer to "Why am I alive?" I believe lives somewhere in there. After all, it's the only thing I've found that truly feels good. It is undeniable that there is God there.

But, you see, I can't say yes to that question "Why?" when I feel like I'm not enough. You can't give away something you do not have. And most of the time I have these nagging thoughts: *I'm not enough, I don't matter, I am too needy.* These thoughts make me uncomfortable. I need love, but I don't trust it. If I drop my game, my Chandler, and show you who I really am, you might notice me, but worse, you might notice me and leave me. And I can't have that. I won't survive that. Not anymore. It will turn me into a speck of dust and annihilate me.

So, I will leave you first. I will fabricate in my mind that something went wrong with *you*, and I'll believe it. And I'll leave. *But something can't go wrong with all of them, Matso.* What's the common denominator here?

And now these scars on my stomach. These broken love affairs.

Leaving Rachel. (No not that one. The real Rachel. The ex-girlfriend of my dreams, Rachel.) They haunt me as I lie awake at 4:00 A.M., in my house with a view in the Pacific Palisades. I'm fifty-two. It's not that cute anymore.

Every house I have ever lived in has had a view. That's the most important thing to me.

When I was five years old, I was sent on a plane from Montreal, Canada, where I lived with my mom, to Los Angeles, California, where I would visit my dad. I was what is called "an unaccompanied minor" (at one point that was the title of this book). It was typical to send kids on planes back then—flying children alone at that age was just something people did. It wasn't right, but they did it. For maybe a millisecond I thought it would be an exciting adventure, and then I realized I was too young to be alone and this was all completely terrifying (and bullshit). One of you guys come pick me up! I was five. Is everybody crazy?

The hundreds of thousands of dollars that particular choice cost me in therapy? May I get that back, please?

You do get all sorts of perks when you're an unaccompanied minor on a plane, including a little sign around your neck that reads UN-ACCOMPANIED MINOR, plus early boarding, kids-only lounges, snacks up the ying-yang, someone to escort you to the plane . . . maybe it *should* have been amazing (later, as a famous person, I got all these perks and more at airports, but every time it reminded me of that first flight, so I hated them). The flight attendants were supposed to look after me, but they were busy serving champagne in coach (that's what they did in the anything-goes 1970s). The two-drink maximum had recently been done away with, so that flight felt like six hours in Sodom and Gomorrah. The stench of alcohol was everywhere; the guy next to me must have had ten old-fashioneds. (I stopped counting after a couple of hours.) I couldn't imagine why any adult would want to drink the same drink over and over again . . . Ah, innocence.

I pushed the little service button when I dared, which wasn't very often. The flight attendants—in their 1970s hot boots and short-shorts—would come by, ruffle my hair, move on.

I was fucking terrified. I tried to read my *Highlights* magazine, but every time the plane hit a bump in the air, I knew I was about to die. I had no one to tell me it was OK, no one to look at for reassurance. My feet didn't even reach the floor. I was too scared to recline the seat and take a nap, so I just stayed awake, waiting for the next bump, wondering over and over what it would be like to fall thirty-five thousand feet.

I didn't fall, at least not literally. Eventually, the plane began its descent into the beautiful California evening. I could see the lights twinkling, streets splayed out like a great sparkling magic carpet, wide swathes of dark I now know were the hills, the city pulsing up toward me as I plastered my little face against the plane window, and I so vividly remember thinking that those lights, and all that beauty, meant I was about to have a parent.

Not having a parent on that flight is one of the many things that led to a lifelong feeling of abandonment. . . . If I'd been enough, they wouldn't have left me unaccompanied, right? Isn't that how all this was supposed to work? The other kids had parents with them. I had a sign and a magazine.

So that's why when I buy a new house—and there have been many (never underestimate a geographic)—it has to have a view. I want the sense that I can look down on safety, on someplace where someone is thinking of me, at a place where love is. Down there, somewhere in that valley, or in that vast ocean out there beyond the Pacific Coast Highway, on the gleaming primaries of the red-tail's wings, that's where parenting is. That's where love is. That's where home is. I can feel safe now.

Why was that little kid on a plane on his own? Maybe fly to Canada and fucking pick him up? That's a question I often wonder about but would never dare to ask.

I'm not the biggest fan of confrontation. I ask a lot of questions. Just not out loud.

For a long time, I tried to find just about anything and anybody to blame for the mess I kept finding myself in.

I've spent a lot of my life in hospitals. Being in hospitals makes even the best of us self-pitying, and I've made a solid effort at self-pity. Each time I lie there, I find myself thinking back through the life I've lived, turning each moment of it this way and that, like a confusing find in an archaeological dig, trying to find some reason why I had spent so much of my life in discomfort and emotional pain. I always understood where the real pain was coming from. (I always knew why I was in *physical* pain at that moment—the answer was, *well, you can't drink that much, asshole*.)

For a start, I wanted to blame my loving, well-intentioned parents . . . loving, well-intentioned, and mesmerizingly attractive, to boot.

Let's go back to Friday, January 28, 1966—the scene is Waterloo Lutheran University in Ontario.

We're at the fifth annual Miss Canadian University Snow Queen competition ("judged on the basis of intelligence, participation in student activities, and personality as well as beauty"). Those Canadians spared no expense to herald a new Miss CUSQ; there was to be a "torchlight parade with floats, bands, and the contestants," plus "an outdoor cookout and a hockey game."

The list of candidates for the honor includes one Suzanne Langford— she is listed eleventh and is representing the University of Toronto. Against her have been arrayed beauties with wonderful names like Ruth

Shaver from British Columbia; Martha Quail from Ottawa; and even Helen "Chickie" Fuhrer from McGill, who had presumably added the "Chickie" to mitigate the fact that her surname was a tad unfortunate just two decades after the end of World War II.

But these young women were no match for the beautiful Miss Langford. That freezing January evening the previous year's winner helped crown the fifth Miss Canadian University Snow Queen, and with that honor came a sash and responsibility: it would now be Miss Langford's job to hand over the crown the following year.

The 1967 pageant was similarly exciting. This year there was to be a concert given by the Serendipity Singers, a Mamas & the Papas–kind of combo that just so happened to have a lead singer called John Bennett Perry. The Serendipity Singers were an anomaly even in the folk-heavy 1960s—their biggest (and only) hit, "Don't Let the Rain Come Down," was a rehash of a British nursery rhyme—even so, it reached number 2 on the adult contemporary list and number 6 on the Billboard Hot 100 in May 1964. But that achievement is somewhat put in perspective because the Beatles famously had the *entire top five*—"Can't Buy Me Love," "Twist and Shout," "She Loves You," "I Want to Hold Your Hand," and "Please, Please Me." No matter to John Perry—he was on the road, a working musician, getting to sing for his supper, and what could be better than having a gig at the Miss Canadian University Snow Queen gala in Ontario? There he was, happily singing, "Now this crooked little man and his crooked cat and mouse They all live together in a crooked little house," and flirting across the microphone with last year's Miss Canadian University Snow Queen, Suzanne Langford. At the time, they were two of the most gorgeous people on the face of the planet—you should see pictures of them from their wedding—you just want to punch them in their perfectly chiseled faces. They didn't stand a chance.

When two people look that good, they just kind of morph into each other.

The flirting turned to dancing once John had finished his gig, and that might have been it, but for the massive, kismetic snowstorm that stalked the evening and made it impossible for the Serendipity Singers to get out of town. So, that's the meet-cute: a folk singer and a beauty queen fall in love in a snowbound Canadian town in 1967 . . . best-looking man on the planet meets best-looking woman on the planet. Everyone there might as well have gone home.

John Perry stayed the night, and Suzanne Langford was quite happy about that, and about a year or two later, after the montage scene, she found herself in Williamstown, Massachusetts, where John is from, and cells inside her were dividing and conquering. Maybe something in those simple divisions went awry, who can say—all I know is, addiction is an illness, and like my parents when they met, I didn't stand a fucking chance.

I was born on August 19, 1969, a Tuesday, the son of John Bennett Perry, late of the Serendipity Singers, and Suzanne Marie Langford, former Miss Canadian University Snow Queen. There was a huge storm the night I arrived (of course there was); everyone was playing Monopoly waiting for me to show up (of course they were). I hit the planet about a month after the Moon landing, and one day after Woodstock ended—so, somewhere between the cosmic perfection of the heavenly orbs, and all that shit down at Yasgur's Farm, I became life, interrupting someone's chance to build hotels on Boardwalk.

I came out screaming, and I didn't stop screaming. For weeks. I was a colicky kid—my stomach was a problem from the very start. My parents were being driven crazy by the amount I was crying. Crazy? Concerned, so they hauled me off to a doctor. This is 1969, a prehistoric time compared to now. That said, I don't know how advanced civilization has to be to understand that giving *phenobarbital* to a baby who just entered his second month of breathing God's air is, at best, an *interesting* approach to pediatric medicine. But it wasn't that rare in the 1960s to slip the parents of a colicky child a major barbiturate. Some older doctors swore by it—and by it, I mean, "prescribing a major barbiturate for a child that's barely born who won't stop crying."

I want to be very clear on this point. I do NOT blame my parents for this. Your child is crying all the time, clearly something is wrong, the doctor prescribes a drug, he's not the only doctor who thinks it's a good idea, you give the drug to the child, the child stops crying. It was a different time.

There I was, on the knee of my stressed mother, screaming over her twenty-one-year-old shoulder as some dinosaur in a white coat, barely looking up from his wide oak desk, tutted under his bad breath at "parents these days," and wrote a script for a major addictive barbiturate.

I was noisy and needy, and it was answered with a pill. (Hmm, that sounds like my fucking twenties.)

I'm told I took phenobarbital during the second month of my life, between the ages of thirty and sixty days. This is an important time in a baby's development, especially when it comes to sleeping. (Fifty years later I still don't sleep well.) Once the barbiturate was on board, I would just conk out. Apparently, I'd be crying, and the drug would hit, and I'd be knocked out, and this would cause my father to erupt in laughter. He wasn't being cruel; stoned babies are funny. There are baby pictures of me where you can tell I'm just completely fucking zonked, nodding like an addict at the age of seven weeks. Which is oddly appropriate for a kid born the day after Woodstock ended, I guess.

I was being needy; I was not the cute smiling baby everyone was hoping for. *I'll just take this and shut the fuck up.*

Ironically, barbiturates and I have had a very strange relationship over the years. People would be surprised to know that I have mostly been sober since 2001. Save for about sixty or seventy little mishaps over the years. When these mishaps occur, if you want to be sober, which I always did, you'd be given drugs to help you along. What drug may you ask? You guessed it: *phenobarbital*! Barbiturates calm you down as you try to get whatever other shit is in your body out; and hey, I started taking one at thirty days old, so as an adult I just picked up where I'd left off. When I'm at a detox, I'm very needy and uncomfortable—I'm sorry to say I'm the worst patient in the world.

Detox is hell. Detox is lying in bed, watching the seconds go by, knowing you are nowhere near feeling OK. When I'm detoxing, I feel like I'm dying. I feel like it will never end. My insides feel like they're trying to crawl out of my body. I'm shaking and sweating. I'm like that baby who wasn't given a pill to make things better. I have chosen to be high for four hours, knowing I will then be in that hell for seven days. (I told you this part of me is crazy, right?) Sometimes, I have to be locked away for months at a time to break the cycle.

When I'm detoxing, "OK" is a distant memory, or something reserved for Hallmark cards. I'm begging like a child for any kind of medication that will help ease the symptoms—a grown man, who's probably looking great on the cover of *People* magazine at the very same time, *begging* for relief. I would give up everything—every car, every house, all the money—just to make it stop. And when detox is finally over, you are bathed in relief, swearing up and down that you will never put yourself through that again. Until there you are, three weeks later, in the exact same position.

It's crazy. I am crazy.

And like a baby, I didn't want to do the inner work for so long, because if a pill fixes it, well, that's easier, and that's what I was taught.

At around my ninth month, my parents decided they had had enough of each other, stashed me in a car seat in Williamstown, and the three of us drove to the Canadian border—five and a half hours. I can just imagine the silence of that car ride. I didn't speak, of course, and the two former lovebirds in the front seat had had enough of speaking to each other. And yet that silence must have been deafening. Some major shit was going down. There, with the distant thrum of the Niagara Falls as a background, my maternal grandfather, the military-like Warren Langford, was waiting for us, pacing up and down, stamping his feet to keep warm, or in frustration, or both. He would have been waving at us as we pulled up, as though we were about to embark upon some kind of fun holiday. I would have been excited to see him, and then, I'm told, my father took me out of my car seat, handed me into my grandfather's arms, and, with that, he quietly abandoned me and my mother. Then, Mom finally got out of our car, too, and me, my mom, and my grandfather stood listening to the waters hurtle over the Falls and roar into the Niagara Gorge and watched as my father sped away, forever.

Seems we weren't going to live together in *a crooked little house* after all. I imagine back then I was told that my dad would be back soon.

"Don't worry," my mother probably said, "he's just going to work, Matso. He'll be back."

"Come on, little chum," Grampa would have said, "let's go find Nanny. She's made your favorite pasghetti for dinner."

Every parent goes off to work, and they always come back. That's just the normal way of things. Nothing to worry about. Nothing that would bring on a colic attack, or addiction, or a lifetime of feeling abandoned, or that I am not enough, or a continual lack of comfort, or a desperate need for love, or that I didn't matter.

My father sped away, to God knows where. He didn't come back from work that first day, nor the second. I was hoping he'd be home after three days, then maybe a week, then maybe a month, but after about six weeks I stopped hoping. I was too young to understand where

California was, or what it meant to "go follow his dream of being an actor"—what the fuck is an actor? And where the fuck is my dad?

My dad, who later in life became a wonderful father, was leaving his baby alone with a twenty-one-year-old woman who he knew was way too young to parent a child on her own. My mother is wonderful, and emotional, and she was just too young. She, like me, had been abandoned, too, right there in the parking lot of the border crossing between the United States and Canada. My mother had gotten pregnant with me when she was twenty years old, and by the time she was twenty-one, and a new mother, she was single. If *I'd* had a baby at twenty-one, I would have tried to drink it. She did her best, and that says a lot about her, but still, she simply wasn't ready for the responsibility, and I wasn't ready to deal with anything, being just born n'all.

Mom and I were both abandoned, in fact, before we'd even gotten to know each other.

With Dad gone, I quickly understood that I had a role to play at home. My job was to entertain, to cajole, to delight, to make others laugh, to soothe, to please, to be the Fool to the entire court.

Even when I lost an entire part of my body. Actually, especially then.

The phenobarbital behind me—its use faded like my memories of my father's face—I plowed on full pelt into a toddlerdom, in which I learned how to be the caretaker.

When I was in kindergarten, some dim kid slammed a door on my hand, and after the great sparkles of blood stopped arcing up like fireworks, someone thought to bandage me up and take me to a hospital. There, it was clear that I had, in fact, lost the tip of my middle finger. My mother was called and sped to the hospital. She came in sobbing (understandably) and found me standing on a gurney with a gigantic bandage on my hand. Before she could say anything, I said, "You don't need to cry—I didn't cry."

There I was already: the performer, the people pleaser. (Who knows—maybe I even did a little Chandler Bing startle/double take just to land the line?) Even at three years old I'd learned I'd have to be the man of the house. I had to take care of my mother, even though my finger had just been sliced off. I guess I'd learned at thirty days old that if I cried, I'd get knocked out, so I'd better not cry; or I knew I had to make sure everyone, including my mother, felt safe and OK. Or, it was just a fucking great line for a toddler to say standing on a gurney like a boss.

Not that much has changed. If you give me all the OxyContin I can stand, I feel taken care of, and when I'm taken care of, I can take care of everybody else and look outward and be in service to someone. But *without* medication, I feel that I would just sputter away into a sea of nothingness. This, of course, means it's pretty much impossible for me to be useful or in service in a relationship because I'm just trying to get to the next minute, next hour, next day. There's that dis-ease of fear, the licorice of inadequacy. A touch of this drug, a drop of that, and I'm OK—you don't taste anything when you're jacked on something.

(Back in the days before 9/11, kids—and curious adults—on planes would sometimes be allowed up to the cockpit to have a look around. When I was about nine, I was brought up to a cockpit and was so mesmerized by the buttons and the captain and all the information that I forgot to put my hand in my pocket for the first time in six years. I had never showed it; I was so ashamed. But the pilot noticed and said, "Let me see your hand." Embarrassed, I showed him. Then he said, "Here, take a look." Turns out he was missing the exact same bit of his middle finger on his right hand.

Here was this man, captaining the whole plane and knowing what

all of those buttons did and understanding all the captivating information in a cockpit, and he was missing part of his finger, too. From
that day forth—I'm fifty-two now—I have never hidden my hand. In
fact, because I smoked for so many years a lot of people noticed it and
people would ask what happened.

At least I got an OK gag out of the incident with the door—for
years I'd complain that since losing half a finger I could tell people only
to "Fuck y—")

I may not have had a father, or all ten fingers, but what I did have was
a fast mind and a fast mouth, even then. Combine that with a mother
who was very busy, and important, and who also had a fast mind and
mouth . . . well, there were times I was happy to lecture my mother
about her lack of attention, and let's just say it didn't go that well. It's
important to note here that I could never get enough attention—no
matter what she did, it was never enough. And let's not forget that
she was doing the work of two people, while dear old dad was busy
wrestling with his own demons and desires in LA.

Suzanne Perry (she kept Dad's name professionally) was basically
Allison Janney from *The West Wing*—a spinmeister. She was the press
secretary for Pierre Trudeau, who was then the Canadian prime minister and a general gallivanter. (The *Toronto Star* captioned a picture
of the two of them this way: "Press aide Suzanne Perry works for one
of Canada's best-known men—Prime Minister Pierre Trudeau—but
she is quickly becoming a celebrity herself; simply by appearing at his
side.") Imagine that: you're a celebrity merely by standing next to Pierre
Trudeau. He was the suave, socially connected PM who had once dated
Barbra Streisand, Kim Cattrall, Margot Kidder . . . his ambassador to
DC once grouched that he'd invited not one but *three* separate girlfriends to a dinner, so there was a lot of spinning needed for a man

so enamored of women. My mom's job therefore meant that she was away at work a lot—and I was left to compete with the ongoing concerns of a major Western democracy and its charismatic, swordsman leader if I wanted a little attention. (I believe the phrase at the time was "latchkey kid"—a bland term for being left fucking alone.) Accordingly, I learned to be funny (pratfalls, quick one-liners, you know the drill) because I *had* to be—my mother was stressed by her stressful job, and already highly emotional (and abandoned), and me being funny tended to calm her down enough that she would cook some food, sit down at the dinner table with me, and hear me out, after I heard *her* out, of course. But I'm not blaming her for working—someone had to bring home the bacon. It just meant I spent a great deal of time alone. (I would tell people I was a *lonely* child, having misheard the phrase "only child.")

So, I was a kid with a fast mind and an even faster mouth, but as said, she, too, had a fast mind and a fast mouth (I wonder where I got it from). We argued a lot, and I always had to have the last word. One time, I was having an argument with her in a stairwell, and she made me feel the most rage I've ever felt in my life. (I was twelve years old, and you can't hit your mother, so the rage turned inward—just like when I was an adult, at least I had the decency to turn into an alcoholic and an addict and not blame other people.)

I've always been abandoned. So much so that I used to ask my grandmother, when a plane went over our house in Ottawa, "Is my mother on that plane?" because I was always worried that she would disappear, just as my father had (she never did). My mother is beautiful; she was a star in every room she entered. And she's certainly the reason I'm funny.

With Dad off in California, Mom, being beautiful and smart and charismatic and the star in every room she entered, would date guys, and they'd date her right back, and sure enough, I'd turn every one of those men into my dad. Once again, when a plane went over our house, I'd ask my grandmother, "Is that [Michael] [Bill] [John] [insert name of Mom's latest beau] flying away?" I was continually losing my father; I was continually being dropped at the border. The roar of the Niagara River was forever in my ears, and not even a dose of phenobarbital could make it mute. My grandmother would coo at me, crack me open a can of Diet Coke, that faint-anise and distant-licorice filling my taste buds with loss.

As for my *real* dad, he would call every Sunday, which was nice. After his stint with the Serendipity Singers, he morphed his performing skills into acting, first in New York, then in Hollywood. Though he was what they sometimes call a journeyman, he was working pretty steadily and would eventually become the Old Spice guy. I saw his face more often on TV or in magazines than I did in reality. (Perhaps that's why I became an actor.) *"What kind of man whistles the Old Spice tune? He's my daddy!"* goes the voiceover from one 1986 ad as a little blond boy with a bowl cut puts his arms around my actual father's neck. *"My practically perfect husband,"* the smiling blond wife intones, and though it's sort of a joke, it was never very funny to me. *"You can count on him, he's a friend. . . ."*

Then, when enough time had passed that it was unseemly, I had a sign that read UNACCOMPANIED MINOR tied around my neck and I was taken to the airport so I could be sent to Los Angeles. Whenever I'd visit him there, I'd realize over again each time that my dad was charismatic, funny, charming, hyperhandsome.

He was perfect, and even at that age, I liked things I could not have.

Bottom line, though, was: my dad was my hero. In fact, he was my *super*hero: whenever we would go for walks, I would say "you be Superman and I'll be Batman." (A smart psychologist might say we played roles instead of Dad and Matthew, because our actual roles were too confusing to me. But I couldn't possibly comment on that.)

Back in Canada once again, the image of his face and the smell of his apartment would fade over the months. Then, it would be my birthday once again, and my mother would do what she could to make up for the fact that my dad wasn't there, and when the too-big cake appeared, covered in many dripping candles, each and every year I'd wish for one thing: in my head I'd whisper, *I want my parents to get back together.* Maybe if my home life had been more stable, or if my dad had been around, or if he hadn't been Superman, or if I hadn't had a fast mind and mouth, or if Pierre Trudeau . . . I wouldn't be so damn uncomfortable all the time.

I'd be happy. And Diet Coke would be delicious instead of just necessary.

Without the proper medicine, for my entire life I was uncomfortable all the time and w-a-a-a-ay screwed up about love. To quote the great Randy Newman, "It takes a whole lot of medicine for me to pretend that I'm somebody else." I guess I wasn't the only one.

"Hi, is Suzanne there?"

"Yes, can I tell my mom who's calling?"

"It's Pierre . . ."

When the phone rang, Mom and I had been in the middle of the *best* day together. We had played games all day long—we even tried to play Monopoly, but it's hard when there's just two of you—and then as night fell, we found *Annie Hall* on our little TV and laughed our asses off at Woody Allen's house under the roller coaster. (I didn't get the sex and relationship jokes, but even at eight years old I could understand the comedy of sneezing away $2,000 worth of some kind of white powder.)

That is my absolute favorite childhood memory—sitting with my mom and watching that movie. But now the prime minister of Canada was calling, so I was about to lose my mom again. As she took the call

I heard her turn on her professional, spinmeister-y voice; the voice of a different person, of Suzanne Perry in fact, not my mom.

I turned the TV off and went to bed. I tucked myself in, and without the need of barbiturates—yet—I uneasily slept till early light illuminated my Ottawa bedroom window.

I remember around this time seeing my mother in the kitchen crying, and I thought, *Why doesn't she just drink?* I have no idea how I got the notion that an alcoholic drink would stop crying. I certainly hadn't had a drink by eight (I'd wait another six years!), but somehow the culture all around me had taught me that drinking equaled laughing and having fun, and a much-needed escape from pain. Mom was crying, so why didn't she just drink? Then she'd be drunk and not feel as much, right?

Maybe she was crying because we moved all the time—Montreal, Ottawa, Toronto—though I spent most of my childhood in Ottawa. I spent a lot of time alone; there would be nannies, but they never lasted that long, so I just added them to the list of people who abandoned me. . . . I just went on being funny, quick, smart-mouthed, just to survive.

By standing next to Pierre Trudeau and looking beautiful, my mother became an instant celebrity, so much so that she was offered the position of anchoring the national news for Global Television, in Toronto.

What an opportunity—this was a job she could not pass up. She was pretty good at it, too, until one day when they were promoting a beauty pageant. My mother said, "I'm sure we'll all be glued to *that* one." It was a funny line—and kind of surreal coming from a beauty pageant winner—but she was fired that night.

I hadn't been happy with the move to Toronto—for starters, I hadn't even been included in the decision. And for the entrée, I would never see my friends again. My mother was also nine months pregnant—by then she had married *Canada AM* host Keith Morrison—yes, him, the one with the hair on NBC's *Dateline.* I had even been picked to give my mother away at the wedding. This was an odd choice—figuratively and literally.

But soon I had a beautiful sister! Caitlin was as cute as could be, and I loved her instantly. But there was now a family growing up around me, a family I didn't really feel a part of. It was around this time that I made the conscious choice to say, *Fuck it—it's every man for himself.* That's when the bad behavior started—I got shitty grades, I started smoking, I beat up Pierre's son (an eventual prime minister himself) Justin Trudeau. (I decided to end my argument with him when he was put in charge of an entire army.) I made the choice to live in my head and not in my heart. It was safer in my head—you couldn't be broken there, not yet anyway.

I changed. The fast mouth appeared, and no one would ever get near my heart. No one.

I was ten years old.

By seventh grade, we were back in Ottawa, where we belonged. I was beginning to see the power of making people laugh. At Ashbury College, my all-boys secondary school in Ottawa, in between being the class cutup I somehow managed to land the role of Rackham, "the fastest gun in the West," in a play called *The Death and Life of Sneaky Fitch,* put on by the school's drama teacher, Greg Simpson. It was a big part, and I just loved it—making people laugh felt like everything. The ripple that turns into a wave, all those parents pretending to be interested in their kids' exploits until—wham!—that Perry kid actually made people laugh. (Of all the drugs, that one is still the most effective, at least when it comes to giving me *joy.*) Being the star of *The Death and Life of Sneaky Fitch* was especially important because it gave me something to excel in.

I deeply cared what strangers thought of me—still do—in fact, it's one of the key threads in my life. I remember begging my mom to paint the backyard blue so people flying in planes overhead, looking down at our yard, would think we had a swimming pool. Maybe there was some unaccompanied minor up there who could look down and be comforted by it.

Even though I was now a big brother, I was also the bad kid. One year I went through all the closets before Christmas to see what my presents were; I was also stealing money, smoking more and more, and getting worse and worse grades. At one point the teachers put my desk facing the wall at the back of the classroom because I talked so much and spent all my time trying to make people laugh. One teacher, Dr. Webb, said, "If you don't change the way you are, you'll never amount to anything." (Should I admit that when I got the cover of *People* magazine I had a copy of it sent to Dr. Webb with a note that read, "I guess you were wrong"? Nah, that would be crass.)

I did.

Making up for my shitty grades was the fact that I was the lead in every play and a nationally ranked tennis player.

My grandfather started teaching me how to play tennis when I was four, and by the time I was eight I knew I could beat him—but I waited until I was ten. I would play for eight to ten hours every day, and spend hours hitting at a backboard, too, pretending I was Jimmy Connors. I would play games and sets, every shot of mine Connors, every return of the backboard John McEnroe. I hit the ball ahead of my body, I would sweep with my strings, I'd put the racket behind me, as though I was placing it in a backpack. I figured it was only a matter of time before I'd be walking out at Wimbledon, nodding sweetly and modestly at the adoring fans, limbering up before going to five sets against McEnroe, waiting patiently while he berated some stuffy British umpire, before nailing a cross-court, backhand passing shot to win the tournament. Then I'd kiss the golden trophy and sip a glass of Robinsons Barley Water, a drink so far from Dr Pepper I would actually love it. Surely, I'd get my mother's attention then.

(The 1982 Wimbledon final, where Jimmy Connors narrowly beat heavily favored John McEnroe, was my favorite match of all time. Jimmy graced the cover of *Sports Illustrated* after his victory, and it's framed and has hung on my wall to this day. I was him, or he was me—either way, on that day, both of us won.)

For actual matches in the real world, I played at Rockcliffe Lawn Tennis Club in Ottawa. You had to wear all whites at the club. At one point, there was a sign out front of the club that read WHITES ONLY until somebody thought that might give the wrong impression. (The sign was quickly changed to WHITE DRESS ONLY and everyone moved on.) There were eight courts, mostly peopled by seniors, and I would spend all day waiting in the clubhouse in case somebody didn't show up and a fourth was needed and I could step in. The older folks loved me because I could get to every ball, but I also had a crazy temper. I'd throw my racket and swear and get all pissed off, and if I was losing badly, I would start sobbing. This usually preceded me coming back to win—I'd be one set down; 5–1 down; love–40 down, *sobbing*, and then I'd come back to win in three. All along I'd be crying but also thinking, *I'm gonna win; I know I'm gonna win.* Winning wasn't as necessary to others.

By fourteen, I was nationally ranked in Canada . . . but that was also the year something else started.

I had my first drink when I was fourteen. I held off as long as I could.

At this point I was hanging out a lot with two brothers, Chris and Brian Murray. Somehow, since third grade we'd developed a way of talking that went, "Could it *be* any hotter?" or "Could the teacher *be* any meaner?" or "Could we *be* more in detention?"—a cadence you might recognize if you're a fan of *Friends,* or if you've noticed how America has been talking for the past couple of decades or so. (I don't think it's an exaggeration to suggest that Chandler Bing transformed the way America spoke.) For the record: that transformation came directly from Matthew Perry, Chris Murray, and Brian Murray fucking around in Canada in the 1980s. Only I got rich off of it, though. Fortunately, Chris and Brian have never busted me for that and are still my dear, hilarious friends.

One night, the three of us were hanging out in my backyard. No one was home; up above, the sun shone through the clouds, none of us knowing that something extremely significant was about to transpire. I was lying in the grass and mud of Canada, and I didn't know anything.

Could I *be* more unaware?

We decided to drink. I forget whose idea it was, and none of us knew what we were getting ourselves into. We had a six-pack of Budweiser and a bottle of white wine called Andrès Baby Duck. I took the wine and the Murrays took the beer. All this took place in the wide open, by the way—we were just in my backyard. My parents weren't home—big surprise there—and off we went.

Within fifteen minutes, all the alcohol was gone. The Murrays were puking around me, and I just lay in the grass, and something happened to me. That thing that makes me bodily and mentally different from my fellows occurred. I was lying back in the grass and the mud, looking at the moon, surrounded by fresh Murray puke, and I realized that for the first time in my life, nothing bothered me. The world made sense; it wasn't bent and crazy. I was complete, at peace. I had never been happier than in that moment. *This is the answer,* I thought; *this is what I've been missing. This must be how normal people feel all the time. I don't have any problems. It is all gone. I don't need attention. I am taken care of, I am fine.*

I was in *bliss*. I had no problems for those three hours. I wasn't abandoned; I wasn't fighting with my mom; I wasn't doing lousy in school; I wasn't wondering what life was about, and my place in it. It took away everything.

Knowing what I know now about the progressive nature of the disease of addiction, it's amazing to me I didn't drink the *next* night, and the next night, too, but I didn't—I waited, and the scourge of alco-holism hadn't gripped me yet. So that first night didn't lead to regular drinking, but it probably sowed the seed.

The key to the problem, I would come to understand, was this: I lacked both spiritual guidelines, and an ability to enjoy anything. But at the same time, I was also an excitement addict. This is such a toxic combination I can't even.

I didn't know this at the time, of course, but if I was not in the act of searching for excitement, being excited, or drunk, I was incapable of enjoying anything. The fancy word for that is "anhedonia," a word and feeling I would spend millions in therapy and treatment centers to discover and understand. Maybe that's why I won tennis matches only when I was a set down and within points of losing. Maybe that's why I did everything I did. *Anhedonia,* by the way, was the original working title of my favorite movie, the one my mother and I had enjoyed to-gether, *Annie Hall.* Woody gets it. Woody gets me.

Things at home just got worse and worse. My mom had a wonderful new family with Keith. Emily arrived, and she was blond and cute as a button. And just like Caitlin, I loved her instantly. However, I was so often on the outside looking in, still that kid up in the clouds on a flight to somewhere else, unaccompanied. Mom and I were fighting all the time; tennis was the only place I was happy, and even then, I was angry, or sobbing, even when I won. What was a fella to do?

Enter, my father. I wanted to know him. It was time for a big geo-graphic.

Yup, Los Angeles, and my father, and a new life were calling, but I was fifteen, and leaving would rupture my home life and my mom's heart. But she didn't ask me if it was OK to marry Keith and move to Toronto and have two kids. . . . And in Canada I was angry, and sobbing, and drinking, and me and my mom were fighting, and I wasn't a full part of the family, and I sucked at school, and who knew if I was going to have to move soon anyway, and on and on and on. And damn it, a kid wants to know his father.

I decided to go. My parents had discussed it and wondered if LA would be better for my tennis career anyway. (Little did I know that in Southern California the best I'd be would be a solid club player, the standard being so much higher in a place where you can play 365 days a year, as opposed to Canada, where you're lucky if you get a couple of months before the permafrost shows up.) But even with that idea, me deciding to go caused a great rift in the fabric of my family.

The night before I made the trip, I was in the basement of our house, where I slept that night only, and it would turn out to be one of the worst nights of my life. Up in the main house, hell was brewing; there was the banging of doors, and hissed conversations, and occasional shouts, and pacing, and one of the kids was crying, and no one could stop it. My grandparents would periodically come down and yell at me; upstairs, my mother was screaming, crying, and then all the kids were crying, and my grandparents were yelling, and the kids were yelling, and I was down there, mute, abandoned, determined, terrified, unaccompanied, and scared. These three very powerful adults would come down to tell me over and over that I was breaking their hearts by leaving. But I had no choice; things had gotten so bad. I was a broken human being.

Broken? Bent.

Early next morning, in what must have been a very difficult drive for her, my mother was kind enough to take me to the airport and watch me fly away from her for the rest of her life. How I had the courage to actually make this voyage is beyond me. I still question whether or not it was the right thing to do.

Still an unaccompanied minor—but a pro by now—I flew to LA to get to know my father. I was so terrified that even the hoopla of Hollywood might not to be able to soothe me. But soon I would see the lights of the city and have a parent once more.

New York

The first thing I did when I got home from those five months in the hospital was light up a cigarette. After all that time, the inhale, the smoke billowing into my lungs, was like the first cigarette I had ever had in my entire life. It felt like a second homecoming.

I was no longer in Pain—the massive surgery on my stomach had caused scar tissue, which in turn caused my stomach to feel like I was doing a sit-up at full stretch 24/7, but it wasn't actually pain. It was more of an annoyance.

But no one needed to know that, so I told everyone I was in pain so I could get OxyContin. Pretty soon the 80 milligrams a day of Oxy-Contin I had conned them into giving me wasn't working anymore, and I needed more. When I asked the doctors for more, they said no; when I called a drug dealer, he said yes. Now all I had to do was figure out a way to get down forty floors from my $20 million penthouse apartment without Erin spotting me. (I bought the place—I swear to God—because Bruce Wayne lived in just such an apartment in *The Dark Knight*.)

Over the next month I attempted to do this four times. I was caught—you guessed it—four times. I was horrible at it. Naturally, the call came down from above that this man needs to go to rehab again. So—

After the explosion of my bowel, I'd been through a first surgery and needed to wear a rather attractive colostomy bag—a look even I couldn't pull off. There was a second surgery pending, to remove the bag, but in between the two surgeries, I was banned from smoking (smokers tend to have much uglier scars, hence the stricture). Not to mention I was missing my two front teeth—a bite into a piece of toast with peanut butter had cracked them and I hadn't had time to fix them yet.

So let me get this straight: you're asking me to quit doing drugs and quit smoking at the same time? I didn't give a fuck about the scars; I am a big smoker; this was too much to ask. What this meant was that I had to go to a rehab in New York, quit OxyContin, and quit smoking, simultaneously, and I was scared.

Once I got to rehab, they gave me Subutex for the detox, so that wasn't that bad. I checked into my room, and the clock started. By day four I was going out of my mind, this had always been the hardest day. I realized how serious they were going to be about this smoking thing, too. It was decided that I could smoke while in detox, but once I moved up to the third floor the smokes had to go.

They insisted, so much so that I was locked in the building so I could not get out. I was on the third floor; all around, New York purred in the distance, going about its business, living life while their favorite sarcastic sitcom star was in hell one more time. If I listened hard enough, I could just hear the subway—the F train, the R train, the 4, 5, 6—deep below me, or maybe it was the rattle of something else, something unbidden and terrifying and unstoppable.

This rehab was prison, I was convinced of it. A real prison, not like the one I had made up before. Red bricks, black iron bars. Somehow, I'd found my way to jail. I'd never broken the law—well, I'd never been caught—nevertheless, here I was, in lockup, pokey, the House of D.

Missing my two front teeth, I even looked like a convict, and every counselor was a guard. They may as well have fed me through a slot in a bolted door.

I hated the whole place—they didn't have anything to teach me. I've been in therapy since I was eighteen years old, and honestly, by this point, I didn't need any more therapy—what I needed was two front teeth and a colostomy bag that didn't break. When I say that I woke up covered in my own shit, I'm talking fifty to sixty times. On the mornings when the bag did not break, I noticed another new phenomenon: when I woke up, I enjoyed about thirty seconds of freedom as I slowly wiped the sleep from my eyes and then the reality of my situation would hit me, and I would burst into tears at a rate that would even make Meryl Streep jealous.

Oh, and I needed a cigarette. Did I mention that?

I was sitting in my room doing God knows what on day four when something hit me, I don't know what. It was like something was punching me from the inside. But even though I had been in therapy for more than thirty years and it had nothing new to teach me, I had to do something to get my mind off nicotine, so I left my cell and headed down the hallway. Aimless, I had no idea what I was doing or where I was going.

I think I was trying to walk outside of my own body.

I knew that all the therapists were on the floor below me, but I decided to skip the elevator and make for the stairwell. I didn't really know what was happening—I can't to this day describe what was going on, except that I was in a sort of panic, confusion, a kind of fugue state, and there was that intense pain again—not Pain, but pretty close to it. Total confusion. And I wanted to smoke so badly. So, I stopped, in that stairwell, and thought about all the years of agony, and the fact that the yard never got painted blue, and Pierre fucking Trudeau, and the fact that I was then, and still am, an unaccompanied minor.

It was like the bad parts of my life were appearing to me all at once.

I'll never be able to fully explain what happened next, but all of a sudden, I started slamming my head against the wall, as hard as humanly possible. Fifteen–love. SLAM! Thirty–love. SLAM! Forty–love. SLAM! Game. Ace after ace, volley after perfect volley, my head the ball, the wall the cement court, all the pain lobbed up but short, me reaching up, smashing my head against the wall, blood on the cement and on the wall, and all over my face, completing the Grand Slam, the umpire screaming, "GAME, SET, AND MATCH, UNACCOMPANIED MINOR, SIX LOVE, NEEDS LOVE, SIX LOVE. SCARED OF LOVE."

There was blood everywhere.

After about eight of these mind-numbing slams, somebody must have heard me, and stopped me, and asked the only logical question:

"Why are you doing that?"

I gazed at her, and looking like Rocky Balboa from every one of those last scenes, I said, "Because I couldn't think of anything better to do."

Stairwells.

2

Another Generation
Shot to Hell

It seemed like the whole world was walking through the arrivals lounge of LAX that summer.

World-class amateur gymnasts, sprinters, discus throwers, pole vaulters, basketball players, weight lifters, show jumpers and their horses, swimmers, fencers, soccer players, synchronized swimmers, media from all around the globe, officials and sponsors and agents . . . oh, and one fifteen-year-old also-amateur tennis player from Canada, they all washed up in Los Angeles during the summer of 1984, though only one was doing a big geographic.

That was the year of the Los Angeles Olympic Games, a golden time of high sun and muscled excellence, of a hundred thousand people packed into the Coliseum and the Rose Bowl, where Mary Lou Retton needed a 10 to win the gymnastics all-around and nailed it, and where Carl Lewis won four gold medals by running really fast and jumping really far.

It was also the year I immigrated to the United States, a lost Canadian kid with a dick that didn't seem to work, heading to Tinseltown to live with his father.

Back in Ottawa, before I'd left, a girl had tried to have sex with me, but I was so nervous that I drank six beers beforehand and couldn't perform. By then I'd been drinking for a few years—it began soon after the time I gave my mother away to that lovely man, Keith.

And I do mean lovely. Keith *lived* for my mother. The only thing that is annoying about Keith is that he always takes my mother's side. He is her protector. I can't tell you how many times my mother has done something that I may have taken issue with and I've been told by Keith that it never happened. Some would call this gaslighting, others would call it gaslighting—it's gaslighting. But my family was held together by one man, and that was Keith Morrison.

Anyway, back to my penis.

I failed to make the correlation between the booze and my private parts not working. And no one could know about this—no one. So, I was walking around the planet thinking sex was something for *other* people. For a long time; years. Sex sounded awfully fun, but it was not in my arsenal. This meant, in my mind and pants at least, that I was (con)genitally, impotent.

If I just go to Los Angeles, I'll be happy. . . . That's what I thought. Seriously—that's what I thought a geographic, long before I even knew what a geographic was, would do for me. I fit right in with the muscled, hypertrained athletes also waiting at the baggage carousels. Weren't we all just bringing some kind of crazy dream to this crazy city? If there were a hundred sprinters, and only three medals per discipline, how much saner could you say they were than me? In fact, I probably had a better chance of making it in my profession than they did in theirs—after all, my dad was an actor, and that's what I wanted to be. All he had to do was help me push on doors already ajar, right? And so what if I came halfway down the pack—I might not get a medal either, but at least I'd get away from Ottawa and a dick that didn't seem to want to work. And a family I wasn't really a part of and on and on.

The initial plan for me had involved sports, too. My tennis had advanced to the point where we seriously considered me enrolling in Nick Bollettieri's Tennis Academy in Florida. Bollettieri was the premier tennis coach—he helped Monica Seles, Andre Agassi, Maria Sharapova, and Venus and Serena Williams among many others—but once in LA, it quickly became apparent that I was going to be a perfectly solid club player, nothing more. I can remember enrolling in a satellite tournament, with my dad and my new family watching (he'd remarried to Debbie, a lovely woman, and the catch of the century, in 1980, and back then they had a very young daughter, Maria), and in my first match I didn't win a *single* point.

The standard in Southern California was off the charts—when it's seventy-two degrees every day, and there are tennis courts seemingly in every backyard and on every street corner, some kid from the icy wastes of Canada—where it's subzero from December through March, if you're lucky—is going to struggle to make an impact. It was kind of like being a really good hockey player in Burbank. And so it turned out: my dreams of being the next Jimmy Connors quickly faded when faced with whipped 100-mph serves coming from bronzed Californian gods who happened to be eleven years old and called Chad, but spelled with a capital *D*.

It was time to look for a new profession.

Despite this swift reality check, I loved LA instantly. I loved the vastness of it, the possibilities of it, the opportunity to start anew—not to mention that the seventy-two degrees every day made a nice change from Ottawa. Plus, when I realized that tennis wasn't going to be how I would make a living, and someone told me people actually get paid to act, I quickly changed career goals. This wasn't as far-fetched as it seemed; for a start, my dad was in show business, and I had a hunch that the attention would light me up like a Christmas tree. I had had a solid training at home; whenever there was tension, or I needed attention, I'd honed my skills at delivering a killer line. If I was performing well, everything was safe, and I was being taken care of. I might have been an unaccompanied minor, but when I got laughs, there was a whole audience—my mother, my siblings, the Murray brothers, kids in school—who would stand and applaud me. It also didn't hurt that three weeks into my sophomore year at a very prestigious and expensive (thanks, Dad) new school, I was cast in the lead role of the high school play. That's right ladies and gentlemen—you are looking at George Gibbs in Thornton Wilder's *Our Town.* Acting came naturally to me. Why wouldn't I want to pretend to be another person?

Jesus Christ . . .

I think my dad had sensed this was going to happen. After I was cast in *Our Town,* I raced home to share the big news and found a book lying on my bed called *Acting with Style.* The inscription inside read:

Another generation shot to hell. Love, Dad.

Acting was another one of my drugs. And it didn't do the damage that alcohol was already starting to do. In fact, it was getting harder and harder to wake up after a night of drinking. Not on school days—it hadn't escalated that far yet. But certainly, every weekend.

But first, I had to get a regular education.

I was the pale Canadian kid with a quick mouth, and there's something about an outsider that piques the curiosity of teenagers—we seem exotic, especially if we have a Canadian accent and can name the entire roster of the Toronto Maple Leafs. Plus, my dad was the Old Spice guy; for years on their TVs, my schoolmates had seen Dad dressed as a sailor on shore leave—replete with peacoat and black sailor cap—slinging that iconic white bottle at clean-shaven bit actors while urging them to "Clean up your life with Old Spice!" It may not have been Shakespeare, but he was famous enough, and he was tall and handsome and very funny, and he was my dad.

Dad was also a drinker. Every evening he'd arrive home from whichever set he'd been on, or *not* been on, pour himself a healthy slug of vodka tonic, and announce, "This is the best thing that's happened to me all day."

He said this about a drink. Sitting next to his son on a couch in Los Angeles. Then he'd have four more and take the fifth to bed.

Dad taught me many good things, too. But he certainly taught me how to drink. It's still no accident that my drink of choice was a double vodka tonic, and my thought every time was, *This is the best thing that happened to me all day.*

There was a difference, though—a big one. Without fail, next morning at seven Dad would be up, bright and breezy; he'd shower and apply his aftershave (never Old Spice), and head out to the bank or his agent or to set—he never missed a thing. Dad was the epitome of a functional drinker. I, on the other hand, was already struggling to wake up and causing whispers with those who drank around me.

I watched my father drink six vodka tonics and live a perfectly functional life, so, I figured it was possible. I figured I'd be able to do the same thing. But there was something lurking in my shadows and my genes, like a creepy beast in a dark place, something I had that my father did not, and it would be a decade before we knew what it was. Alcoholism, addiction—you call it what you want, I've chosen to call it a Big Terrible Thing.

But I was George Gibbs, too.

I don't remember what my classmates thought of this newbie showing up with his pale skin and Canadian brogue, but I didn't care. SparkNotes describes Gibbs as "an archetypal all-American boy. A local baseball star and the president of his senior class in high school, he also possesses innocence and sensitivity. He is a good son . . . [but for] George [to] stifle his emotions is difficult, if not impossible."

So, pretty much dead-on, then.

At home, though, my dad had vodka all over the house. One afternoon, when he and Debbie were gone, I decided to take a big swig of vodka. As the warm spice of it jangled down my throat and innards, I felt that well-being, that ease, that sense that everything was going to be fine, I saw the clouds from my backyard in Ottawa and I figured I'd head out into LA, to walk in this bliss, this seventy-two-degree heaven, the star of the school play wandering like a drunk Odysseus through the star-studded streets. Clancy Sigal, writing for the London *Observer* about the 1984 LA Olympics, noted that whenever he visited the city, he sensed that he was "passing through a soft membrane that seals Los Angeles off from the real, painful world." Here I was, too, slipping through that soft, vodka-softened membrane, into a place where there was no pain, where the world was both real, and not . . . and yet, as I turned a corner, something else hit me that had never occurred to me before—death, fear of death, questions like "Why are we all here?" "What's the meaning of all this?" "What's the point?" "How do we all arrive at this?" "What are human beings?" "What is air?" All these questions poured into my brain like a tidal wave.

I was just rounding a fucking corner!

The drink, and that walk, opened a chasm in me that's still there. I was so troubled; I was an extremely screwed up guy. The questions cascaded like alcohol into a glass; all I'd done was what Sigal had done—I had arrived in Los Angeles, along with gymnasts and sprinters and horses and writers and actors and wannabes and has-beens and Old Spice actors, and now, a great void had opened up beneath me. I was standing at the edge of great pit of fire, like "The Pit of Hell" in the Karakum Desert of central Turkmenistan. The drink, and that walk, had created a thinker, a seeker, but not some soft-focus, Buddhist crap—one who was on the edge of a deep crater of flames, haunted by the lack of answers, by being *unaccompanied,* by wanting love but being terrified of abandonment, by wanting excitement, but being unable to appreciate it, by a dick that didn't work. I was face-to-face with the four last things: death, judgment, heaven, and hell, a fifteen-year-old boy brought up close to the face of eschatology, so close he could smell the vodka on its breath.

Years later, my father, too, would take his own meaningful walk: he had had a bad night on the drink where he fell through some bushes or something, and he talked to Debbie about it the following morning and she said, "Is this the way you want to live your life?" And he said, no—then he went for a walk and quit drinking and hasn't had a drop since.

Excuse me? You went for a walk and quit drinking? I have spent upward of $7 million trying to get sober. I have been to six thousand AA meetings. (Not an exaggeration, more an educated guess.) I've been to rehab fifteen times. I've been in a mental institution, gone to therapy twice a week for thirty years, been to death's door. And you went for a fucking walk?

I'll tell you where you can take a walk.

But my dad can't write a play, star on *Friends,* help the helpless. And he doesn't have $7 million to spend on anything. Life has its trade-offs, I suppose.

This begs the question—would I trade places with him?

Why don't we get to that one later?

On the jukebox, I'd put a few dimes in and play "Don't Give Up" by Peter Gabriel and Kate Bush over and over; sometimes I'd slip in

"Mainstreet" by Bob Seger, or "Here Comes the Sun" by the Beatles. One of the reasons we loved the 101 Coffee Shop was because they kept the jukebox up-to-date; plus, it felt like old Hollywood in there, with its caramel-colored leather booths and the sense that at any moment someone super famous might walk in—you know, to pretend that fame didn't change anything.

By 1986, I was pretty sure fame would change everything, and I yearned for it more than any other person on the face of the planet. I *needed* it. It was the only thing that would fix me. I was certain of it. Living in LA you would occasionally bump into a celebrity, or you'd see Billy Crystal at the Improv, make note of Nicolas Cage in the next booth, and I just knew they had no problems—in fact, all their problems had been washed away. They were famous.

I'd been auditioning steadily and had even gotten a gig or two—most notably, in the first season of *Charles in Charge*. I played Ed, a preppy, plaid-sweater-and-tie-wearing square who confidently intoned his one main line: "My father's a Princeton man, and a surgeon—I'd like to follow in his footsteps!" But it was work, and TV, and without much more thought I found that I was already skipping school to hang out in diners with girls who liked my accent and my quick patter and my budding TV career and my ability to listen to them. Thanks to my training back in Canada, I knew I was able to listen to and help women in crisis. (If you're a woman and you are in duress and you sing a song about it, I will listen to it over and over and over.) So there I was, in the 101 Coffee Shop, holding court with a gaggle of young women, quick with a line and a smirk and a willing ear; I'd ditched the preppy, *Charles in Charge* look as soon as I'd left the Universal lot in Studio City and was dressed like any cool teen in the mid-1980s: denim jacket over a plaid shirt, or probably wearing a Kinks T-shirt before going home to listen to Air Supply.

When you're nearly sixteen, days seem endless, especially when you're charming a bunch of young women in a greasy spoon in Holly-wood. I must have been really on that day, too, because as I joked around, a middle-aged guy walked past the booth and put a note on a napkin in front of me on the table and walked away and right out the door. The girls all stopped chattering; I looked at the guy's back as he left, then did a prototype of Chandler's double take, getting more laughs.

"Well, read it!" one of the girls said.

I carefully picked up the note as though it were covered in poison, and slowly opened it. In spidery handwriting it said,

I want you to be in my next movie. Please give me a call at this number. . . . William Richert.

"What does it say?" another girl said.

"It says, 'Could you be more handsome and talented?'" I said, deadpan.

"No," the first girl said, "it does *not!*"

The tenor of her disbelief caused another round of laughter as I said, "Oh, thanks *very* much," but once the laughter died down, I said, "It says, 'I want you to be in my next movie. Please give me a call at this number. William Richert.'"

One of the girls said, "Well, *that* sounds legitimate. . . ."

"Right?" I said. "This movie is going to be shot in the back of a windowless van."

At home that evening, I asked my dad what to do. He was on his third vodka tonic—there was just enough cogency left in his tank to get a useful answer. By now, he was starting to get a little frustrated by the fact that my career was beginning to percolate; he wasn't jealous, but he was aware that I was younger than he was, and that the road was rising to meet me, and that if I played my cards right, I might have a better career than the one he was having. That said, he never showed anything but support—there was no "Great Santini" going on here. My dad was my hero, and he was proud of me.

"Well, Matty," he said, "can't hurt to call."

But whatever my dad said, I knew I'd call that number. I'd known it when I first read the note. This was Hollywood, after all—that's supposed to be how it happens, right?

It turned out that William Richert didn't want to make a movie in the back of a van.

Richert had been watching me perform for the girls that day in the 101 and had seen enough of *The Matthew Perry Show* to want to cast me in a movie he was making based on his novel *A Night in the Life of Jimmy Reardon*. The novel and the movie are set in Chicago in the early 1960s; Reardon is a teenager who is being forced to go to business school when all he really wants to do is get enough money to buy a plane ticket to Hawaii, where his girlfriend lives. I was to play Reardon's best friend, Fred Roberts, who, like Ed in *Charles in Charge,* was well-off and a bit snobby, and suffered from chronic virginity. (I could relate.) I ditched the preppy look once again, as Fred was to be dressed in a gray felt flat cap and leather jacket over a dress shirt and tie, oh, and black leather gloves. In the movie, the character of Reardon sleeps with my girlfriend, but that's OK, because playing Reardon would be someone it would be a privilege to be cheated on by.

The list of geniuses who were ahead of their time is too long to detail here—suffice to say, near the top of any such list should be my costar in *A Night in the Life of Jimmy Reardon,* River Phoenix. This movie was my first job, and I'm acutely aware it would be a better story if the movie was a huge hit, but all that really matters is that I learned how to make a film, and I got to know River, who personified beauty in every way. There was an aura around that guy. But he made you feel too comfortable to even be jealous of him. *Stand by Me* had just come out—which he *excelled* in—and when you walked into a room with him, his charisma was such that you instantly became part of the furniture.

The movie was shot in Chicago, so there I was, just turning seventeen years old, and heading to the Windy City, sans parents, sans anything, once again an unaccompanied minor, but this time it felt like freedom, like what I was born to do. I had never been so excited in my life. It was in Chicago, and on this movie, and with River Phoenix, that I fell deeply in love with acting—and the cherry on top of this deeply magical time was that River and I became firm friends. He and I drank beer and shot pool on North Rush Street (*The Color of Money* had just come out, and pool was the thing to do). We had a per diem; we flirted with girls, though that's as far as it went for me because, well, you know.

River was a beautiful man, inside and out—too beautiful for this world, it turned out. River was a better actor than me; I was funnier. But I certainly held my own in our scenes—no small feat, when I look back decades later. But more important, River just looked at the world in a different way than we all did, and that made him fascinating, and charismatic, and, yes, beautiful, but not in a Gap ad kinda way (though he was that, too)—in a there-is-no-one-else-in-the-world-like-him kind of way. Not to mention he was rocketing to stardom, yet you would never know it.

And somewhere in all that magic, River Phoenix and I managed to shoot a movie together.

Later, River would say that he wasn't happy with his performance in *Jimmy Reardon,* claiming he hadn't been the right person for the role. But to me he was the right person for every role. He could do anything. I remember seeing him in the movie *Sneakers*—he was making choices no one else would make. Not to mention holding his own with legends like Robert Redford and the wonderful Sidney Poitier. (If you haven't seen it, you should—it's highly entertaining.)

The movie *we* made would eventually tank at the box office, but it didn't matter. We'd been somewhere beautiful and magical, even if it was just North Rush Street in freezing Chicago. And it was the best experience of my life—I knew it, too. My work was done in about three weeks, but they (probably River, actually) liked me so much that they kept me on the movie till the end. Things didn't get better than this.

One night, alone in my tiny room at the Tremont hotel, as things were drawing to a close, I knelt down and said to the universe: "Don't you ever forget this."

And I have not.

But magic never lasts; whatever holes you're filling seem to keep opening back up. (It's like Whac-A-Mole.) Maybe it was because I was always trying to fill a spiritual hole with a material thing. . . . I don't know. Either way, when it came to the last day of shooting, I sat on my bed in my Chicago hotel room and cried. I sobbed and sobbed because I knew even then I would never again have an experience like that—my first movie, far from home, free to flirt and drink and hang out with a brilliant young man like River Phoenix.

I would sob again seven years later on Halloween 1993, when River died in front of the Viper Room in West Hollywood. (I heard the screaming from my apartment; went back to bed; woke up to the news.) After his passing, his mom wrote, in reference to drug use, "the spirits of [River's] generation are being worn down," and by then, I was drinking every night. But it would be years before I understood exactly what she meant.

With *Jimmy Reardon* in the can, I flew back to LA from Chicago and returned to planet Earth in the form of high school. I was still auditioning for tons of things but wasn't getting much traction. I was booking mostly comedy stuff, and I ended up guest starring on just about everything. My grades still sucked, though. I graduated with a 2.0 average, exactly. All that I asked for my graduation was that my mother and father both attend, which they kindly did. The incredibly awkward dinner that followed seemed only to underline the fact that the child they shared was destined to be uncomfortable as a default, even though he was also usually the funniest person in the room. But that night at dinner I was only the third funniest, and the third most beautiful. At least a childhood dream of them being together had come true, if for one night only, and even then, if only in embarrassing silences and barbs passed back and forth like some angry cosmic joint.

I am grateful to my parents for attending that dinner—it was an incredibly kind and completely unnecessary thing for them to do. But it crystallized something for me that I had not anticipated. It was *right* that they weren't together. They were not to be. They were correct to be apart. They both subsequently found the person they were meant to be with. And I am incredibly happy for both of them. Matty no longer needed to make the wish that his parents would be together.

It would be decades before they were in the same room together again. And then, for a very different reason.

The acting roles, and the quick mind and mouth, and the friendship with River, and the denim jacket over plaid shirt all combined to help me land a beautiful girlfriend named Tricia Fisher. (Eddie Fisher and Connie Stevens's daughter—that's right, Carrie Fisher's half sister. This girl was no stranger to charm.)

The rhyming poetry of her name alone should have made her irresistible—plus, I was eighteen now, and was pretty sure everything worked, except when I was in the company of another human being. I carried impotence around with me like a great ugly secret, like I carried around everything else. Accordingly, as my relationship with Tricia Fisher deepened, thoughts naturally turned to a physical consummation, but I announced confidently that like a Roman Catholic, I wanted to wait—not many eighteen-year-old males say that, by the way, nor should they. This, of course, caught her interest. When she pressed me on why, I said something about "commitment" or "the future" or "the state of the planet" or "my career," anything, in fact, to avoid telling her that I was softer than the caramel-colored booths at the 101 Coffee Shop when push came to shove. And I couldn't let push come to shove or my secret would be out.

My firmness, at least in my conviction to wait, lasted two months. But dams burst, and the make-out sessions that didn't lead anywhere were beginning to cause us both to hyperventilate. Tricia Fisher made up her mind.

"Matty," she said, "I've had enough of this. Let's go."

She took my hand and led me to the bed in my tiny studio apartment in Westwood.

I was horrified, and also excited, though I was still haunted by an inner dialogue of fear:

—Maybe this time, and with someone I care deeply for, my previous inabilities will dissolve. . . . Dissolve—bad word.
—Should I have a stiff drink beforehand? Well, stiff's the problem, pal.
—Maybe it won't be as hard as I feared. Not as hard? Matty, stop doing that. . . .

Before this brief dialogue could turn into a threepenny opera, Tricia had disrobed both of us and pulled us into bed. I distinctly remember the foothills of lovemaking as pure bliss, but like a neophyte mountaineer, I feared that beyond a certain base camp, no amount of oxygen would help me get any higher. And so it proved to be. How else to put it?—I just couldn't get that thing to work right. I thought of everything, spinning complex, erotic images through my addled brain, hoping to land on something—*one thing, that's all it will take!*—that would firm up my commitment to future bliss. Nothing worked; nothing. Horrified yet again, I forsook the loving arms of Tricia Fisher and padded my slim, naked body over to a chair in the apartment. (It was like you could bend me in half if you wanted to.) I sat there, soft, and sad, my two hands cupped over my lap like a nun's during Vespers, doing my best to cover my embarrassment and maybe a tear or two.

Tricia Fisher was once again having none of it.

"Matty!" she said. "What the hell is going on? Don't you find me attractive?"

"Oh, no, of course I find you attractive!" I said. The physical issues were bad enough, but worse, I could feel an escalating sense of abandonment slipping in through the windows of that room. What if Tricia left me? What if I wasn't enough, like I always wasn't enough? What if I was destined to be unaccompanied again?

I was desperate; I really liked her; and I really wanted to believe that love could save me.

There was only one thing to do. I had to tell her everything.

"Tricia," I said, "back when I was in Ottawa, I was so nervous about making out with a girl that I drank six beers. . . ." I left nothing out; told Tricia the whole, shameful tale, and I ended by admitting that I was impotent, and always would be, that it was no use, there was nothing to be done, that my desire for her could never be matched by anything solid, anything worthy of the name. But I was desperate for her not to abandon me, too, so if there was anything I could do to keep her, all she had to do was ask and on and on and on I went, burbling like a little river in the spring.

Dear Tricia Fisher—she let me babble on and on, as I tried my best to convince her that no matter how beautiful she was—and she was very beautiful indeed—it didn't matter: I was destined to repeat that night in Ottawa for the rest of my days.

Eventually, I wound down, and took a deep breath. Tricia said very calmly, very simply, "Come with me. That's never going to happen again."

With that, she walked over to me, took my hand, led me back to bed, laid me down, and sure enough . . . sheer glory, for two whole minutes! That night, by the dint of a miraculous universe and the ministrations of a beautiful young woman who deserved better, I finally first misplaced my virginity then lost it altogether, and impotence has not been part of my vocabulary since, just as she promised it wouldn't be. Everything about me—at least physically—works just fine.

And how, pray tell, did you manage to pay such a debt, Mr. Perry, such an onerous debt to the woman who saved your life in one of the most meaningful ways imaginable?

Why, good reader, I paid that debt to Tricia by sleeping with almost every woman in Southern California.

(On one such date back then, with another eighteen-year-old, at one point the woman stopped dinner and said, "Let's go back to your house and have sex."

Sex still being relatively new to me I agreed right away. We went to my apartment and as we crossed the threshold, she stopped me and said, "Wait wait wait! I can't do this! You have to take me home."

Which of course I did.

The following day, I felt bothered by what had happened, and already in therapy, I shared the story with my therapist.

"I'm going to tell you a story and it's going to help you," he said. "When a woman comes over to your place, and she takes her shoes off, you are going to get laid. If she leaves them on, you won't."

I was eighteen then; I am fifty-two now; and he has been right 100 percent of the time. There have been times I've cheated a little and left a pair of shoes at my doorstep as a kind of hint that this is where the shoes go. But that therapist's insight has been correct every single time—if a woman keeps her shoes on, it's a make-out session at best.)

Years later, Tricia and I would date again, while *Friends* was at its peak. She didn't abandon me, but old fears crept up, and I ended the relationship. I only wish I could truly feel that she didn't abandon me, truly believe that. Maybe things would be better. Maybe vodka tonic wouldn't have become my drink of choice.

Maybe everything would be different. Or maybe, not.

But to Tricia, and those after her, I thank you. And to all the women that I left, simply because I was afraid that they were going to leave me, I deeply apologize from the bottom of my heart. If I only knew then, what I know now. . . .

Matman

"This is the pitch," I said. "Ya ready?"

Adam said, "Sure! Lay it on me!"

I took a long drag of my Marlboro, pushed the phone closer to my cheek, gave a long exhale of tar and nicotine and pain, and began selling.

"OK," I said. "It's about this guy. You'd recognize him. His name is Matt and he's about fifty years old. And he's very very famous from doing a super beloved TV show years ago. But now, when the movie starts, we meet him and he's got a pot belly—there are piles of empty pizza boxes in his apartment, all piled up like that totem in *Close Encounters of the Third Kind,* you know, the one they made out of mashed potatoes . . . anyway, his life is a little bit of a mess. He is lost. Then, out of the blue, a distant relative of his dies and leaves him $2 billion. And he uses the money to become a superhero."

"I love it!" says Adam.

Then he said, "Did you really inherit two billion dollars?"

Adam's a funny guy.

"No, no!" I said. "It's just the character who inherits the money.

Does any of that spark anything with you? Because if it does, what's our next move? You're the big shoulders."

"I'm not really the big shoulders," Adam said, though we both know he is. I appreciated his modesty, but modesty won't get you even a "fuck you" in Hollywood.

"What do you mean?" I said. "Of course you're the big shoulders. . . ."

This was, after all, Adam McKay, the guy who directed *Anchorman* and *Step Brothers* and a bunch of other big stuff. At the time we were chatting, he was making *Don't Look Up,* that movie about a giant asteroid heading toward Earth, you know, the one that stars Leonardo DiCaprio, Jennifer Lawrence, Timothée Chalamet, Mark Rylance, Cate Blanchett, Tyler Perry, Jonah Hill, even Ariana Grande *and* Meryl Streep—amazing cast.

I was in *Don't Look Up* at one point, too, and even though I was also heading to rehab in Switzerland, I nevertheless went to Boston to shoot my bit. While there, I pitched a line to Adam that he loved and which became the blow to the scene, which is what you're always hoping for (he ended up not using the scene—shit happens; no bigs). The point being, Adam McKay and I got along really well, and here he was, loving my pitch.

At the time I was in pain from the scar tissue from the surgeries, so I needed pain meds, but I'd get addicted to them, of course, which would only cause more damage to my insides . . . but feeling a bit better, I was happy recently when I got a call from Adam. We were just chatting, but in Hollywood there's no such thing as just chatting, so I figured what the hell—why is he calling me? And when he never seemed to get to his point, I seized the moment and I pitched him my idea.

"Anyway, Mr. Big Shoulders," I said, ignoring his false modesty, "what do you think?"

You know when there's a pause in a conversation that in hindsight you wish could have lasted forever so you don't have to hear the rest of it?

"I don't think you're talking to the person you think you're talking to," "Adam" said.

"What? Well, who is this?" I said.

"It's Adam McLean. We met six years ago. I'm a computer salesman."

If you've seen *Don't Look Up,* you'll know that at the end . . . well, let's just say that when I realized it was Adam McLean, not Adam McKay, a huge fucking asteroid smacked into my brain.

I have history in this kind of shit, too. Years earlier, Bruce Willis won the People's Choice award for Best Actor for *The Sixth Sense* and asked me to present it to him. That night, backstage, I met Haley Joel Osment and M. Night Shyamalan, and spoke to both of them for about ten minutes.

Six months later, I was with some friends at the Sunset Marquis Hotel, and who should walk in but M. Night Shyamalan.

"Hey, Matthew," he said, "long time no see! Can I sit down?"

Can he sit down? He had just written and directed *The Sixth Sense.* He was the next Steven Spielberg, of course he can sit down! I was a few drinks in and having a good time (this was when alcohol alone still worked for me).

Eventually my friends filtered out, and it was just M. Night and me, sitting there, kickin' it. I remember making a mental note that we were not talking show business at all, just talking about love and loss and girls and LA and all the other stuff people chat about at bars. He seemed to be having a really good time, too—laughing at all of my dumb jokes—and I began to think, *Hey, this guy likes me! He must be just a huge* Friends *fan or something, because he really seems super focused on everything I'm saying.*

I usually never do this—I've been burned by this line of thinking way too many times—but I began to have wild fantasies about what this could do for my career. He told me that there was another bar that had just opened across town and asked if I wanted to go with him. Did I want to go with him? He was M. Night Fuckin' Shyamalan! Of course I wanted to go with him.

We went to the valet, picked up our cars, and I followed him across town to this new place, all the while certain that I was going to be the star of his next, huge movie—yeah, there was going to be a new, awesome, twisty movie and the trick ending was going to be me!

My head was doing cartwheels. I can't explain why—he just seemed like he loved me, and my work, and I was just drunk enough to think that this was going to be a life-changing night. As we took our seats at the new place, I felt comfortable [read: drunk] enough to say that we should work together sometime. All at once, a strange look came across his face, and I remember immediately regretting having said it. He excused himself to go to the bathroom, and while he was gone, someone I knew a bit came up to me asked me how my night was going.

I said, "Well, I've been hanging out with M. Night Shyamalan all night and I'm telling you, the guy loves me." My buddy was impressed . . . that is, until M. Night returned from the bathroom.

"Matty," my pal said, looking closely at M. Night, "could I have a word in private?"

This was weird as fuck, but drink will make almost anything plausible, so I stepped away from my magical evening with M. Night for a moment.

"Matty," my friend whispered, "that is *not* M. Night Shyamalan."

This revelation caused me to attempt to fully focus my vodka-softened eyes for a moment, and through the gloom of the dark bar I squinted hard at N. Night Shyamalan.

Not.

Even.

Close.

Turns out, "M. Night" was actually just an Indian gentleman who looked the tiniest bit like M. Night Shyamalan (maybe it was N. Night Shyamalan?), and who was, in reality, the maître d' at Mr. Chow Beverly Hills, a hip restaurant in LA that I frequented . . . and that I no longer frequent, because I told its maître d' that we should work together sometime. *What kind of a night did he think he was having?* I thought.

3

Baggage

I lived in a perpetual state of *Groundhog Day.* It's my favorite movie for a reason.

Every evening, I would head to the Formosa Café on Santa Monica Boulevard in West Hollywood with my friends. There were two signs over the bar: the one under all the headshots read WHERE THE STARS DINE. The other read WINE BY THE GLASS, but we didn't drink by the glass—we drank by the pint and the quart and the gallon . . . and vodka, not wine.

"We" was Hank Azaria, David Pressman, Craig Bierko, and me. We had formed our very own mini–Rat Pack.

I'd met Hank first, when I was sixteen. We were at the CBS lot auditioning for a pilot starring Ellen Greene (of *Little Shop of Horrors*). We both got cast, and he played my uncle in the pilot. We got along so well that when I left the nest to move out on my own, I moved into a studio apartment in his building. He was already a seriously funny guy, and by the time I met him he was doing a ton of voiceover work. That gig would eventually lead him to becoming an incredibly wealthy guy, but back at the start of it, all we wanted was fame. Fame, fame, fame, that's all we wanted. And girls, and erm, fame. It was all we cared about because, at least for me, I figured being famous would fill the great hole that was endlessly growing inside of me.

But being prefamous, it was a hole I filled with alcohol.

I was drinking all the time—I spent my college years drinking at the Formosa—in fact, in drinking I got a 4.0 GPA and was Alkoól Beta Kappa. Love of alcohol had indeed become the helmsman of my life, but I don't think I realized just how much it controlled me until one night when I was out with my girlfriend at the time, Gaby. Gaby would go on to write for *Veep* and a bunch of other stuff and be a friend for life, but that night, she and I and a group of friends went to a magic show in Universal City. I remember ordering some specialty drink, simmering with alcohol, to sip on while the guy produced rabbits out of hats, or whatever, but eventually the endless lines of silk scarves out of sleeves grew wearisome, and we all headed back to Gaby's apartment to hang out. Gaby didn't have any alcohol at home, which is, of course, totally fine, but for me at the age of twenty-one, all of a sudden this creeping feeling came over me for the first time. I felt my blood on fire for more to drink; I really wanted another drink, and I could think of nothing else.

It was that night when I first felt the *obsession* for alcohol. I noticed that no one else seemed even the slightest bit fazed by the lack of drink at Gaby's—but I had that overpowering pull, like a great magnet and I was just little shards of iron. I was freaked-out by this, especially as it was me and only me who seemed to be struggling. So, I decided to not go find more to drink that night . . . but it left me unable to sleep, uncomfortable, tossing and turning, lost to it. Restless, irritable, and discontented until the sun finally rose.

What was happening to me? What was wrong with me? Why was I the only person there who had been dying for another drink? I couldn't tell anyone this was happening, because even I didn't understand it. I think for many years my drinking was a secret to people—well, at least the extent of it. Certainly back then. I was just a college-age kid wasting the equivalent of his college years on booze and women and making my guy friends, and women, laugh. What was there to admit?

But what no one knew was I was drinking alone—that remained a secret. How much I drank when I was drinking alone depended entirely on the year. Eventually I'd work my way up to that party bottle with the handle—killed that in two days, by myself. But that night of the magic show, even then I was freaking out. What's going on? I've never experienced this feeling before in my life. Why can't I think of a single fucking solitary thing except a drink? If you're at a bar, you just order another drink . . . but when it's the middle of the night, you don't tend to lie wide awake wishing you had one in your hand. That was new. That was different. That was terrifying. And that was a secret.

Ten years later, I read the following words in the Big Book of Alcoholics Anonymous: "Drinkers think they are trying to escape, but really they are trying to overcome a mental disorder they didn't know they had."

Eureka!—someone understands me. But reading that was both wonderful and horrible. It meant I wasn't alone—there were others who thought like me—but it also meant I was an alcoholic and would have to quit drinking one day at a time, for the rest of my life.

How was I ever going to have fun again?

I can't decide if I actually like people or not.

People have needs, they lie, cheat, steal, or worse: they want to talk about themselves. Alcohol was my best friend because it never wanted to talk about itself. It was just always there, the mute dog at my heel, gazing up at me, always ready to go on a walk. It took away so much of the pain, including the fact that when I was alone, I was lonely, and that when I was with people, I was lonely, too. It made movies better, songs better, it made *me* better. It made me comfortable with where I was instead of wishing I was somewhere—anywhere—else. It made me content to hang out with the woman in front of me rather than continually wondering if life would be better if I were dating someone else. It took away being an outsider in my own family. It removed the walls all around me, except one, even if for a while. It allowed me to control my feelings and, in doing so, control my world. Like a friend, it was there for me. And I was fairly certain I would go crazy without it.

And I'm right about that, by the way—I would have gone crazy without it.

It made me want to be a completely different person. To give it up seemed impossible. Learning to move forward in life without it was tantamount to asking someone to go about his or her day without breathing. For that, I will always be grateful to alcohol. It finally beat me into a state of reasonableness.

According to Malcom Gladwell, if you did anything for ten thousand hours, you could be an expert. This made me an expert in two areas: 1980s tennis and drinking. Only one of those subjects is important enough to save a life.

I'll let you guess which one.

But when I wanted to feel less alone among people, it was Hank Azaria, David Pressman, and eventually Craig Bierko I chose.

Weirdly, I'd played a character with the surname Azarian on *Beverly Hills, 90210*. Getting a guest spot on episode nineteen of the twenty-two-episode first season was a big deal. *Beverly Hills, 90210* hadn't yet reached cultural phenomenon status by the time I played Roger Azarian, Beverly Hills High tennis star and the son of a hard-charging, distant, businessman father—but the themes in that episode (teen depression, suicide, and learning disabilities) marked it out as a show that wouldn't shy away from real shit, however privileged its milieu.

The episode, which borrowed its title from T. S. Eliot of all people ("April Is the Cruelest Month"), opens with me hitting the crap out of some tennis balls, showing off my Canadian-ranked form, my big, whipped forehands and aggressive backhand winners, showcasing the fact that I could really play. I was even using a throwback, Björn Borg–style wooden Donnay racket with the tiny head, which I manage to break in the scene by hitting too hard. Jason Priestley, in the role of Brandon Walsh, noting my thinly veiled rage, proceeds to ask me how many rackets I go through in a week, and in an art-imitating-life moment, I say, "Depends on whose face I see on the ball."

I couldn't escape stairwells, even when I was playing a fictional character on a TV show. By the end of the episode, I've shared a screenplay with Brandon, gotten drunk, held a gun to my own face, and ended up in a locked psychiatric ward—only the gun bit was play-acting, the rest was Method.

I wasn't yet twenty-two. For a few years I'd been a guest actor, doing a series here, a series there, guest starring roles.

The point was, I was working. My first biggish break had come when I was cast in *Second Chance*, though my casting was overshadowed by who *wasn't* cast.

I still think *Second Chance* had a great premise: a forty-year-old guy called Charles Russell dies in a hovercraft accident (because that happens *all* the time) and goes to see Saint Peter in his office. If the light shines gold on Charles as he stands in judgment, he goes to heaven; if it shines red, he goes to hell—but if it shines blue, as it does in Mr. Russell's case, he was called a Blue Lighter, meaning, they didn't know what to do with him. So, Saint Peter decides to send him back to Earth to meet his fifteen-year-old self and guide him through a life of better decision-making. That way, by the time he once again boards a hovercraft at forty, when he dies the second time, because he's been a better person, the light will change from a we-don't-know-what-to-do-with-you blue to a we're-sold, welcome-to-eternity gold. Can you think of a more perfect premise for a father-son acting team? And my father and

I duly auditioned. Then, disaster—I got a green light to be the son of a Blue Lighter, and Dad got no light at all.

"They want you. They don't want me," Dad said when he heard the news. I guess I threw him a hard-to-read look—after all, I'd gotten a huge part, even if he hadn't, so I imagine my face combined sorrow for him and glee for me—so much so that he said, "Do I have to *repeat* it? They want *you*. They *don't* want me."

My father's hurt feelings aside, I had just booked my first TV show. I was making five grand a week; I was seventeen years old. My ego was off the charts; I thought I was the shit, just like everyone thought *Second Chance* was. It came in as number 93 of the ninety-three ranked shows that season. For the final nine episodes after the initial thirteen, the whole Saint Peter / Blue Lighter stuff had been forgotten and the show just followed me and my pals in our various adventures. So, it didn't matter that the show remained ninety-third in a list of ninety-three— someone important had liked me enough to build a show around me, which only increased my ego to epic proportions. And might well have set me up for success later.

My father dealt with this news by not attending a single taping ex- cept the very last one. He had his reasons, I suppose.

Accordingly, I was able to score various guest roles after that, and two years later I got another series, this time in a show starring Valerie Bertinelli. The show, called *Sydney,* followed the exploits of Valerie as a private eye (!), and I played her fast-talking brother—that's all you'll ever need to know about those thirteen episodes (*Sydney* was canceled after one half season). But despite its failure to ignite audiences, I'll never forget two things about *Sydney.*

First, Valerie's lawyer/love interest in the show was played by an ac- tor named Craig Bierko—almost immediately after meeting Craig on set, I called Hank Azaria and said, "He sounds the way we do!" which was the highest praise I could give someone. But before I could truly get to see how funny Craig was, there was the second thing I should tell you about *Sydney*—during filming, I fell madly in love with Valerie Bertinelli, who was clearly in a troubled marriage and truly getting off on two of the funniest guys on the planet adoring her and heaping their attention on her.

Valerie Bertinelli—those seven syllables once stirred every part of my soul and other parts.

In the early 1990s, there was no one more attractive than Valerie. Not only was she stunning and vivacious, but she also had this great, booming, adorable laugh, which Craig and I longed to hear all day long. Now that Craig and I were cast, it was as if Valerie had two new clowns to play with, and we threw ourselves into those roles with abandon. The three of us had a lot of fun.

But for me, being on *Sydney* and playing the fool with Valerie was more than just fun—it was serious shit. I was having to hide my love for her as we worked (this wouldn't be the last time this happened), which was desperately difficult. My crush was crushing; not only was she way out of my league, but she was also married to one of the most famous rock stars on the planet, Eddie Van Halen. Back when we were making *Sydney,* Eddie's band, Van Halen, were in the middle of a string of four, back-to-back, number one albums—they were arguably the biggest band on the planet in the late 1980s, early 1990s, and Eddie was arguably the greatest rock guitarist on the planet at the time, too.

As for me, well, I was always able to get laid because I made women laugh, but I knew that being funny always came in second to musicians. (In the world of music, there's a hierarchy, too—it's my contention that bass players tend to get laid first, because they're stolid and cool and their fingers move in gentle yet powerful ways [except for Paul McCartney; he never got laid first]; drummers come next because they're all power and grit; then guitarists because they get those fancy solos; then, weirdly, the lead singer, because even though he's out there up front, he never quite looks fully sexy when he has to throw his head back and reveal his molars to hit a high note.) Whatever the correct order, I knew I was way behind Eddie Van Halen—not only was he a musician, which means he was able to get laid more easily than some-one who is funny, but he was also already married to the object of my desire.

It is important to point out here that my feelings for Valerie were real. I was completely captivated—I mean, I was obsessed with her and harbored elaborate fantasies about her leaving Eddie Van Halen and living out the rest of her days with me. I was nineteen and lived in a one-bedroom apartment on Laurel Canyon and Burbank (called Club California, mind you). But fantasies and first loves don't know about real estate, they don't know about real *anything*.

I didn't stand a fucking chance. Of course.

That said, there was one night . . . I was over at Valerie and Eddie's house, just hanging out and gazing at Valerie, trying to make her laugh. When you made her laugh, you felt ten feet tall. As the night pro-gressed, it was clear that Eddie had enjoyed the fruits of the vine a little too hard, one more time, and eventually he just passed out, not ten feet away from us, but still. This was my chance! If you think I didn't actually have a chance in hell you'd be wrong, dear reader—Valerie and I had a long, elaborate make-out session. It was *happening*—maybe she felt the same way I did. I told her I had thought about doing that for a long time, and she had said it right back to me. "Heaven" eventu-ally wrapped up, and I hopped in my black Honda CRX and headed back to Club California with a hard-on that could have propped up the Leaning Tower of Pisa, and a nineteen-year-old head flooded with dreams of a life spent with the object of my affection/obsession.

I told Craig Bierko about this the following day, and he passed on some desperately needed advice and reality, though it was advice I wasn't ready to take.

"Be careful," he said. *He's just jealous,* I thought as I prepared for the following day of work, but this time with Valerie as my new girlfriend.

The following day at work did not go as I expected it would. Valerie made no mention of what had happened and was behaving—as she should have been—like this was just a normal day. I quickly got the hint and also played the role I was supposed to, but inside I was devastated. Many a tearful night and spending the bulk of my daytimes sleeping off hangovers in my tiny trailer—not to mention hours and hours of watching Craig's part get bigger as Valerie's love interest on the show— all made for a very sad disillusioned teenager. The show did very badly, and I was so grateful that four weeks after that fateful night, *Sydney* got canceled, and I didn't have to see Valerie anymore.

She, of course, had done nothing wrong, but having to see her every day and pretend I was fine about everything reminded me too much of what I had to do every day with my mother back in Ottawa, Canada.

I have spent my life being attracted to unavailable women. It doesn't take a psychology degree to figure out that this had something to do with my relationship with my mother. My mother captivated every room she entered. I vividly remember being at some fancy ballroom when I was about six years old, and when my mom came in, every head in the room turned. I wanted her to turn and look at me in these moments, but she was working and could not—it took me only thirty-seven years to work that out.

Ever since then I have been addicted to "the turn." Once the turn happened, I could start making a woman laugh and making her want me sexually. Once the sex was done, reality set in, and I realized I didn't know these women at all. They were available, so I had no need for them. I had to get back out there and try to make them make the turn. That's why I slept with so many women. I was trying to re-create my childhood and win.

I knew none of this at the time, of course, and just thought something had gone wrong with them. Surprise surprise, everyone—Canadian actor-boy had some major mommy issues.

But I was nineteen, and life quickly moved on for everyone. A year later, Van Halen released the aptly titled *For Unlawful Carnal Knowledge,* and I went back to trying to pick up women at the Formosa. And trying to re-create "the turn" as often as humanly possible.

Sometimes it worked; but every time, I left at 1:40 A.M. to rush to the nearest liquor store so that I could score more vodka and keep drinking deep into the night. I'd sit there, emptying the bottle (eventually the one with the handle), watching *The Goodbye Girl* or even the Michael Keaton movie *Clean and Sober* (figure *that* one out), until just like Eddie Van Halen, I passed out. A needling thought had begun to enter my brain, too—not a huge one, but one nonetheless: *You are drinking every night,* though this thought was quickly washed away by the next drink.

And every next day, I'd manage to drag myself to lunch, where I would meet Craig Bierko, to this day, by far the fastest comic mind I have ever seen. I thought my mind was fast, but no, it was Craig Bierko. Hank Azaria became the richest one of the group, because he had been doing a voice on *The Simpsons* since 1955. I was to be the most famous, and David Pressman was to be a journeyman actor just like his dad, Laurence Pressman, and the craziest. David loved to do things like run naked into a supermarket shouting, "I have horrible problems, someone please shave me!" and then run out. (He did this well into his forties; I sometimes joined him in disrobing in public, though I quit in my mid-thirties because I'm the mature one.)

To this day no one has made me laugh as hard as Craig Bierko. Being funnier than Hank, David, and me as a threesome was pretty much impossible, but Craig managed it. Being funnier than Hank and me without David was also unheard of, but Craig managed that, too. We would go out to lunch, and Craig would say something that was so funny that fifteen minutes after lunch had finished and I was driving home, I would have to pull over to the side of the road because I would still be laughing, and Craig would drive by, see me laughing, and know why. There was no one funnier than Craig. No one.

The other thing that drove our friendships, besides trying to be the quickest, the funniest, was fame—we were all absolutely desperate to be famous. Hank, being the voice of *The Simpsons,* had the most lucrative gig, but it was not the Al Pacino career he longed for. As for me, well, I had done plenty of TV, but nothing that had even remotely brought me fame . . . and fame, fame, fame, that's all that any of us cared about. In between the laughter—and after we'd shared the latest stories of auditions gone awry or scripts we'd read and hated—the quieter moments were filled with a profound worry, a quiet yearning and fear that we would never make it, that fame would just somehow pass us by. We were four strong egos, four funny men, the bon mots flying about like shrapnel, but the battle raged on: the battle for *fame.*

I held firm in my belief that fame would fill that unaccompanied hole in me, the one that Valerie refused to fill. But now it was just me and vodka attempting and failing this seemingly impossible task. When fame finally happened, well . . . we're coming to that.

I once made out with David Pressman, or tried to, though I didn't mean to, either way.

When we were in our early twenties, he and I and a couple of other guys headed east to Vegas to do the Vegas thing. We basically had no money, but that had never before stopped four idiots heading to Sin City. I think I had about two hundred bucks in my pocket; the four of us rented one motel room off the Strip, with two beds. I shared a bed with David; in the middle of the night, I guess I was dreaming about Gaby, my ex, and was inching closer and closer to David, saying things like "Aw, baby," and "You smell so good," and "I promise I'll be quick." He, too, was mercifully asleep, but his subconscious had the where-withal to keep saying, "NO!" and "back up!" and "leave me the fuck alone!" Eventually I started kissing the back of his neck, which caused us both to startle awake—seeing the horrified look on his face I said, "Aw, just forget it," and scuttled back to my side of the bed.

Clearly, we all needed some release.

The first night we hit the tables, and somehow, I lucked into some-thing, winning $2,600 at blackjack, which was the most cash any of us had ever had.

It was time to spend it unwisely.

I lifted up my arms and, like a king, exclaimed, "I'm getting every-one laid!"

A cabdriver took us way out of town to a place called Dominions, a place he promised us would satiate our needs (he received, presumably, a cut for every set of foolish young men he deposited at Dominions in the desert). To even gain ingress to this fine establishment, we were informed by a man with no neck that somebody had to drop at least a grand, and as I'd done well on the tables, that privilege fell to me. In fact, I ended up plopping down $1,600 on a single bottle of champagne, at which point we were each escorted to a separate, boxy room, where a young lady awaited each of us.

I figured the $1,600 I'd already spent would be good for what I hoped would come next, but I was sadly mistaken. In fact, I wasn't going to be taken at all unless I proffered another $300, which I duly did, but before I could graduate to the business end of the evening, David Pressman and the other two guys appeared at my door, needing their own $300 stipend. Their financial needs met, I returned to the matter at hand. (It didn't occur to me to do the math, but here it is in case you need it: I started with $200, won $2,600, dropped $1,600 on the champagne, and ponied up an additional $300 each, for a total of $2,800—everything I had.)

With the financial commitments in place, the young lady proceeded to start dancing at me, a ways off at the other side of the room, and though she gyrated in a perfectly acceptable, if slightly "Roxbury Girls" manner, I was ready to take our relationship to the next level.

"What the hell is going on?" I said, obliquely.

"What?" she said.

"What? We're supposed to be having sex!" I said. "I've spent a small fortune in here!"

Then she explained to me for some reason that I could arrange the pillows wherever I wanted to.

"That's wonderful, and I'm excited about the pillow thing—I really am—but aren't we supposed to be doing something else right about now?" I asked/begged.

"Are you the police?" she asked.

"No!" I said, though I was beginning to wonder if I should call them to report a fraud. "I paid you all that money. We had a deal—"

"Oh!" she said, interrupting me. "That was just for the dance. . . ."

At that point, a rapping on the door alerted me to the fact that each of my cronies had faced the same, disappointing fate. But as we were thoroughly out of money by this point, with tears in our eyes, four taken (though *not* taken) losers stepped out into the inky black of the Mojave and began the long walk back to the motel.

One of my friends, Nick, did get to take his girl to *Young Guns II* the following day, so that's something. And there were a lot of unanswered questions in the original *Young Guns*.

*   *   *

In 1994, Craig Bierko was the hot item in that particular pilot season. All of us were running around auditioning for the latest slate of sitcoms and dramas, but Craig was the one everyone wanted. This, and he was quicker with a line than me. He was also much better-looking than me, but let's not go into any more of that—we don't want a crying author on our hands. I should have hated him, but funny always wins, so I decided to keep loving him.

I was twenty-four, and already I was missing 50 percent of my auditions. I was tailing out as an actor. Drinking was slowly but surely winning the war against auditions, and no one was really interested in me anyway. I wasn't getting any movies, and the roles I got on TV were hardly setting the world alight. I was hungover half the time, the rest of the time I was on my way to lunch or the Formosa. My manager sat me down one day and told me that the people I aspired to be—Michael Keaton, Tom Hanks—all possessed the attitude I was shooting for. But they both also looked great, and he was getting daily feedback from casting directors and producers that I looked like a mess.

Hank, too, was starting to get worried that he was wasting his life away and stopped coming to the Formosa and the funny lunches—he was always very serious about his body and his career.

I shouldn't have been surprised, but around that time, I got a phone call from my then–business manager.

"Matthew, you are out of money."

"How about a little warning?" I said, scared to death. "Did it occur to you that a few months ago you could have given me a heads-up? You know, via a call in which you said, 'Hey, *Matthew,* your funds are looking a bit *anemic,*' instead of waiting till I was now broke?"

There was silence on the other end of the line, as though keeping tabs on someone's income *before* they were broke was an entirely new concept for a business manager.

Fortunately, I had just enough juice in me to book a part in a terrible pilot. Hanging up with my now former business manager, I called my agents and told them I was out of money, I needed a job, something, anything, and it had to be right then.

If, gentle reader, you're imagining that's how I got *Friends,* you might want to cool your jets. That call led to the show that almost *stopped* me from getting *Friends.*

L.A.X. 2194 was a "sci-fi comedy" about baggage handlers at Los Angeles International Airport. You could really stop there, but there's more: those numbers in the title give away the twist—it was set two hundred years in the future, and the air travelers would be aliens. The show would star Ryan Stiles as an automaton office manager with a weird accent (seriously, Ryan is a hilarious actor, but what was that accent?), and me as the poor guy who had to be the lead in this mess and sort out the baggage issues for the arriving aliens, who happen to have been played by Little People in ridiculous wigs.

If all this sounds underwhelming, please know that it was way worse than that. I had to wear a futuristic shirt for a start. Despite my misgivings (to repeat, it was a "comedy" about baggage handlers set two hundred years in the future where the aliens are played by Little People), the pilot paid me $22,500, so I was set for drinks and food at the Formosa for a while . . . but it did something else, too: because I was attached to *L.A.X. 2194,* I was thereby off the market for all other shows.

Then, disaster struck, and I don't mean *L.A.X. 2194* got picked up for a season—that never happened, thank God. What did happen was a script for a new show called *Friends Like Us* became the hot read of the season. Everyone who read it knew it was going to be great; I read it and immediately called those same agents who'd gotten me *L.A.X. 2194.*

"You have to get me on *Friends Like Us,*" I said.

"Not gonna happen," my agents said. "You're attached to the baggage handlers show. They've already measured you for the futuristic shirt and everything."

I was devastated. When I read the script for *Friends Like Us* it was as if someone had followed me around for a year, stealing my jokes, copying my mannerisms, photocopying my world-weary yet witty view of life. One character in particular stood out to me: it wasn't that I thought I could *play* "Chandler," I *was* Chandler.

But I was also Blaine in *L.A.X. 2194. Fuck me, is everyone kidding? Am I the least lucky person on the planet?*

It only got worse. Because *Friends Like Us* was the hot ticket of the season, everyone was reading it, everyone was auditioning for it, and everyone, it seemed, decided that the part of Chandler was exactly like me and came to my apartment to ask me to help them with their auditions. A few even went a long way, based on my choices and my choices alone. Hank Azaria thought it was so good he auditioned for it twice, for the role of Joey. That's right—he auditioned for it, got passed on, begged and pleaded to go in again, and got passed on again. (Later, Hank would be Phoebe's romantic interest for a few episodes, performances for which he won an Emmy. I did 237 episodes and won nothing.)

I ended up knowing the script for *Friends Like Us* pretty much off by heart because I'd practiced it so much with my pals—in fact, there were times I just acted Chandler out for them and told them to copy what I'd done, so sure was I that it was the right way to play him. And still I would call my agents every three or four days begging for a chance.

Now, we are forgetting about Craig Bierko, the hottest ticket in town. One morning, Craig called Hank and me to breakfast, and as we walked in we saw Craig sitting at a table with two scripts open in front of him.

"Guys," Craig said, "I've been offered two shows—Jim Burrows, the hottest director in Hollywood, is directing both. One is called *Best Friends,* and the other is that one called . . ."

Wait, don't say it, please don't say it . . .

". . . *Friends Like Us.*"

He had been offered the role of Chandler. It made my head explode.

"And I need you to tell me which one to take."

My first instinct was to tell him to take his jobs and go fuck himself. But he was a close friend, so Hank and I both obliged. The three of us read those two scripts that morning, though I already knew *Friends Like Us* off by heart, and it was clear which one he should take. My heart sank, because I knew I was Chandler, but I also wasn't an asshole. I was crushed. We both told Craig to do *Friends Like Us.*

(This made me think of an exchange from my episode on *Beverly Hills, 90210*:

BRANDON: *What about friends?*

ROGER: *Friends? My father says those are the only ones you can't trust.*

BRANDON: *Do you always listen to him?*

ROGER: *No.*)

Lunch was winding down and it was time for Craig to tell his agents where his head was at. Hank made his goodbyes and went to the gym, because he was always going to the gym, and I went with Craig as he looked for a pay phone. (No cell phones folks; this was 1994.) The nearest one was outside a Fred Segal store (the same store that weirdly also features in my episode of *Beverly Hills, 90210*). Craig threw a few coins in the machine, tapped in the numbers, and waited. Eventually they patched him through.

And then, I stood two feet away from Craig and listened to him pick THE OTHER SHOW! I couldn't believe my fucking ears. So, the new lead of *Best Friends* and I parted ways. I raced home to make another plea to get an audition for *Friends Like Us.*

A few weeks later I went to the taping of the pilot for *Best Friends*—it was funny; Craig was funny, and the lead, which is what he really wanted. Perfectly fine, cute show. But the final role available during the entire pilot season of 1994, Chandler in *Friends Like Us*, was still not cast. And I was still attached to the fucking futuristic baggage handler show!

You know how sometimes the universe has plans for you that are hard to believe, how the world wants something for you even though you've done your best to close off that avenue?

Welcome to my 1994.

NBC producer Jamie Tarses—oh, sweet, magical, much-missed Jamie Tarses—who was helping to develop *Friends Like Us,* at NBC— apparently turned to her then-husband, Dan McDermott, a Fox TV producer, one night in bed.

"Hey, is the show *L.A.X. 2194* going to get picked up?" Jamie reportedly said.

Dan said, "No, it's *awful*—for a start, it's about baggage handlers in the year 2194. They wear futuristic vests. . . ."

"So, is Matthew Perry available? A safe second position?" Jamie said. (That's Hollywood-speak for "available.") (Ironically, Jamie and I dated for several years much later, after she got divorced.)

A couple of days later I got the phone call that would change my life.

"You're meeting Marta Kauffman about *Friends Like Us* tomorrow."

And this is no lie: I knew right then and there just how huge it was all going to be.

Marta Kauffman, along with David Crane, was the person most responsible for what would become *Friends.* Next day, a Wednesday, I read as Chandler for her, and I broke all the rules—for a start, I didn't carry any pages of the script (you're supposed to carry the script with you when you read, because that way, you're acknowledging to the writers that it's just a work in progress). But I knew the script so well by this point. Of course, I nailed it. Thursday, I read for the production company, and nailed it, and Friday I read for the network. Nailed it again. I read the words in an unexpected fashion, hitting emphases that no one else had hit. I was back in Ottawa with the Murrays; I got laughs where no one else had.

I was cheering up my mother.

And Chandler was born. This was my part now and there was no stopping it.

The pilot season of 1994 had cast its final actor: Matthew Perry as Chandler Bing.

That phone call at Fred Segal's, and Craig's desire to be the star of his own show, rather than be part of an ensemble, saved my life. I don't know what would have happened to me had the call gone the other way. It is not out of the realms of possibility that I may have ended up on the streets of downtown LA shooting heroin in my arm until my untimely death.

I would have loved heroin—it was my opiate addiction on steroids. I've often said that taking OxyContin is like replacing your blood with warm honey. But with heroin, I would imagine, you *are* the honey. I loved the feeling of opiates, but something about the word "heroin" always scared me. And it is because of that fear that I am still alive today. There are two kinds of drug addicts, the ones who want to go up, and the ones who want to go down. I could never understand the coke guys—why would anyone want to feel more present, *more* busy? I was a downer guy, I wanted to melt into my couch and feel wonderful while watching movies over and over again. I was a quiet addict, not the bull-in-a-china-shop kind.

Sure, without *Friends,* I may have had a career as a sitcom writer—I'd already written a pilot called *Maxwell's House,* but though I had some skills, it hadn't sold. But there was no way I could have been a journeyman actor. I wouldn't have stayed sober for that; it was not worth not doing heroin for that. *Friends* was such a good and fun job that it curtailed everything for a while at least. I was the second baseman for the New York Yankees. I couldn't fuck that up. I would never forgive myself. . . .

When you're earning $1 million a week, you can't afford to have the seventeenth drink.

About three weeks before my audition for *Friends,* I was alone in my apartment on Sunset and Doheny, tenth floor—it was very small, but it had a great view, of course—and I was reading in the newspaper about Charlie Sheen. It said that Sheen was yet again in trouble for something, but I remember thinking, *Why does he care—he's famous?*

Out of nowhere, I found myself getting to my knees, closing my eyes tightly, and praying. I had never done this before.

"God, you can do whatever you want to me. Just please make me famous."

Three weeks later, I got cast in *Friends.* And God has certainly kept his side of the bargain—but the Almighty, being the Almighty, had not forgotten the first part of that prayer as well.

Now, all these years later, I'm certain that I got famous so I would not waste my entire life trying to get famous. You have to get famous to know that it's not the answer. And nobody who is not famous will ever truly believe that.

Dead

I bought her a ring because I was desperate that she would leave me. I didn't want to be this injured and alone during Covid.

I was high on 1,800 milligrams of hydrocodone when I asked her to marry me.

I had even asked for her family's blessing. Then I'd proposed, high as a kite. And on one knee. And she knew it, too. And she said yes.

I was in Switzerland at the time, at yet another rehab. This one was at a villa on Lake Geneva with its own butler and chef, the kind of luxurious place where you were guaranteed to not meet anybody else. (Thereby pretty much defeating the purpose of every rehab I had ever heard of.) But what it lacked in fellow sufferers it made up for in the easy availability of drugs, which again, unfortunately, did not differentiate it from other high-priced rehabs. I could make millions if I sued these places, but it would divert more attention to the situation, which I didn't want to do.

I did my usual trick, complaining about intense stomach pain, when in fact I was OK (it still felt like I was constantly doing a sit-up—so it was very uncomfortable—but it wasn't Pain). So, they'd give me hydrocodone—as much as I could actually feel—which turned out to be 1,800 milligrams a day. To put that in perspective, if you broke your thumb, and had a kind doctor, he or she would probably prescribe you five 0.5-milligram pills.

Not enough to put a dent in this guy.

I was also doing ketamine infusions every day. Ketamine was a very popular street drug in the 1980s. There is a synthetic form of it now, and it's used for two reasons: to ease pain and help with depression. Has my name written all over it—they might as well have called it "Matty." Ketamine felt like a giant exhale. They'd bring me into a room, sit me down, put headphones on me so I could listen to music, blindfold me, and put an IV in. That was the hard part—I'm always a little dehydrated because I don't drink enough water (big surprise), so finding a vein was no fun. I was like a fucking pincushion by the end of it. Into the IV went a smidge of Ativan—which I could actually feel—and then I was on a ketamine drip for an hour. As I lay there in the pitch-dark, listening to Bon Iver, I would disassociate, see things—I'd been in therapy for so long that I wasn't even freaked-out by this. Oh, there's a horse over there? Fine—might as well be. . . . As the music played and the K ran through me, it all became about the ego, and the death of the ego. And I often thought that I was dying during that hour. *Oh, I thought, this is what happens when you die.* Yet I would continually sign up for this shit because it was something different, and anything different is good. (Which just so happens to be one of the last lines of *Groundhog Day.*) Taking K is like being hit in the head with a giant happy shovel. But the hangover was rough and outweighed the shovel. Ketamine was not for me.

Back in my room, the butler had laid out more clothes I wouldn't change into, the chef had prepared yet another healthy meal I wouldn't touch, and I went back to looking at Lake Geneva a lot, completely fucking high. But not the good kind of high. A loopy drunk feeling that I did not enjoy.

I was also now, somehow, engaged.

At some point, the rehab geniuses decided that to help my stomach "pain," they'd put some kind of weird medical device in my back, but they'd need to do surgery to insert it. So I stayed up all night, taking 1,800 milligrams of hydrocodone ahead of the next day's surgery. In the operating room they gave me propofol, you know, the drug that killed Michael Jackson. I learned then and there that Michael Jackson didn't want to be high, he wanted to be out. Zero consciousness. And yet another masterful talent taken from us by this terrible disease.

I was given the shot at 11:00 A.M. I woke up eleven hours later in a different hospital.

Apparently, the propofol had stopped my heart. For five minutes. It wasn't a heart attack—I didn't flatline—but nothing had been beating.

If I may be so bold, please pause your reading of this book for five minutes—look at your phone, starting now:

[Insert five minutes of you time]

That's a long fucking time, right?

I was told that some beefy Swiss guy really didn't want the guy from *Friends* dying on his table and did CPR on me for the full five minutes, beating and pounding my chest. If I hadn't been on *Friends,* would he have stopped at three minutes? Did *Friends* save my life again?

He may have saved my life, but he also broke eight of my ribs. As I lay there in agony, the following day the head doctor waltzed in, all full of himself and said, "You will get no ketamine here, and if you need to go to a rehab, there is one we can send you to."

"I'm already in a fucking rehab!" I screamed, and in a rare show of physical anger, I knocked over the table next to me, which was covered in medical supplies. This scared the doctor, and he promptly left the room. I apologized for the mess I had made and got the hell out of there.

(The rehab I was speaking of had already done a rapid detox, but they put me under for the wrong two days—the first two [it should have been days three and four]. By the time I came around, the detox fully hit, and I'd gone from 1,800 milligrams to bupkis. Not much a butler and a chef can do about that.)

Those eight broken ribs were, by the way, much the same injury that the New Orleans Saints' quarterback Drew Brees suffered in a game in November 2021 against the Tampa Bay Buccaneers. Brees would break three more the following week and puncture his lung—just to be better than me—but then he missed four games, so I'd argue we're at least even. Which makes me feel tough.

Right in the middle of all this madness (but prior to the rib thing) I took a meeting with Adam McKay about a big movie called *Don't Look Up*. There was no Chandler, that day—I wasn't on. I couldn't get it up for that. We just talked for a while, and as I walked out, I said, very calmly, "Well, I'd love to help you in any way I can with this thing."

Adam said, "I think you just did."

I got the call the following day that he was hiring me—this would be the biggest movie I'd gotten ever. It promised to be a little calm within the storm. I was to play a Republican journalist and was supposed to have three scenes with Meryl Streep. Yes, that's right. I got to do a group scene (with Jonah Hill among others) in Boston where the movie was filmed—I was on 1,800 milligrams of hydrocodone then, too, but nobody noticed. But with the broken ribs, there was no way I could continue, so I never got to do my scenes with Meryl. It was heartbreaking, but I was in too much pain. God knows how Brees continued to throw a football, but you don't get to do a scene with Meryl Streep with broken ribs. And I couldn't smile without it hurting like fuck.

Being in *Don't Look Up* didn't work out because my life was on fire, but I learned an important lesson: I was hirable in something big without putting on a show. In that meeting, Adam and I had just been two men talking. I will treasure that moment, that day, that man. What a good guy. And I sincerely hope our paths cross again (I'll be sure to check it's actually him next time).

When it came time to leave Switzerland, I was still on 1,800 milligrams of Oxy every single fucking day. I was told that once back in Los Angeles I'd still be able to get that much—and I needed it, just to stay level. As ever, this was not me getting high; this was purely maintenance, so I didn't go through agonies. I flew back on a private jet—there was no way I could fly commercial, given that everyone in the world recognized my damn face—and it cost me a cool $175,000 to do so. Back in LA, I went to see my doctor.

"I need eighteen hundred milligrams a day," I said. No point beating around the bush.

"Oh no," she said, "we're not giving you that at all—cancer patients only get a hundred milligrams." This only upped my gratitude that I didn't have cancer.

"But the doctor in Switzerland told me that's what I'd be on when I got home."

"Oh, they'll consult," she said, "but I'm in charge now. Here's thirty milligrams."

This would not do. I would get incredibly sick.

There was only one thing for it: that very same night, I booked another $175,000 private jet and flew right back to Switzerland.

"I need you to combine my morning and evening dose."

"*Ich verstehe kein Englisch,*" the Swiss nurse said.

This was going to be a problem. My pressing need to change the rules, versus her lack of English. This was all done in some weird German-English game of charades.

I don't need a pill at six o'clock in the morning. I need it when it's scary at night. I can't find the center of the fear—it's general. Also, I can't sleep, so there's a negotiation every single night with myself. My mind races. The ideas come so fast. I get auditory hallucinations, too—I hear voices and conversations and sometimes, I even talk back. Sometimes, too, I'll think that somebody wants to hand me something, and I put my hand out to get that nothing from no one. Sober or not, this troubled me a bit. On top of everything else, I was crazy? It's not schizophrenia, just a damn load of voices. The voices, I'm told, do not make me a crazy person. They are called auditory hallucinations and they happen to people all the time.

There is no cure for the voices. Of course there isn't. Actually, I can think of a cure, it's called, "being somebody else."

Either way, I needed those pills as one shot, at night, without saving any for the morning.

"Morning. Evening. Together," I said, miming eight pills in my hand, not one.

"*Nee, keine Ahnung,*" she said.

"Tomorrow morning. No pill. Now instead," I said, extremely slowly.

"*Ich habe keine Ahnung, was Sie brauchen.*"

You and everyone else—no one knows what I need.

Back in LA one more time, trying to sober up, I think, *Wait . . . how did I get engaged? There are dogs living in my house. How did this happen?*

I had asked her parents, begged for her hand while high, and put up with the dogs. That's how scared I was of being abandoned.

4

Like I've Been There Before

It was so special it felt like we'd all been together in a previous life or something. Or in a future life, but certainly this one. This was a real day. But a day that dreams were made of.

For the longest time I didn't really want to talk too much about *Friends.* Partly that was because I'd done plenty of other stuff, too, but all anyone ever wanted to talk about was Chandler—it's like James Taylor talking about "Fire and Rain" (a gruesome little tale if you've ever heard what that's about). It's like a band who've written a brilliant new album but all anyone wants to hear when they play live is the hits. I always admired Kurt Cobain's refusal to play "Smells Like Teen Spirit," or Led Zeppelin's refusal to play "Stairway to Heaven." *The New York Times* once said that "*Friends*... sticks to [Perry] like a sweaty shirt." They weren't right about that—in fact, that's just fucking cruel—but they weren't the only ones to think it. I was so good at something, yet I was being penalized for it. I left my blood, sweat, and tears onstage every Friday night—we all did. And that should be a good thing, not something that says we can only excel at *that.*

I'm not complaining. If you are going to be typecast, that's the way to do it.

But in recent years, I've come to understand just what *Friends* means to people. And we knew from the very start that it was something very, very special.

I was the last actor to be cast in the entire pilot season of 1994—in fact, I got the gig on the actual final day of pilot season.

With *L.A.X. 2194* thankfully in the rearview mirror, I was free to be Chandler Bing. The following Monday after the Friday I was hired was day one of my new life—this was big, and I guess we all felt that way, because we all showed up dead on time. Well, Matt LeBlanc was first, every single day; Aniston last, every single day. The cars got nicer, but the order stayed the same.

We sat around the table, and all met each other for the first time. That is, except me and Jennifer Aniston.

Jennifer and I had met through mutual acquaintances about three years earlier. I was immediately taken by her (how could I not be?) and liked her, and I got the sense she was intrigued, too—maybe it was going to *be* something. Back then I got two jobs in one day—one was *Haywire,* an *America's Funniest Home Videos*–type show, and the other was a sitcom. So I called Jennifer and I said, "You're the first person I wanted to tell this to!"

Bad idea—I could feel ice forming through the phone. Looking back, it was clear that this made her think I liked her too much, or in the wrong kind of way . . . and I only compounded the error by then asking her out. She declined (which made it very difficult to actually go out with her), but said that she'd love to be friends with me, and I compounded the compound by blurting, "We can't be *friends!*"

Now, a few years later, ironically we *were* friends. Fortunately, even though I was still attracted to her and thought she was so great, that first day we were able to sail right past the past and focus on the fact that we had both gotten the best job Hollywood had to offer.

Everyone else was brand-new to me.

Courteney Cox was wearing a yellow dress and was cripplingly beautiful. I had heard about Lisa Kudrow from a mutual friend, and she was just as gorgeous and hilarious and incredibly smart as my friend had said. Mattie LeBlanc was nice and a cool customer, and David Schwimmer had had his hair cut really short (he had been playing Pontius Pilate for his theater troupe in Chicago) over his hangdog face and was incredibly funny right away; warm and smart and creative. After me, he was the guy who pitched the most jokes—I probably pitched ten jokes a day and two of them got in. They weren't just jokes for me; I'd pitch jokes for everybody. I'd go up to Lisa and say, "You know, it might be funny if you tried to say this . . ." and she'd try it.

The director, Jimmy Burrows, was the best in the business, too—he'd directed both *Taxi* and *Cheers*. He knew instinctually that Job One for us was to get to know each other and generate chemistry.

Immediately, there was electricity in the air.

I'd always wanted to be the only funny one. But now, at the ripe old age of twenty-four, I quickly realized that it's better if everyone is funny. I could already tell that this was going to be big; I knew it from the start, but I didn't say anything out loud. Partly that was because it isn't unheard of for an actor to fuck up a table read so badly that they were politely asked to leave before a minute of shooting took place. But that would be tomorrow—for now, Jimmy took the six of us to Monica's apartment set and told us just to talk to each other. And so we did—we talked and joked, about romance, our careers, our loves, our losses. And the bond that Jimmy knew would be critical had begun.

The six of us ate lunch together, outside on a beautiful spring day. As we ate, Courteney—the only established name of the group back then—said, "There are no stars here. This is an ensemble show. We're all supposed to be friends."

Given her status—she'd been on *Family Ties* and in *Ace Ventura* and in a guest spot on *Seinfeld* and had danced with Bruce Springsteen in the video for "Dancing in the Dark"—she could have been everything and everybody; she could easily have said "I'm the star." Hell, she could have had her lunch somewhere else, and we would have to have been fine with it. Instead, she simply said, "Let's really work and get to know each other." She said it's what she'd noticed about how it worked on *Seinfeld,* and she wanted it to be true about *Friends,* too.

So we did what she suggested. From that first morning we were inseparable. We ate every meal together, played poker. . . . At the start, I was full-on the joke man, cracking gags like a comedy machine whenever I could (probably to the annoyance of everyone), trying to get everybody to like me because of how funny I was.

Because, why else would anybody like me? It would take fifteen years for me to learn that I didn't need to be a joke machine.

That first afternoon we were assigned dressing rooms, which eventually didn't matter because we were never in them. We were always together. As we all walked to our cars and said goodbye that first evening, I remember thinking, *I'm happy.*

This was not an emotion I was altogether used to.

That night I called my friends (except for Craig Bierko, given what had happened) and told them what a wonderful day I'd had. I then spent yet another night "at college" (the Formosa), as was my custom. I remember saying that night that I was on a show that was so good it was better than anything I could have dreamed of writing myself. . . . My friends were all so happy for me, but even then, I could sense a shift.

Maybe I was growing out of this Formosa thing? I had a life-changing job that I had to—hell, desperately *wanted* to—report to in the morning, so I drank far less than usual. My apartment even had a Lifecycle in the back, and I used it every day, dropping about ten pounds of baby/alcohol fat between the pilot and the first episode.

That night I went to bed thinking, *I can't wait to get back there tomorrow.* Next morning, as I drove from Sunset and Doheny over the Cahuenga Pass to the Warner Bros. lot in Burbank, I realized that I was leaning toward the windshield as I drove. I wanted to be there.

That would be true for the next decade.

Day two was big. We reported to a new building—Building 40—for our first table read. I was nervous and excited, and yet confident, too. I had always been good at table reads. But there was still the looming thought that anyone could be fired and replaced (Lisa Kudrow, for example, had originally been cast as Roz on *Frasier* but had been fired during the rehearsal process by none other than . . . *Friends* director, Jimmy Burrows). If jokes didn't land, or something was off, well, anybody could be replaced before they'd even properly found their way to their dressing room.

But I *knew* Chandler. I could shake hands with Chandler. I *was* him. (And I looked a hell of a lot like him, too.)

That day, the room was packed—in fact, it was standing room only. There were writers, executives, network people. There must have been a hundred people in the room, but I was a song-and-dance man, and this is where I excelled. We got reacquainted with Marta Kauffman, David Crane, and Kevin Bright—the people behind the show, and who had hired us—and almost instantly we all felt they were our parental figures.

Before the table read began, we all went around the room introducing ourselves and saying what we did for the show. Then it was time to read. How would it go? Would the chemistry we'd only just started to create show up, or were we just six young hopefuls making believe that this would be our big break?

We needn't have worried—we were ready, the universe was ready. We were pros—the lines flew out of our mouths. No one made a mistake. All the jokes landed. We finished to thunderous applause.

Everyone could smell money.

The cast could smell fame.

After the read the six of us piled into a van and were brought to the actual set at stage 24 to begin rehearsing. But it was the run-through at the end of the day that sealed the deal—the jokes, the chemistry, the script, the direction, everything was magical. All the elements seemed to meld into one hilarious, cogent, powerful whole. And we all knew it.

This show was going to work, and it was going to change everyone's lives forever. I swear there was a popping sound; if you listened really closely, you could hear it. It was the sound of people's dreams coming true.

It was everything I thought I wanted. I was going to fill all the holes with *Friends Like Us*. Fuck Charlie Sheen. I was going to be so famous that all the pain I carried with me would melt like frost in sunlight; and any new threats would bounce off me as though this show was a force field I could cloak myself in.

There is an unwritten law in show business that to be funny, you had to either *look* funny, or be older. But here we were, six attractive people, all in their twenties, all knocking every joke out of the park.

That evening, I drove home on a cloud. There was no traffic; all the lights were green; a trip that should have taken half an hour took fifteen minutes. The attention that I always felt had eluded me was about to fill every corner of my life, like a room illuminated by a flash of lightning. People were going to like me now. I was going to be enough. I mattered. I wasn't too needy. I was a star.

Nothing was going to stop us now. No one walking into a ballroom would have to turn around and notice me. All eyes would be on me now, not the pretty woman walking three feet in front of me.

We rehearsed the rest of the week, and it was then that we began to notice something else. I have been an actor since 1985 and that has never happened before or since, and it was beautiful: the bosses were not in the least tyrannical. In fact, it was a truly creative atmosphere. We could pitch jokes, and the best joke won, no matter where it came from. The craft services lady said something funny? Put it in, it didn't matter. So, not only was I there as an actor, but my creative juices were flowing, too.

The creators took each of us out for lunch, too, to get to know us, so they could incorporate some aspects of our real personalities into the show. At my lunch I said two things: one, that even though I considered myself not unattractive, I had terrible luck with women and that my relationships tended toward the disastrous; and two, that I was not comfortable in any silence at all—I have to break any such moment with a joke. And this became a built-in excuse for Chandler Bing to be funny—perfect for a sitcom—and Chandler wasn't much good with women, either (as he shouts at Janice as she leaves his apartment, "I've scared ya; I've said too much; I'm awkward and hopeless and desperate for love!").

But think of a better character for a sitcom: someone who is uncomfortable in silence and has to break the silence with a joke.

This was all too true, both for Chandler, and for me. Fairly early in the making of *Friends* I realized that I was still crushing badly on Jennifer Aniston. Our hellos and goodbyes became awkward. And then I'd ask myself, *How long can I look at her? Is three seconds too long?*

But that shadow disappeared in the hot glow of the show. (That, and her deafening lack of interest.)

On tape nights, nobody made a mistake. We might have run scenes over if a joke didn't land—all the writers would huddle together and rewrite—but mistakes? Just never happened. So many shows have blooper reels, but there are only a few for *Friends*. From the pilot on . . . in fact, that pilot was error-free. We were the New York Yankees: slick, professional, top of our game from the very start. We were ready.

And I was talking in a way that no one had talked in sitcoms before, hitting odd emphases, picking a word in a sentence you might not imagine was the beat, utilizing the Murray-Perry Cadence. I didn't know it yet, but my way of speaking would filter into the culture across the next few decades—for now, though, I was just trying to find interesting ways into lines that were already funny, but that I thought I could truly make dance. (Marta Kauffman was later to say that the writers would underline the word not usually emphasized in a sentence just to see what I would do with it.)

Even when there were issues with the characters, we were able to work them out to the point where the solutions created their own iconic moments.

When I first read the script, I knew it was different because it was so character driven and smart. But early on, Matt LeBlanc was concerned that because he was this kinda cool, macho, ladies' man in the script, Rachel, Monica, and Phoebe wouldn't be friends with him, wouldn't like him that much, and that made his character less believable.

It didn't help that Matt was very good-looking—he had leading man looks, even to the point where I was a little jealous of that when I first saw him. But he was so nice and funny that any jealousy I had soon disappeared—but still, he hadn't been able to find the right way into his character. He was the one character in the show that had not been properly defined—he was described as a cool, Pacino-type, out-of-work actor, so that's how he was playing it, but it still wasn't working. At one point during a wardrobe session, he put on brown leather pants, which were thankfully nixed by everyone, especially Marta, who was in charge.

Then came the moment early in the run where he has an exchange with Courteney about a woman he's been seeing and how the sex wasn't working out. Courteney asks him if he's thought of being there for the girl, and Joey just simply doesn't understand the concept. That was the moment he turned from being a ladies' man to a loveable, useless, dumb puppy. He underlined this by doing a running joke of things being repeated to him and him not following them. He had found his position in the show, which was basically as a big dumb brother to Rachel, Monica, and Phoebe. Everyone was in place.

Occasionally Matt would come into my dressing room, mostly during season one, and ask me how to say his lines. And I would tell him, and he would go downstairs, and he would nail it . . . but he gets Most Improved Player because by season ten, I was going into his room and asking *him* how he would say certain of *my* lines.

This was all to come. For now, we were filming shows ahead of our fall 1994 air date. And as yet, no one knew who we were.

With the shows in the can, all that was left to find out was our time slot. NBC knew they had something special, so they put us right between *Mad About You* and *Seinfeld*. It was the perfect spot; plum. This was before streaming, so your time slot was crucial. It was still the days of appointment TV, when folks would rush home to catch the 8:00 P.M. show or the 9:00 P.M. show. And people organized their lives around their shows, not the other way round. So, 8:30 P.M. on a Thursday, between two huge shows, was a massive deal.

We flew to New York on the Warner Bros. jet for the "upfronts." The upfronts are when a show is presented to the affiliates. It was on this trip that they told us the name of the show was now *Friends* (when they renamed it I thought it was a horrible idea—I never said I was a smart person), and *Friends* was a smash with the affiliates, too—everything was lining up. In New York we were celebrating, getting drunk, partying; then on to Chicago for more upfronts, more partying.

Then we had to wait a summer before the show first aired. I filled that summer with three notable things—gambling in Vegas at the behest of Jimmy Burrows; a trip to Mexico on my own; and a make-out session in a closet with Gwyneth Paltrow.

I was back in Williamstown, Massachusetts, when I met Gwyneth. She was doing a play there, and I was visiting my grandfather. At some big party we slipped off into a broom cupboard and made out. We were both still unknown enough that it didn't make it to the tabloids, but with that in mind, it fell to Jimmy Burrows to give me a reality check.

After the upfronts it was clear the show was going to be a hit, so Jimmy flew us all to Vegas on the jet—we watched the pilot of *Friends* on the way—and once we arrived, he gave us each $100 and told us to go gamble it and have fun, because once the show aired in the fall, we'd never be able to do it again.

"Your lives are going to utterly change," Jimmy said, "so do some things in public now because once you're as famous as you're about to be, you'll never be able to do them again." And that's what we did; we six new friends got drunk and gambled and wandered through the casinos, just six close strangers on a weekend trip, unknown to anyone, no one asking for autographs or photos, none of us being chased by paparazzi, a million miles from what was coming, which was every single moment of our lives being documented in public for all to see forever.

I still wanted fame, but already I could taste a wild and weird flavor in the air—would fame, that elusive lover, really fill all the holes I carried around with me? What would it be like to not be able to put twenty on black in some harsh-lit casino, a vodka tonic in my hand, without someone shouting, "Matthew Perry just put twenty on black, everyone, come and see!" This was the last summer of my life when I could make out at a party with a beautiful young woman called Gwyneth and no one, save Gwyneth and I, cared.

Would the payoff be worth it? Would giving up a "normal" life be worth the price paid, of people digging through my trash, clicking pictures through telephoto lenses of me at my worst, or best, or everything in between?

Would I ever again be able to anonymously replicate my twenty-first birthday, when at the Sofitel across from the Beverly Center, I'd drunk seven 7 and 7s, poured a bottle of wine into a huge brandy snifter—you know, the one they put on the piano for tips—ordered a cab, gotten into the back of the cab with the snifter, still sipping the wine, tried to give directions to my home when I could only pronounce the letter *L,* only for the guy up front to yell, "What the fuck are you doing?" because he wasn't a cabdriver—it was just some random car?

Most important, would these holes get filled? Would I want to trade places with David Pressman or Craig Bierko, or they with me? What would I tell them down the line when my name became a shorthand for stand-up comedians and late-night hosts, a shorthand that meant "addict"? What would I tell them when complete strangers hated me, loved me, and everything in between?

What would I *tell* them?

And what would I tell God when he reminded me of my prayer, the one I'd whispered three weeks before I got *Friends.*

God, you can do whatever you want to me. Just please make me famous.

He was about to keep one half of the bargain—but this also meant he could do whatever he wanted with me as the other half. I was completely at the mercy of a God who was sometimes merciful, and sometimes thought it was perfectly fine to put his own son on a fucking cross.

Which way would he choose for me? Which one would Saint Peter pick? The gold, the red, or the blue?

I guess I was about to find out.

With Jimmy Burrows's words about impending fame still ringing in my ears, I figured I should take one last trip as an anonymous person.

Late in the summer of 1994 I flew alone to Mexico. I'd recently broken up with my girlfriend, Gaby, and decided to go on a booze cruise, solo. In Cabo, I wandered about, getting drunk and calling girls in LA from my room. Then, each night on the cruise, I'd head to some kind of weird party where everybody was all nervous until they brought out a jug of booze, then it was on. I was lonely; I didn't get laid; it was hot in Cabo but cold inside me. I could feel God watching me, waiting. The most unnerving part was, I knew God was omniscient, which meant that he knew, already, what he had in store for me.

Friends premiered on Thursday, September 22, 1994. It initially hit number 17 in the rankings, which was really good for a brand-new show. The reviews were mostly stellar, too:

> "Friends" . . . promises to be . . . offbeat and seductive. . . . The cast is appealing, the dialogue is pitch-perfect 1994. . . . "Friends" comes as close as a new series can get to having everything.
>   —*The New York Times*

"Friends" has so many good moves that there's really nothing to dislike. It's all so light and frothy that after each episode you may be hard-pressed to recall precisely what went on, except that you laughed a lot.

—*Los Angeles Times*

A game cast delivers the barrage of banter with an arch coyness that suggests they think they're in some Gen X Neil Simon play.

—*People*

If fans of "Mad About You" and "Seinfeld" can handle the age difference, they should feel right at home with the six as they sit around riffing on life, love, relationships, jobs and each other.

—*The Baltimore Sun*

A couple of reviews hated it:

One character says he dreamed he had a telephone for a penis and when it rang, "it turns out it's my mother." And this is in the first five minutes. [It's a] ghastly creation . . . so bad. . . . The stars include that cute Courteney Cox, formerly funny David Schwimmer, Lisa Kudrow, Matt LeBlanc and Matthew Perry. They all look nice, and it's sad to see them degrading themselves.

—*The Washington Post*

Anemic and unworthy of its Thursday-night time slot.

—*Hartford Courant*

But then, Dick Rowe, an A&R man from Decca, in turning down the Beatles, told Brian Epstein in 1961 that "guitar groups are on their

way out." I wonder how those reviewers feel now, having dissed arguably the most beloved show of all time. They really missed the boat
on that one. Had they also hated *Seinfeld? M*A*S*H? Cheers? St. Else-
where?*

We were not on our way out. We were the very definition of prime
time, when prime time still mattered. The gold rush of television. Even
more important than the great reviews, we'd dropped only about 20
percent of the audience for *Mad About You,* which was an incredibly
strong performance for a new show. By episode six, we were beating
Mad About You, which meant we were a smash hit. Pretty soon we hit
the top ten, then the top five, and we wouldn't leave the top five for a
decade. This is unheard of, still.

So here it was—*fame.* Just as we'd predicted, *Friends* was huge, and
I couldn't jeopardize that. I loved my co-actors, I loved the scripts, I
loved everything about the show . . . but I was also struggling with my
addictions, which only added to my sense of shame. I had a secret, and
no one could know. And even making the shows could be painful. As I
admitted at the reunion in 2020, "I felt like I was gonna die if [the live
audience] didn't laugh. And it's not healthy for sure. But I would sometimes say a line, and they wouldn't laugh, and I would sweat and—and
just, like, go into convulsions. If I didn't get the laugh I was supposed
to get, I would freak out. I felt like that every single night."

This pressure left me in a bad place; and I also knew that of the
six people making that show, only one of them was sick. The fame I'd
yearned for had arrived, though—in London it was as if we *were* the
Beatles, with people outside our hotel rooms screaming—and the show
ended up covering the globe.

In late October 1995—between the airing of episodes five and six
of season two—I flew to New York to notch my first appearance on the
Late Show, when going on Letterman was the pinnacle of pop culture

fame. I was in a dark suit—at one point, Letterman would finger my lapel and describe it as "late 1960s, British Invasion, kinda mod."

"Ladies and gentlemen, this man is on the number one show in America, please welcome Matthew Perry."

I sauntered out a star. I had made it. But I was so nervous I could barely stand, which was why I was quite happy to be sitting.

I shook hands with Mr. Letterman and dove into my well-rehearsed routine, a long description of a typical *Gilligan's Island* episode. I somehow swung it so that I'd told the same story to Yasser Arafat, who was staying in my hotel (it was during the fiftieth anniversary of the UN, and everyone was in town). This was just the kind of bizarre, wordy story Letterman loved. The laughs landed—I even got Dave to crack a few times—and my earth-shattering fear had been properly hidden.

Everything was good. Everything was golden. I had just turned twenty-five. I was in the biggest sitcom on the planet; I was in a hotel in New York, watching as world leaders were hustled into elevators by flanks of security, putting on a thousand-dollar suit ahead of joshing it up with Dave Letterman.

This was fame. And just beyond the glare of the city, beyond the skyscrapers and the faint stars twinkling beyond the midtown skies, God looked down on me, just waiting it out. He's got all the time in the world. Fuck, he invented time.

He wouldn't forget. Something was looming. I had an idea what it was, but I did not know for sure. Something to do with drinking every night . . . but just how bad was it going to be?

The juggernaut was just getting going, though. The show was a cultural touchstone; we were getting mobbed everywhere we went (David Schwimmer would later tell the story that he was accosted by a gaggle of young women on the street who physically pushed his girlfriend out of the way to get near him). By late 1995, right around the time of the Letterman appearance, I also had a new, and very famous, girlfriend of my own. But before we get there, I had some unfinished business with the "other" Chandler.

I didn't hear from Craig Bierko for two years after I got Chandler—he had moved to New York, and we lost touch.

Best Friends, the show he chose over *Friends Like Us,* had gone nowhere. (Later, Warren Littlefield, former network president of NBC, wrote in his memoir about Craig not choosing *Friends,* "Thank God! There was something Snidely Whiplash about Craig Bierko. He seemed to have a lot of anger underneath. The attractive leading man who you love and can do comedy is very rare.") He was working steadily—he'd eventually star in *The Music Man* on Broadway and *The Long Kiss Goodnight* with Geena Davis and Sam Jackson, among a lot of other really awesome stuff—but the divergence of our fortunes had left our friendship in flames.

I missed him. He was still the quickest comedic mind I'd ever met, and I loved that—and much else—about him. I could no longer go to the Formosa to just hang out, either; I missed that life, too. I'd taken to drinking alone in my apartment because that was safest. The illness was deepening, but I couldn't see it, not then. And if anyone saw how much I was drinking, they might be alarmed and ask me to stop. And stopping was, of course, impossible.

One day, though, Craig Bierko called me out of the blue. He wanted to come by and see me. I was delighted, but apprehensive. You know that feeling when you end up dating someone your best friend had a crush on? It felt like that; I'd taken the role he could and should have taken, and everything had gone gold for me, then platinum, then some other rare metal as yet undiscovered.

I had no idea how a meeting with my former friend would go. Marta Kauffman would later comment, "We saw a countless number of actors [for Chandler], but things happened as they were supposed to happen." But I couldn't say anything like that to Craig, because the thing that was supposed to happen—the miracle—had happened to me, not to him. (That had been his choice, not mine.)

When he got to my apartment, the tension was high. Craig spoke first.

"I want you to know that I am very sorry for not speaking to you for two years," he said. "I simply could not handle that you got rich and famous doing a role that I turned down. We were both good enough to get that role, and yeah, so, I just could not handle it. . . ."

I heard him out; there was a silence. The traffic on Sunset was backing up all the way to the Fred Segal on La Cienega.

I decided I wouldn't mention Fred Segal.

I hated what I was *actually* about to say, but I had to say it.

I said: "You know what, Craig? It doesn't do what we all thought it would. It doesn't fix anything." (What a sobering thought for a twenty-six-year-old who had only ever wanted fame and had only just realized that fame hadn't filled the holes at all. No, what had filled the holes was vodka.)

Craig stared at me; I don't think he believed me; I *still* don't think he believes me. I think you actually have to have all of your dreams come true to realize they are the wrong dreams.

Later, when I was promoting *Studio 60 on the Sunset Strip*, I told *The Guardian*, "I've been on the least-watched show in the history of television [*Second Chance*, in 1987] and the most-watched [*Friends*] and none of it really did what I thought it was going to do to my life."

Given everything, there is no way I wouldn't change places with Craig, and David Pressman, and the guy in the gas station down the block—I'd change places with all of them in a minute, and forever, if only I could not be who I am, the way I am, bound on this wheel of fire. They don't have a brain that wants them dead. They slept fine at night. I don't expect that would make them feel any better about the choices they made, the way their lives went.

I would give it all up not to feel this way. I think about it all the time; it's no idle thought—it's a coldhearted fact. That Faustian prayer I made was a stupid one, the prayer of a child. It was not based on anything real.

But it became real.

I have the money, the recognizability, and the near-death experiences to prove it.

Zoom

Finally, back in LA, from Switzerland. It was Covid time. Everything everywhere was shut down. We'd all closed ourselves off in little rooms, terrified of death. My head was clearing up, though, and I was once again in a battle for sobriety.

The pandemic was slightly easier for me to handle for two reasons. (1) It was happening outside of my head. And (2), it gave me a pretty damn good excuse for hiding out in my 10,400-square-foot apartment on the entire fortieth floor of the Century Building in Century City.

My ribs had started to feel a bit better at least and I was sobering up. That meant that I was slowly beginning to realize that I was engaged, lived with a woman and two dogs. Needless to say, I was not ready for any of this. You live with me? We live together? We have kids' names picked out, the whole nine yards, which is the name of a movie I once made?

You went down on one knee to propose, which really hurt your stomach, remember?

I didn't remember—needless to say, we broke up.

5

No Fourth Wall

You know how during Covid some people felt like they were living the same day over and over and over again?

Here's the day I wish I could live over and over again (this is the Groundhog Day of my Groundhog Day). In fact, I wish I could relive it every day for the rest of my life. But I cannot. So, the only way to get past it is to tell it like a story, see if that helps.

(This of course will not bring it back.)

It was New Year's Eve 1995, Taos, New Mexico. All afternoon we'd been playing football in the snow. Me, and my girlfriend, Julia Roberts, and a bunch of our friends. She was the biggest movie star in the world, and I was on the number one show on TV.

The courtship had initially been conducted via fax. Somewhere in the world, there is a stack of faxes about two feet long—a two-foot-long courtship, filled with poems and flights of fancy and two huge stars falling for each other and connecting in a beautiful, romantic way.

At the time, I was walking on air. I was the center of it all and nothing could touch me. The white-hot flame of fame was mine—I kept passing my hand through it, but it didn't burn yet; it was the inert center. I had not learned yet that fame would not fill the hole, but at the time it filled it just nicely, thank you very much.

Season one of *Friends* had been a smash hit, and I had basically floated into season two. I'd done Letterman; I was slated to do Leno. We'd hit the cover of *People* magazine and *Rolling Stone* magazine when both were a big deal. Now, the movie offers were coming in. Why would they not? I was getting anything I wanted. Million-dollar movie offer here, million-dollar movie offer there. I was no Julia Roberts, but there was only one of those.

Then something that only happens to famous people happened. Marta Kauffman approached me and said that I should probably send flowers to Julia Roberts.

You mean the biggest-star-in-the-universe Julia Roberts?

"Sure, great, why?" I said.

Turned out Julia had been offered the post–Super Bowl episode in season two and she would only do the show if she could be in my story line. Let me say that again—she would only do the show if she could be in *my* story line. (Was I having a good year or what?) But first, I had to woo her.

I thought long and hard about what to say on the card. I wanted it to sound professional, star to star. (Well, star to much bigger star.) But I wanted something a tad flirty in there, too, to match what she had said. I'm still proud of what I settled on. I sent her three dozen red roses and the card read:

> The only thing more exciting than the prospect of you doing the show is that I finally have an excuse to send you flowers.

Not bad right? I was afraid to go to sleep at night, but I could pour on the charm when called for. But my work here was far from done. Her reply was that if I adequately explained quantum physics to her, she'd agree to be on the show. Wow. First of all, I'm in an exchange with the woman *for whom lipstick was invented,* and now I have to hit the books.

The following day, I sent her a paper all about wave-particle duality and the uncertainty principle and entanglement, and only some of it was metaphorical. Alexa Junge, a staff writer on the show, told *The Hollywood Reporter* many years later that "[Julia] was interested in [Matthew] from afar because he's so charming. There was a lot of flirting over faxing. She was giving him these questionnaires like, 'Why should I go out with you?' And everyone in the writers' room helped him explain to her why. He could do pretty well without us, but there was no question we were on Team Matthew and trying to make it happen for him."

In the end, all our efforts worked. Not only did Julia agree to do the show, but she also sent me a gift: bagels—lots and lots of bagels. Sure, why not? It was Julia fucking Roberts.

Thus began a three-month-long courtship by daily faxes. This was pre-internet, pre–cell phones—all our exchanges were done by fax. And there were many; hundreds. At first, it was the edges of romance: I sent her poems, asked her to name the triple crown line on the Los Angeles Kings, that kind of thing. And it wasn't like we weren't both busy—I was shooting the most popular show on the planet, and she was shooting a Woody Allen movie, *Everyone Says I Love You,* in France. (Of course she was.) But three or four times a day I would sit by my fax machine and watch the piece of paper slowly revealing her next missive. I was so excited that some nights I would find myself out at some party sharing a flirtatious exchange with an attractive woman and cut the conversation short so I could race home and see if a new fax had arrived. Nine times out of ten, one had. They were so smart—the way she strung sentences together, the way she saw the world, the way she articulated her unique thoughts, all was so captivating. It wasn't uncommon for me to read these faxes three, four, sometimes five times, grinning at that paper like some kind of moron. It was like she was placed on this planet to make the world smile, and now, in particular, me. I was grinning like some fifteen-year-old on his first date.

And we had never even spoken yet, much less met each other.

Then early one morning, something changed. Julia's fax veered romantic. I called a friend and said, "I'm in over my head. You have to come over right away. Tell me if I'm wrong."

When he arrived, I showed him the fax and he said, "Yup, you are not wrong. You are most certainly in over your head."

"What am I supposed to send back?"

"Well, how do you *feel*?"

"Oh, fuck off," I said, "just tell me what to say."

So, "Cyrano" and I compiled and sent a fax that veered romantic, too. Then we stood there, by the fax machine, looking at each other. Two men just staring at a machine.

After about ten minutes, the jarring sound of the fax machine—all bongs and whirrs and hissing messages from outer space—filled my apartment.

"Call me," it said, and her phone number was at the bottom.

I picked up the phone and called Julia Roberts. I was nervous as hell, as nervous as my first appearance on Letterman. But the conversation went easy—I made her laugh, and man, what a *laugh*. . . . She was clearly extremely smart, a big intellect. I could tell already that she was easily in the top three of storytellers that I had ever met, too. Her stories were so good, in fact, that at one point I asked her if she had written them out ahead of time.

Five and half hours later, as we came to a close, I realized I wasn't nervous anymore. After that we could not be stopped—five-hour conversations here, four-hour conversations there. We were falling; I wasn't sure into what, but we were falling.

It was clear that we were in deep smit.

One Thursday, my phone rang again.

"I'll be at your house at two P.M., Saturday."

Click.

And there we had it.

How did she even know where I lived? What if she didn't like me? What if the faxes and the phone calls were all really cute but when it came to real life, she didn't want me anymore?

Why can't I stop *drinking?*

Sure enough, at 2:00 P.M. that Saturday, there was a knock on my door. *Deep breaths, Matty.* When I opened it, there she was, there was a smiling Julia Roberts on the other side.

I believe I said something like:

"Oh, *that* Julia Roberts."

Even in moments like this, the jokes just flew by. Craig would have said it faster, but he wasn't there. She laughed that Julia Roberts laugh, the one that could launch a thousand ships. And any tension seemed to just vaporize.

She asked me how I was doing.

"I'm feeling like the luckiest man in the word. How are *you* doing?"

"You should probably invite me in now."

I did let her in, both figuratively and literally, and a relationship began. We would already be a couple by the time we started filming the *Friends* Super Bowl episode.

But before we filmed it, it was New Year's Eve, in Taos. It was about to be 1996. I was dating Julia Roberts. I'd even met her family. She picked me up in her orange Volkswagen Beetle, after flying me there privately. I thought I had money. *She* had money.

We'd played football in the snow all day. Later, Julia looked at me, looked at her watch—11:45 P.M.—took my hand, and said, "Come with me."

We jumped in this big blue truck and drove up a mountain, snow swirling around. I had no idea where we were going. We seemed to be heading up into the very stars themselves. Eventually, we reached a mountaintop, and for a moment the weather cleared, and we could see New Mexico and beyond, all the way back to Canada. As we sat there, she made me feel like the king of the world. A gentle snow was falling, and with that, 1996 began.

In February, Julia went on Letterman, and he pressed her on whether or not we were dating. She had just guest starred in the *Friends* episode "The One After the Super Bowl." That episode—replete as it was with guest stars like Julia, Jean-Claude Van Damme, Brooke Shields, and Chris Isaak, among others—was viewed by 52.9 million people, the most watched show ever to follow a Super Bowl. The ad revenue alone was staggering—more than half a million dollars for thirty seconds of airtime. The show was now solidly NBC's major cash cow.

(And yet, I can still recall a couple of nights thinking, *I wish I was on* ER *instead of* Friends. I could never get enough attention. The problem was still there, my fingerprint, the color of my eyes.)

We'd filmed Julia's part of the double episode a few days after New Year's—January 6 to 8. They'd written lines for me like, "Back then, I used humor as a defense mechanism—thank God I don't do that anymore," and "I've met the perfect woman." Our kiss on the couch was so real people thought it *was* real.

It was. She was wonderful on the show, and our chemistry seemed to seep off televisions all across America.

To answer Letterman, Julia yet again proved her smarts by fucking with everyone:

"Yes, I've been going out with Matthew Perry, and for some reason, maybe because I did the Super Bowl show, people think it is the Matthew Perry from *Friends*. But, in fact, it's this haberdasher I met in Hoboken. But Matthew Perry from *Friends* is nice, too, so I don't mind that mistake."

Me at thirty-eight years of age

Baby feeding baby

Even then I knew: always
lead with a drink

(*Opposite page*) A little boy and his dad. I have always loved this picture, see? There were plenty of good things, too!

I have always been great with kids. Man, I wish I had one of my own.

(Above) My childhood
in a nutshell

Here I am, hopefully
catching something

Here I am with my wonderful sister Maria, who grew up to be a mother of two and a psychiatrist. I assume she has ditched the sweater.

(Below) My youngest sister, Madeline, my brother Will, and me, hiding my teeth

(Bottom) These kids grew up and saved my life

My devilishly handsome father and a very confused boy wondering why my father was marrying another woman. I was ten. Cool bowl haircut I was sporting.

Imagine what I'm thinking in this picture. At my mother's wedding to Keith Morrison. (Those are my grandparents, and that's Keith's son.)

This is me "giving my mom away"

My mom with Pierre Trudeau, the prime minister of Canada *(Photo by Boris Spremo/ Toronto Star via Getty Images)*

(Below) For my fourteenth birthday, my dad got me a dancer named "Polly Darton." You can't make this stuff up.

It starts

My growing-up-way-too-fast sister. Note to the reader: if I had a goatee, I was on Vicodin or any other kind of opiate.

(Below) My dad and me at Boston Garden, playing celebrity hockey. My father was in heaven. I was a Kings fan, but don't tell anyone that.

(Above) Me and my amazing grandmother. I always smiled that way to hide my front teeth, which were slightly out of place. You can see them in *Fools Rush In*. But after that, a studio made me fix them for a movie.

On the set of *Three to Tango* with my sister Madeline, both of us wishing it were a better movie

(*Above*) Madeline and I are obviously comfortable with each other

Here's a picture of Madeline not lying on me (*Steve Granitz/WireImage*)

See? I've always had the legs of a dancer.

(Above, left) In 2002, I was nominated for an Emmy Award for Outstanding Lead Actor in a Comedy Series. I brought my mom. (Vince Bucci/Getty Images)

(Above) Got nominated for everything for The Ron Clark Story; lost everything to Robert Duvall. What a hack. (©TNT/Courtesy Everett Collection)

(Left) First TV show ever. Second Chance. Couldn't have been worse. (Copyright © 20th Century Fox Licensing/Merchandising/Everett Collection)

(Below) This is the show that almost lost me Friends (© YouTube)

(*Above*) With the beautiful River Phoenix
(*Courtesy Everett Collection*)

Me and my ex-girlfriend Rachel. Man, you
don't get prettier than that. (*Gregg DeGuire/
WireImage*)

(*Below*) This is the one photo ever taken of
us where I'm not staring at Rachel
(*Chris Weeks/WireImage*)

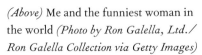

(Above) Me and the funniest woman in the world *(Photo by Ron Galella, Ltd./ Ron Galella Collection via Getty Images)*

(Above, right) Me with Salma Hayek (and Jon Tenney) in my first starring role, in *Fools Rush In (Photo by Getty Images)*

(Center, right) Me with the coolest man in the universe *(© 2000 Warner Photo by Pierre Vinet/MPTV Images.com)*

(Right) The *LA Times* said I gave a "tired performance" in *Seventeen Again*. But that was the whole point— I was supposed to seem tired. *(© 2009 New Line Cinema/Photo by Chuck Zlotnick)*

(Above) Me and the beautiful Lauren Graham (AP Photo/Dan Steinberg)

Me pretending to not be in love with Valerie Bertinelli (Photo by Jim Smeal/Ron Galella Collection via Getty Images)

(Below) Me enjoying my pal, Bradley Whitford (MPTVImages.com)

Best job in the entire world *(Neil Munns/PA Wire/Press Association Images)*

My first and last 8 x 10

She also called me "awfully clever and funny and handsome."
Everything back then was a yes.

Once we'd wrapped season two, in April I headed to Vegas to shoot
my first major movie. I was being paid a million dollars to star in *Fools
Rush In,* with Salma Hayek. To this day, it's probably my best movie.

If I were doing that movie now, I would travel with three people,
mostly because I am scared to be alone. But back then, it was just me.
I wasn't filled with fear the way I would be now. I think that's why
they send young people off to war. They are *young*—they aren't scared;
they are invincible.

Don't get me wrong, I was nervous about making *Fools Rush In.*
There I was, in Vegas, with a $30 million movie on my shoulders. On
the first day, I was being driven home and said to the driver, "You have
to pull over." He did, and I threw up from fear, right there by the side of
the road.

On a movie, not only is the work done slower, but it also only works
if you really are actually feeling what you're trying to portray as a feeling. This deeper work can be hard to transition to, and I found it more
difficult, because on movies you tend to shoot scenes out of order.

I remember on day two of *Fools Rush In* we were shooting a scene at
the obstetrician's office, hearing our baby's heartbeat for the first time. I
had no idea how to get the feeling for it, given that I'd just met Salma.
Later, I remember there was a scene that called for me to cry. I was
very scared about that, too. I thought about it all day long and worried
about it all night. I ended up by pulling it off, somehow. The trick is
easy—you think of something that makes you feel really sad. But the
timing is difficult, because you have to do it at exactly the right time,
and you have to do it over and over again.

That day, I had been crying all day on the set of *Fools Rush In.* I went up to Andy Tennant, the director, and said, "We've been doing this for ten hours, man. I've got nothing left in me."

Andy said, "We need it two more times, buddy."

The prospect of this made me burst into tears. We both laughed and agreed that there must be a little more in the tank. (I actually find dramatic acting easier to do than comedic acting. I look at a scene and think, *I don't have to be funny? This will be a snap.* I have been nominated for four Emmys in my life so far. One in comedy, and three in drama.)

But I was starting to come up with some fun strategies to tap into real feelings and to be more of a leading man than a funny sitcom actor. At noon at the Stratosphere Hotel in Vegas they have a big firework show—I told Salma to look at the hotel then because that was how *my* character felt when he first met *her* character.

Salma had tried her best, too—she came into my trailer at the start of the shoot and said, "Let's just spoon a little bit."

I did my best Chandler impression—the double-take-and-sardonic-stare thing—and said, "Oh, *OK*! Let's just spoon a *little* bit!"

Salma always had a very elaborate and lengthy idea about how to do a scene, but her long-winded ideas weren't always helpful. There's one scene in which I'm professing my love for her. She suggested that we don't look at each other—rather, we should look out at our future together. After listening to this nonsense for about twenty minutes, I finally said: "Listen, Salma," I said, "I'm telling you I love you in this scene. You look wherever you want, but I'm going to be looking at *you*."

Throughout the making of the movie, I had been going through the script and pitching jokes to Andy Tennant, who was a very smart and incredibly nice guy. He sat on me—I was bouncing around doing my funny little things, and he would take me aside and say, "You don't have to do that. You're interesting enough to watch without doing that."

That line of thinking allowed him to pull out of me one of the best performances of my career. Could this be a different way of saying *Matty, you're enough,* the words I've been longing to hear my entire life? (Andy went on to direct dozens of movies, including *Hitch,* starring Will Smith. Nice guys don't finish last, I guess.)

Andy was also open to hearing pitch ideas. One day my friend Andrew Hill Newman was visiting me on set and came up with the line, "You are everything I never knew that I always wanted." I wrote it out and handed it to Andy Tennant, who loved it, and it became the most famous line in the movie. And movie-wise, probably the best line I ever said.

One day during shooting there had been a bunch of people in the background on Lake Mead on Jet Skis, and I asked if I could ride one during the lunch break. But this was the start of the movie, and I was told it was too dangerous.

But everything back then was a yes . . . so I just said, "Erm, you have to say yes to that."

So, I headed out onto Lake Mead. The sun was high; the blue water crackled like a flame. As I zoomed around on the Jet Ski, in the distance I could see the Hoover Dam, where the climax of the movie would be shot, and Mount Wilson hovering over everything like a warning. But everything in my life was perfect. I had the most beautiful, famous woman in the world as my girlfriend; I was on the number one TV show in America; I was making a lot of money shooting a movie that could only be a number one box-office smash. I revved that Jet Ski hard, feeling the loose-soft connection to the water, turning this way and that, the chop bumping me up and down on the seat, my right hand turning and turning and turning, pushing that machine to its limit.

And then I turned the Jet Ski hard right, but my body went straight on. I was airborne, and then I was not airborne. Once I surfaced, I looked back to where I'd started, and there stood forty people on the shoreline, the entire crew, who had been watching me risk the entire movie, and who now all dove into Lake Mead to get me.

When I got back to shore, I knew I was hurt. That night, there was a big scene to shoot—the birth-of-the-baby scene, the key moment—and I had to be right for it. But everything was hurting; I had especially fucked up my neck. The crew knew I was struggling, so they called a doctor, who came by my trailer and handed me a single pill in a plastic package.

"Take this when you're done," the doctor said. "Everything will be fine."

I stashed that pill in my pocket, and I swear to God I think if I'd never taken it, none of the next three decades would have gone the way they did. Who knows? I just know it was really bad.

My character in *Fools Rush In* is a real estate developer who drives a red Mustang. The scene that night went on and on, but just before dawn we wrapped. I could sense the sun edging closer to the horizon.

"Hey, can I drive that Mustang home to Vegas, do you think?" I asked.

I'm amazed, after the Jet Ski debacle, that they said yes to anything right then. But they did.

The first light of that Nevada day was creeping over Mount Wilson when I left the lot. I put the top down of that Mustang and swallowed the pill. I thought about Julia; I thought about flying across Lake Mead, not a care in the world. I thought about my childhood, but it didn't hurt, not then. As the pill kicked in, something clicked in me. And it's been that click I've been chasing the rest of my life. I thought about fame and Craig Bierko and the Murray brothers and *Friends*. The summer was coming up, all pink cirrus clouds and soft, desert air.

This was my pink sky. I felt so good that if a locomotive hit me, I would simply turn to the engineer and say, "It happens, brother." I was lying in the grass in Canada in my backyard, surrounded once again with Murray puke. I couldn't believe how good I felt; I was in complete and pure euphoria. The pill had replaced the blood in my body with warm honey. I was on top of the world. It was the greatest feeling I'd ever had. Nothing could ever go wrong. As I drove that red Mustang convertible to my rented house in Vegas, I remember thinking, *If this doesn't kill me, I'm doing this again.* This is a bad memory, of course, because of what followed, but it was also a good memory. I was close to God that morning. I had felt heaven—not many people get that. I shook hands with God that morning.

Was it God, or someone else?

My first move when I got home that morning was to get in touch with that doctor and tell him that the pill had worked for the pain (I decided to leave that God part out). I went to sleep, and when I woke up, forty more of those pills had been delivered to my house. Eureka!

Be careful, Matty, something that feels that good must come with consequences. I know the consequences now—boy, do I ever. But I didn't know them then. I wish that was all there was to say about *Fools Rush In.* Fun, inside-baseball stories about how movies get made. Hate to burst the celebrity-industrial complex bubble, but there are real lives going on, too, behind the glamour and the martini shots and the A-cameras. However, what no one could tell was that someone's life, probably the least likely candidate, was about to plummet into the gates of hell.

A year and a half later, I was taking fifty-five of those pills a day. I weighed 128 pounds when I checked into Hazelden rehab in Minnesota, my life in ruins. I was in raw fear, certain I was going to die, having no idea what had happened to me. I wasn't trying to die; I was just trying to feel better.

Of course, "Matthew Perry is in rehab" became a huge news story. I was not even granted the opportunity to work out my problems in privacy. Everyone knew. It was on the covers of all the magazines—I didn't even get the anonymity everyone else got. I was terrified. I was also young, so I bounced back quickly. Within twenty-eight days, I was back on my feet again and looking healthy.

This was a big news story, too, but nowhere near the size of the other one.

Making movies is a completely different animal from making TV. On *Friends,* if you were sad about something you'd play it up, as though you're the saddest person in the world—basically, for the back row of the live audience. There's sort of a wink to the audience in your performance, too, as if to say, "Hey, everybody, watch this. You're going to enjoy this." When you do a sitcom, it's like you're doing a one-act play every week. There are three hundred people in the audience, and you have to open up to them.

Film work is much, much slower—there's a master shot and then a closeup, and then an even *closer* closeup. And if your character was sad, you played him sad. There was no winking—this was the pros, baby. But on *Friends* we even *rehearsed* quickly. I remember Alec Baldwin guest starring once and saying, "You guys are going so fast!"

There were guest stars all the time, which meant we always had to think on our feet. Sean Penn was one of my favorites—he appeared in two episodes in season eight and nailed it. His story line called for me to be dressed up as a pink bunny rabbit (it was Halloween), so at the end of the table read, I said, "I've always dreamed of working with Sean Penn, but I never thought I'd have to wear a pink bunny rabbit suit to do so."

Despite not having an actual fourth wall of the apartment, *Friends* never broke the metaphorical fourth wall, either. The closest we ever got was with Sean—I had pitched a tag (the brief end scene after the main story has landed) that had me backstage in the bunny rabbit suit. Sean walks by and I say, "Sean, can I talk to you for a second?"

"Sure, Matthew, what's up?"

"Well, I've been really giving this a lot of thought. And I think you're a good person to talk to about this." I'm smoking as I say this, and as I put the cigarette out with my huge bunny foot, I say, "I've been looking to transition myself into dramatic work."

Sean Penn looks me up and down for about five beats and just says, "Good luck."

It got a great laugh at the table read. But it broke a rule we never broke in ten years. Even someone as powerful as Sean Penn and me looking ridiculous in a huge pink bunny costume could not get the go-ahead to break the fourth wall. It stayed in place. Right where it should be.

Everybody had their particular years on *Friends* when the whole world was talking about their character. David Schwimmer's was the first season; season two, it was Lisa; seasons five and six were Courteney and me; Jen was seasons seven and eight, and Matt (Most Improved Friend) was nine and ten. Some of them won Emmys for those seasons and all of us should have won more than we did, but I think there's a bias against attractive rich people with an apartment that's way too big for reality in New York City . . . except, as I always pointed out, there was no fourth wall.

During that first year—David's year—he showed up one day at my dressing room. He had brought an original hangdog expression to his character and was just damn funny. He was also the first one of us to shoot a commercial, be on *The Tonight Show,* buy a house, get his own movie. He was the hot guy that first year, and rightly so. He had been hilarious.

That day in my dressing room, he sat down opposite me and started in.

"Matty," he said, "I've been thinking. When we renegotiate our contracts, we should do it as a team. We should all get paid the same amount." He was by far the one in the best position to negotiate. I could not believe what he was saying. Needless to say, I was thrilled. I was perfectly happy to take advantage of his generosity of spirit.

It was a decision that proved to be extremely lucrative down the line. David had certainly been in a position to go for the most money, and he didn't. I would like to think that I would have made the same move, but as a greedy twenty-five-year-old, I'm not sure I would have. But his decision served to make us take care of each other through what turned out to be a myriad of stressful network negotiations, and it gave us a tremendous amount of power. By season eight, we were making a million dollars per episode; by season ten we were making even more. We were making $1,100,040 an episode, and we were asking to do *fewer* episodes. Morons, all of us. We had David's goodness, and his astute business sense, to thank for what we had been offered. I owe you about $30 million, David. (We were still morons.)

Being on *Friends* was one of those unicorn situations where the news just kept getting better and better. But off-screen, things weren't going so well. In late April 1996, I went on Jay Leno and admitted I was single. Dating Julia Roberts had been too much for me. I had been constantly certain that she was going to break up with me—why would she not? I was not enough; I could never be enough; I was broken, bent, unlovable. So instead of facing the inevitable agony of losing her, I broke up with the beautiful and brilliant Julia Roberts. She might have considered herself slumming it with a TV guy, and TV guy was now breaking up with her. I can't begin to describe the look of confusion on her face.

I decided to party in Cape Cod with the Murray brothers. I have no idea why I chose Cape Cod, or why the Murray brothers came with me. I imagined it was just a new place to barhop. It was there that I noticed that something had changed, though—a new dynamic was at play. Girls were coming up and talking to me; the days of nervously approaching women with mediocre lines were over. I just stood in a corner, a vodka tonic in hand, and they came to me.

None of them were Julia Roberts, though.

I've detoxed over sixty-five times in my life—but the first was when I was twenty-six.

My Vicodin habit had now kicked in badly. If you watch season three of *Friends,* I hope you'll be horrified at how thin I am by the end of the season (opioids fuck with your appetite, plus they make you vomit constantly). In the final episode, you'll see that I'm wearing a white shirt, and tan slacks, and both look at least three sizes too big for me. (Compare this to the difference in how I look between the final episode of season six and the first of season seven—the Chandler-Monica proposal episodes. I'm wearing the same clothes in the final episode of six and the first of seven [it's supposed to be the same night], but I must have lost fifty pounds in the off-season. My weight varied between 128 pounds and 225 pounds during the years of *Friends.*)

You can track the trajectory of my addiction if you gauge my weight from season to season—when I'm carrying weight, it's alcohol; when I'm skinny, it's pills. When I have a *goatee,* it's *lots* of pills.

By the end of season three, I was spending most of my time figuring out how to get fifty-five Vicodin a day—I had to have fifty-five every day, otherwise I'd get so sick. It was a full-time job: making calls, seeing doctors, faking migraines, finding crooked nurses who would give me what I needed.

It had taken me a while to realize what was happening. At the start, I'd been taking something like twelve a day, and then went cold turkey one day, and felt absolutely terrible. *Something's really wrong with me,* I thought, but I kept going and kept going. *I'll finish the season of* Friends *and then I'll get treatment for this.*

I almost killed myself by that decision. Had the season lasted another month, I would no longer be here.

I was never high while I was working. I loved those people—I wanted to always step up for them, and I was the second baseman for the New York Yankees. But addiction wakes up before you do, and it wants you alone. Alcoholism will win every time. As soon as you raise your hand and say, "I'm having a problem," alcohol sneers, *You're gonna* say *something about it? Fine, I'll go away for a while. But I'll be back.*

It never goes away for good.

I had quickly booked another movie, *Almost Heroes,* a comedy starring Chris Farley and directed by Christopher Guest. They paid me $2 million for that. We shot it in the shitty part of Northern California, up near Eureka. Farley was just as funny as you'd imagine, though his addictions, plus mine, meant that we barely were able to even finish the fucking thing. I was shooting *Friends* and *Almost Heroes* at the same time, and I was tired. The pills were not doing what they used to do. I had to take a certain number just to not feel sick all the time.

Eating got in the way of the high, too, so I never ate. Plus, I was always so sick I didn't want to eat. I was constantly vomiting. This was fine in private, but not great when you are in the middle of the woods talking to Christopher Guest. *You are going to throw up in thirty seconds. Better figure out a way to excuse yourself and fast.* I vomited behind trees, behind rocks, in ladies' rooms. I had heard tell of people looking through their own vomit for chunks of pills that they could take again, but I couldn't bring myself to do that. I already had so many doctors on the payroll I was rarely in that kind of need anyway. But I did have two towels next to my toilet—one to wipe away the vomit and one to wipe away the tears. I was dying, but I couldn't tell anyone about it.

Then, Chris Farley died. His disease had progressed faster than mine had. (Plus, I had a healthy fear of the word "heroin," a fear we did not share.) I punched a hole through Jennifer Aniston's dressing room wall when I found out. I had to promote *Almost Heroes* two weeks after he died; I found myself publicly discussing his death from drugs and alcohol.

I was high the entire time.

No one knew—not my family, my friends, no one. I was impossibly sick all the time. I would try to quit every now and then—three days here, four days there—but it just made me so sad and sick that it was impossible to sustain.

I was home one night, trying to make sense of all of it, when a call came in from an ex-girlfriend.

"I know there is something wrong with you," she said. "And I am taking you to a doctor."

I crumbled. I told her everything. I had never cried that much in my life. The secret was out. Someone else knew.

I saw a doctor the next day. He told me to go to Hazelden.

"They have a big lake, there," the doctor said, and I figured, *It's Minnesota—close enough to Canada. At least I'll feel at home in the shitty weather.*

But I was scared out of my mind. This was real, now. I was on my way to rehab. I was twenty-six years old.

I went to Hazelden to kick pills and managed to learn precisely nothing.

The plan was that before I trekked up to Minnesota I'd go through a rapid detox. In a rapid detox they put you out for two or three days

and fill you with antagonists for opiates. By the end of it, you're supposed to be sober. (By the way, I know now that it doesn't work, even
though it's still used as a treatment.)

So, I did the rapid detox and *then* went up to Hazelden, but once
I arrived, I felt like death. What they say about opioid detoxes is they
can't kill you, but they can make you wish that you were dead. (The
detoxes that *can* kill you are alcohol and benzos.) I was in my room at
Hazelden and I was incredibly sick—I kicked like a fucking dog. Legs,
arms, jerking and herking in sheer terror. I was continually begging for
some relief, only to be told "you're detoxed, just relax."

But I was not detoxed—I'd merely gone from fifty-five Vicodin a
day to zero Vicodin a day, basically cold turkey. I became what was
called a "wall hugger"—to even move a few steps I had to grab onto the
nearest wall.

I know now that if I hadn't done the rapid detox, I would have
been given something to ease the agony, but they thought I'd detoxed, so they let me be. Going from fifty-five to nothing shows I was
at least a fucking strong person I suppose, but it was the purest form
of hell.

About ten days into my stay, I was in a group session when everything got a little fuzzy. I'm told I kept saying "I'm fine, totally fine,"
but I was not fine. My childhood training—that I could never be a bad
boy—was so strong I guess that even while having a grand mal seizure
I had to make sure I didn't rock the boat.

When I woke up from the seizure, I was back in my room, and all
the staff had gathered, terrified. Not knowing what had happened, and
clearly still deeply confused, I said, "Oh my God, I can't believe you
guys came to California to see me. That's so nice!"

"You're not in California," someone said, "you're in Minnesota. You
had a grand mal seizure."

I stayed for another two weeks, and by the end of it, I felt like I ran the place, I was the king of the place. And the way I managed that was simply to imitate Michael Keaton in *Clean and Sober*.

I was young enough that I put some weight on, played a bunch of tennis, and stopped taking pills. But inside I knew I was going to drink again. Once I felt better, I headed back to California—I wasn't back to normal, but I felt fine. But as I said, I had learned precisely nothing about what was wrong with me. I hadn't learned about AA, or how to live a sober life; I'd just gotten off the Vicodin. For those of you watching, this was the beginning of season four—the best I ever looked on the show. Still not good enough for Jennifer Aniston, but pretty fucking good.

Back in Cali, I lasted sixty-eight days and then I had my first drink, my theory being that drinking wasn't the thing that had almost killed me. It was opiates that almost killed me; vodka had only ever filled the holes, and as the holes were still there, something had to fill them.

I drank every night until 2001.

The run-up to Hazelden had been probably the best year of my life, the best year anyone could ever wish for. The joys of fame had not quite worn off, though if I'd died then, my headstone would have read either: HERE LIES MATTHEW PERRY—HE BROKE UP WITH JULIA ROBERTS or, COULD I *BE* MORE STUPID AND DEAD?

In 1999, I fell hard for a woman I was working with on a movie. (I was starting to have a track record of falling for women who were famous, just as my mother had been in Canada.) All the walls dropped, and I was just myself . . . and then she picked somebody else to be in love with.

I've been able to get most people I've wanted, but this one still hurts. Which just shows that the exception proves the rule: when I can get someone, I have to leave them before they leave me, because I'm not enough and I'm about to be found out, but when someone I want doesn't choose me, that just proves I'm not enough and I've been found out. Heads they win, tails I lose. Either way, to this day if someone mentions her name, my stomach clenches. The fear that drives my every waking minute had come true. She had even mentioned that my drinking was a problem—just another thing that addiction has cost me. You would think that might knock somebody sober, but it actually made it worse. I lit candles all over my house, drank, watched the movie we were in together, torturing myself, alone, heartsick, trying to get over it. Failing.

I was bloated and looked awful, and it was dangerous.

I remember realizing when I was in ninth grade in Ottawa that Michael J. Fox had both the number one movie and the number one TV show at the same time, and even then, at the age of fourteen, steam came out of my ears with envy. Later, I told *The New York Times,* "You want the attention, you want the bucks, and you want the best seat in the restaurant." Fast-forward to the hiatus between seasons five and six of *Friends* and I found myself filming *The Whole Nine Yards,* and sure enough, when it came out in early 2000, I had the number one TV show and the number one movie.

Me? I was taking so many pills that I couldn't leave my bedroom. So, in a moment when you'd think Matthew Perry would be celebrating and being the toast of the town, I was just handling drug dealers and living in dark rooms and misery.

In nature, when a penguin is injured, the other penguins group around it and prop it up until it's better. This is what my costars on *Friends* did for me. There were times on set when I was extremely hungover, and Jen and Courteney, being devoted to cardio as a cure-all, had a Lifecycle exercise bike installed backstage. In between rehearsals and takes, I'd head back there and ride that thing like the fires of hell were chasing me—anything to get my brain power back to normal. I was the injured penguin, but I was determined to not let these wonderful people, and this show, down.

But still, the addiction ravaged me—one time, in a scene in the coffeehouse when I'm dressed in a suit, I fell asleep right there on the couch, and disaster was averted only when Matt LeBlanc nudged me awake right before my line; no one noticed, but I knew how close I'd come.

But I always showed up, and always had the lines.

And then I got pancreatitis. I was thirty years old.

It was during hiatus. I was alone, again, there was nothing going on—no movie to shoot, nothing, just slow, tar-like time, slipping down the LA canyons toward the endless sea. I was just sitting at home for months drinking—alone so I could drink; drinking, therefore alone. (As I said, alcoholism is desperate to get you on your own.) I was watching the movie *Meet Joe Black* on repeat, even though it's about the character Death (me), trying to figure out what love is. Perfect. But it was as if I were Joe Black myself, repeatedly being asked, "What do we do now?" I was like death—I'd drink, watch the movie, pass out, wake up, drink, watch that movie, pass out.

Then, out of nowhere, I felt a knife slide into my stomach, just like that. It pierced the membrane, twisted a little, its serrated edge catching on the veins, heating my blood to boiling and beyond. As that knife got deeper and deeper, I heard myself screaming in pain, an animal being ripped to shreds up in the canyons.

I called my sort-of girlfriend at the time, the wonderful Jamie Tarses, and managed to say, "There's something *wrong*."

Jamie was an angel from God—she drove straight over to my house, poured me into a car, and drove me to the nearest hospital.

In the ER I was screaming, "You gotta pump my stomach! You gotta pump my stomach!"

The doctor just stared at me.

"I don't need to pump your stomach. It's not food poisoning."

"Then what the fuck is it?" I wailed.

"You have pancreatitis," he said. "Which is something you can only get from drinking too much."

There are a few causes of pancreatitis, actually—you can have an autoimmune disease, or an infection, or gallstones, but mostly you get it from drinking a fuck-ton of alcohol. Pancreatitis at the age of thirty was unheard of. Yay for me! Another record.

"Fuck that," I said, "no. I don't drink too much. . . ." It could have been shame; it could have been denial. I think they're hard to tell apart. Whatever it was, I made Jamie drive me home.

After about an hour at my house, I knew something was still seriously wrong, so this time we went to a different hospital, but got the same answer.

For thirty days and nights I was in the hospital, fed fluids through an IV (the only way to treat pancreatitis was to leave the pancreas completely alone, which meant I could not eat or drink anything for about thirty days); and for every one of those nights, I'd fall asleep with Jamie Tarses by my side—she had a bed moved in, the whole bit—so I'd wake up to find her there, too. (I still believe Jamie was a messenger from a benevolent God, and that none of us were worthy of her—I know I wasn't.) We'd watch *The West Wing* over and over while I smoked—yes, I smoked in my hospital room. It was a different time, or I was so fucking famous at the time that it didn't matter. At one point they caught me and told me to stop. But I was desperate, so I checked myself out of the hospital, had a cigarette, and then checked myself back in.

It took seven hours to go through intake again. It was worth it.

To ease the pain they hooked me up to a machine that administered regular amounts of a drug called Dilaudid. It is an opioid that changes the brain's relationship to pain—if only it came in human form. But I loved Dilaudid—it was my new favorite drug, and I would have stayed in that hospital for a hundred days if they kept administrating it. For those thirty days I had Jamie at my side, and I was high and happy. Especially happy when I signed the deal for seasons six and seven, the deal that, owing to David Schwimmer's selfless and brilliant idea, brought us $50 million. I signed that contract with a feeding tube in my arm and Dilaudid flowing through my brain.

But they were onto me—clearly, I was asking for too much of the wonder drug.

"You're fine," one doctor said. "Your pancreatitis is over. You have to go home. Tomorrow."

"You mean you're not going to give me Dilaudid *tonight*?"

"No," he said, "we are *not*."

Somehow, I got through the night, but nobody knew what to do with me.

Enter, stage left, my father. Bless him, he offered to have me live with him and his family in Ojai, a town northwest of LA.

"Come live with us," he said, "go to some AA meetings. Get yourself straight."

It was an OK option, and with nothing else to do, I headed back to my home on Chelan Way in the Hollywood Hills to pick up some things. I was sober, but I had just been on Dilaudid for thirty days, so I was still a little out of it. Jamie waited while I packed a bag, then I followed her in my green Porsche out along the winding roads in the Hills. As I made my first left onto Chelan Drive there was a courier van right in the middle of the road coming toward me, so I swerved and pumped the brakes, but the car hit some grass and just kept going and I drove into the stairs leading up to a house, demolishing them, and then on into the living room. Fortunately, no one was home, but the car was a wreck, and so were the stairs.

Fucking stairwells once again.

I did the right thing and waited for the cops to arrive. I kept glancing up at the sky, wondering when the next cartoon anvil was going to fall on my head. I was there long enough for someone to take a picture and sell it to *People* magazine—my car in a house, me on the way to staying with my father in Ojai.

It was like I was fifteen again, living with my dad in California. A car would come to pick me up every day to take me to film *Friends*. But it wasn't too long until I picked up Vicodin again, and then started fucking drinking again, and liking it again. To quote my therapist, "Reality is an acquired taste," and I had failed to acquire it. I was sneaking both drugs and alcohol into my dad's house, and his wife was so angry that eventually my father very calmly approached me and told me that I had to leave.

Oh, I'll leave, but neither of you will ever see a dime of my money, ever, I thought, but I did not say.

I returned for the next season of *Friends* high as a kite, and everyone knew that something had to be done.

I had already heard about methadone, a drug that promised to remove a fifty-five-a-day Vicodin habit in one day with one little sip. The only catch was, you had to drink that little sip every day, or you would go into serious withdrawal. *Sounds good to me,* my desperate mind thought. I got on the drug immediately and was able to return to *Friends* the next day, sharp as a tack.

I had been told that methadone had no side effects. This was not true. In fact, it was the beginning of the end.

Otherwise, everything else was going great. *Friends* was still as successful as ever. And then another cast member came to my trailer. It wasn't David this time, and it wasn't good news.

"I know you're drinking," she said.

I had long since gotten over her—ever since she started dating Brad Pitt, I was fine—and had worked out exactly how long to look at her without it being awkward, but still, to be confronted by Jennifer Aniston was devastating. And I was confused.

"How can you tell?" I said. I never worked drunk. "I've been trying to hide it. . . ."

"We can smell it," she said, in a kind of weird but loving way, and the plural "we" hit me like a sledgehammer.

"I know I'm drinking too much," I said, "but I don't exactly know what to do about it."

Sometimes I wasn't OK to drive to set (I never worked high, but I certainly worked hungover) and I'd take a limo—that will get you some dubious looks from people, let me tell you. Everyone would ask me if I was all right, but nobody wanted to stop the *Friends* train because it was such a moneymaker, and I just felt horrible about it. My greatest joy was also my biggest nightmare—I was this close to messing up this wonderful thing.

Eventually I got a sober companion at work with me, but it wasn't really helping. One day I had taken some kind of medication and had drunk the night before, and it all kicked in during a run-through in front of everyone. But there was a curious twist to this one: I was hammered but didn't know it, so I thought there was nothing to hide. I didn't know that I was wasted, but I was slurring. Folks couldn't understand a word that came out of my mouth. But I had no idea.

Once again, I went back to my dressing room and everybody from the show was there.

"What are you going to do, Matty?" they said.

"It's medication, I'll fix it. I'm sorry."

I didn't drink that night and the next day I showed up to work, but I was on thin ice.

I called my manager.

"Yeah," he said, "they're onto you."

The writers, the cast—fuck, *everybody*—knew, so I said, "You gotta get me a movie. Right now. Get me out of here."

Once again, my idea was to pull a geographic. I still thought if I removed myself from the situation I was in, I would be able to quit all the drugs and drinking and come out fighting. (All I was actually doing was tripling my workload while the drinking and drugs continued to escalate.) Because wherever you go, there you are. This also reminded me of the time I'd begged for a pilot and had gotten *L.A.X. 2194*. Back then I'd had enough juice to get a pilot and thereby enough money to drink at the Formosa; now, as the new century dawned, I had enough juice to be able to score a movie if I wanted it. *Serving Sara* would be filmed in Dallas, and I have no idea why I thought that would be the perfect place to get sober. . . .

Serving Sara was a bad movie, but it was made much worse by how bad I was in it.

I was in terrible shape, and I was overextended. I was working four days a week on the movie and then flying on a private jet back to Los Angeles to do *Friends*. On the plane I'd have a water bottle filled with vodka that I'd sip from continually as I read over my lines. (In fact, if you're keeping score at home, I was actually on methadone, Xanax, cocaine, and a full quart of vodka a day.) One day in Dallas I showed up to do a scene only to realize that we'd filmed it a few days earlier. Things were unraveling.

Jamie Tarses—beautiful, amazing, caring, genius Jamie Tarses—flew out to Texas and was basically my nurse, but I was still drinking and taking all the drugs and trying to hide it from her. One night we were watching TV and she turned to me, and she said, "It looks like you're disappearing."

A window opened—the slightest crack, but open.

"I don't want to disappear," I whispered. "Stop everything."

I called my manager, I called my father, I called everybody.

"I'm completely fucked-up," I said. "I need help. I need to go to rehab."

Serving Sara shut down, something that later cost me $650,000. Small price to save my life. *Friends* postponed my scenes. And off I went to a detox center in Marina del Rey this time, on the west side of LA. I was a car going two hundred miles an hour that just hit a brick wall; a green Porsche hitting a stairwell. (Fucking *fucking* stairwells.)

The first day they said, "Go to your room; you're not taking any more drugs," but they may have well said:

"Go to your room and just don't breathe anymore."

"But I have to breathe to live."

"No. People have done it before. People have gone in there and stopped breathing."

That's exactly what it felt like.

I spent one month there. One night during my stay, I was smoking a cigarette and it was raining and there was a light bulb swinging in the smoking section. And I said out loud, "This is what hell is. I'm in hell."

It was in del Rey when I finally picked up the Big Book of Alcoholics Anonymous. About thirty pages in I read: "These men were not drinking to escape; they were drinking to overcome a craving beyond their mental control."

I closed the book and began to weep. I'm weeping now just thinking about it. I was not alone. There was an entire group of people who thought the way I did. (And William Silkworth had written this line on July 27, 1938.) It was an amazing moment and a terrible moment all at the same time. What this line meant was that I was never going to be alone again. It also meant that I was an alcoholic and would have to stop drinking and drugging right now, and every day, one day at a time, for the rest of my life.

The folks at Marina del Rey said, "This guy is *hard-core*. Thirty days is not going to do it for him. He needs long-term treatment." So, from there they sent me to a Malibu rehab, where I spent the first twelve days not sleeping at all. My liver enzymes were off the charts high. But after about three months I started to get better—I took part in the groups and "did the work," as they say.

I was living in rehab when Monica and Chandler got married. It was May 17, 2001.

Two months earlier, on March 25, 2001, I'd been detoxing one night when the powers that be decided to give us all the night off to watch the Academy Awards. I was lying there, sweating and twitching, filled with fear, barely listening, when Kevin Spacey stepped up to the podium and intoned:

"The nominees for best performance by an actress in a leading role are:

Joan Allen, in *The Contender*;
Juliette Binoche, in *Chocolat*;
Ellen Burstyn, in *Requiem for a Dream*;
Laura Linney, in *You Can Count on Me*;

and

Julia Roberts, in *Erin Brockovich*."

Then he said,
"And the Oscar goes to . . . *Julia Roberts!*"
I watched as Julia kissed her boyfriend at the time, the actor Benjamin Bratt, and walked up the steps to receive her award.

"Thank you, thank you, ever so much," she said. "I'm *so* happy. . . ." As she made her speech, a voice rose in that room in that rehab, urgent, sad, soft, angry, pleading, filled with longing and tears, arguing with the universe while God calmly tapped his cane on the hard, cold world.

I made a joke.

"I'll take you back," I said. "I'll take you back."

The whole room laughed, though this was not a funny line in a sitcom. This was real life now. Those people on the TV were no longer my people. No, the people I was lying in front of, shaking, covered in blankets, were my people now. And I was lucky to have them. They were saving my life.

On Julia's big night in Hollywood, I crawled into bed and stared at the ceiling. There would be no sleep for me that night. Just thoughts racing through my head like someone had fired a bullet into a tin can. *That blue truck, that mountaintop. All the blue trucks, all mountaintops, gone, vanished like ether in a vacuum of fear.* I was incredibly happy for her. As for me, I was just grateful to have made it one more day. When you are at the bottom, the days are long.

I didn't need an Oscar, I just needed one more day.

Holes

Addiction is like the Joker. It just wants to see the whole world burn.

6

Bruce Willis

After three long months of rehab, I was feeling better.

Back on my feet, I was very excited to live a life that was not completely ruled by my alcoholism and addiction. I had stopped drinking and drugging. And my cravings for each had disappeared. Something way, way bigger than me was in charge now. Miracles do happen.

The first move I made was driving to Jamie Tarses's house.

"I need time to process being sober," I said to her, "and that's going to take up all my time. I'm incredibly grateful for all the wonderful things you did for me."

I could see her face losing color.

"But . . . I can't be in a relationship right now," I said.

So, to be clear: in order to adequately pay sweet, wonderful Jamie back for two years of giving up huge portions of her own very busy and important life by basically being my nurse, I ended our relationship. Jamie Tarses was one of the most magical, beautiful, smart . . . oh so smart. I loved the way her mind worked. And I broke up with her. Proving that getting sober didn't make *me* any smarter—in fact it may have made me a colossal idiot. Jamie was probably the most amazing person I had ever met, and she loved me. But I wasn't ready for that.

What I said to Jamie that day was all bullshit, of course. I was newly sober, I was a huge star, and I wanted to sleep with every single girl in Southern California.

And, I did. [Insert cartoon anvil landing on my head here.]

Because of this huge star thing, I had no problem getting dates. And this is how I opened each and every one of them.

"Hi, sorry I'm late.

"You look great by the way. I've been really excited to finally meet you." [Pause for appropriate positive response.]

"But I don't want to get off on the wrong foot here," I would continue. "I want to be as transparent as possible. I am an open book. Ask me anything—I will tell you the truth."

More warmth would here be shared; on a good day, she would tend to be nodding along, loving my transparency, my emotional pitch, my very air of suave involvement.

Then, I'd bring the hammer down.

"I'm not sure what you are looking for, but if it's any kind of emotional attachment, I am not your man." [Pause to let this sink in.]

"I'm not going to call you every day," I went on, "and I'm not going to be your *boyfriend*. But if it's fun you're looking for, I. Am. *Your*. Man."

That great twentieth-century philosopher Cyndi Lauper was right as it turned out—girls do in fact just want to have fun. But in case the message wasn't entirely clear, I added some salt to the heady stew I was ladling out.

"I'm an extremely passionate person," I said, a little abashedly, in case they thought I protesteth too much. "In fact, I'm a bit of a romantic. Even beating up the elliptical machine, all I do is listen to songs about women in some kind of duress.

"But I am not looking for, or available for, any kind of emotional relationship," I repeated, just in case the message had been a tad fuzzy. "I just got out of a long-term relationship and had just gotten sober and I am not looking to be in one now."

And then it was time to nail the landing.

"Oh, did you want to look at your menu?" I'd say. "I hear the food here is fantastic."

It is amazing to me how many women signed up for this after all that. I presume many of them thought they could change me. What's that you say? Oh yes, I did get the occasional abrupt walkout, of course. A few women would say, "Well, I'm not interested in that at all," and would just get up and leave. (No surprise that those were the ones that I was *really* interested in.)

But for the most part my speech worked to a tee.

I use the word "worked" loosely. Because I barely need to point out that the best you could say about all this was that at any point you could exchange my head for a donkey's ass and no one would see the difference. Not only had I just broken up with the greatest woman on the planet, what I was proposing was just a giant fucking waste of time. Sex is great and everything, but I think I would be a much more fulfilled person now if I had spent those years looking for something more.

In a life riddled with mistakes, this may have been my biggest one. And mistakes are hard to undo.

During that time, I met at least five women that I could have married, had children with. Had I done so just once, I would not now be sitting in a huge house, overlooking the ocean, with no one to share it with, save a sober companion, a nurse, and a gardener twice a week—a gardener I would often run outside and give a hundred dollars to so he'd turn his fucking leaf blower off. (We can put a man on the moon, but we can't invent a silent one of those things?)

Natasha Wagner was one of these women. Not only is she beautiful, smart, caring, and sexy, she's also the daughter of Natalie Wood and Richard Gregson (and raised by Robert Wagner, and then by Robert Wagner and Jill St. John after her mother's tragic death). Natasha had it all; she was perfect! But I wasn't looking for *perfect,* I was looking for *more.* More, more, more. So, because I'd done the speech at her, and then not properly dated her, we parted ways, and I was left to find even more perfect women when in fact I'd already found them.

A few years later I was driving on the Pacific Coast Highway one day in some kind of fuck-off-everybody car, a car so amazing that I now cannot for the life of me remember what make it was. I had the top down; the glistening sun was picking the edges of the surf out in the ocean and turning it into a slippery silver. Dudes on surfboards lounged around waiting for The One, which never came; I knew exactly how they felt.

Then, my phone rang. It was Natasha. She had fallen for me after one of these dates, so she had had to go—*that's the rule, Matty, that's the rule!*—but somehow, even though I'd jettisoned her, she was still a friend.

"Hey, Matty!" she said in her inimitably sunny way. She was as bright as the sun on the ocean, always. Sometimes I had to look away just to get my bearings back.

"Hey, Natasha! How are you?" I said. It was so lovely to hear from her. "What's going on with you?"

Perhaps, if she was calling me, there was a chance that we . . . ?

"I'm a mother!" she announced. "I just had a baby girl. Clover!"

"Oh . . . ," I said, then quickly recovered, or thought I did. "That's fantastic news, babe. I love that name, too!"

We talked for a little while longer, then we got off the phone. And then, out of nowhere, the fuck-you-everybody car was pulling over—

because *I* was pulling it over—and I lurched to a stop on the verge. The sun was still high, the surfers were up on their boards, but I was utterly thunderstruck with emotion. The giant wave everyone was looking for was happening in my head.

"She could have had that child with me," I said, to no one, as I sobbed like a newborn myself.

I was so sad and alone. I cried for about forty-five minutes until, gradually, a new thought came, like clouds across the sky above an ocean:

Jesus, this is quite a reaction. . . .

It behooved me to work out why I'd broken down so hard. I sat there, wondering, and wondering, until I finally realized what the fuck had I been doing: I'd been looking for an hour or two of pleasure with every woman ever invented when there was so much life I was missing. Is this why I got sober? To sleep with women? Surely God had something better in store for me than that.

I would need to find out, and fast. Natasha's life was blossoming while mine was turning into one huge mistake.

When I try to work out how sobriety and addiction work for me, I keep coming back to this line: *I'm capable of staying sober unless* anything *happens.*

Some quiet days, when I was sober, I'd think back to the recent past and wonder why I'd ever picked up pills or drugs after getting clean. When I was sober, strong, and feeling like a normal person, I'd sometimes have a fantasy of putting on a baseball cap and shades and heading off to mingle with the regular people poking around the La Brea Tar Pits or standing next to some celebrity's star on the Walk of Fame, just to see what it's like. Not in the sense of "I'm a star, I'm better than them"; no, in the sense of "Oh, so this is what a sober life feels like."

But I was still so often just a tourist in sobriety. It was so hard to put down roots in it. Why was it so hard for me, when I'd seen hundreds around me do it with impunity?

I was dating literally everyone and anyone in LA, but I'd also met a woman in New York I really liked. I was not faithful to her, but I loved her. I was newly sober, and famous, and I wanted to fuck everybody in Los Angeles County; many reciprocated my desires. My speech worked far more than it had the right to. But the woman I loved in New York was like a good mom—a great caretaker and so beautiful, so of course I was drawn to her and, of course, I screwed it up. But it wasn't all bad—in LA, I was also working to help other alcoholics get sober—sponsoring people, answering calls whenever needed, imparting advice. *Friends* was a juggernaut, too, and I didn't have to worry about fucking *that* up—I was clean, and I was about to have *my* season, the one where everyone was talking about Chandler. (Nine was the only year I was completely sober for a *Friends* season. Care to hazard a guess as to which was the only year I got nominated for an Emmy for best actor in a comedy? Yup, season nine. If that doesn't tell you something, nothing will. What did I do differently that season? I *listened.* I didn't just stand there and wait for my turn to speak. Sometimes in acting, it's more powerful to listen than to talk. I have tried to incorporate that in real life, too. *Know more, say less.* That's my new mantra.)

The two years flew by; maybe this is what normal people feel. Maybe I'd found my calling; beyond *Friends,* beyond movie stardom, beyond everything, I was here to help people get and stay sober.

And then, something happened, and *I'm capable of staying sober unless* anything *happens.*

One of the women I'd used the speech on had grown attached to me, and as we know, dear reader, if that happens, I have to backpedal.

So, that's what I did. I said, "I *don't* love you. I warned you when I met you. . . . Remember the speech, when I asked you about the menu?"

But it was too late. Some kind of agony-hook was in her; it was my fault. *Is this why I got sober? To sleep with women? And then hurt them? Surely God had something better in store for me than that.*

She was staying at the Beverly Hills Hotel at the time, and I went to see her, but she could not be consoled. She reminded me of my mother—no matter how much charm I used, no matter which funny thing I said, I could not help her pain.

Eventually, she stormed off into the bathroom, leaving me alone in the room. On the side table, there was a knocked-over bottle of Vicodin. Three of the pills had spilled out under the glare of the bedside lamp. She was locked in the bathroom, screaming; I couldn't take care of the situation. This was the *anything* that was happening. So, I took three of the pills, and somehow made it through the night, but I had thereby ended two years of sobriety.

I was in deep, deep shit again. Because once you puncture the membrane of sobriety, the phenomenon of craving kicks in, and you're off to the races one more time.

It was impossible for me to get back. I graduated quickly to getting my own pills. And then I was drinking again. I was knowingly surfing down a long slide to oblivion. But it was bigger than me—there was literally nothing I could do about it.

Looking back, all I would have had to do was to tell someone about it, but that would mean I would have to stop. But stopping was not an option.

At one point in 1999, I was sitting alone in my way-too-big house at the top of Carla Ridge, yet another house with a beautiful view, this time of the Los Angeles Basin. Down there, somewhere, normal Los Angeles life was going on (Tar Pits; Walk of Fame)—up here, I was just waiting it out—drink in one hand, a steady flow of Marlboro Lights in the other. We were five seasons into *Friends*; Ross and Rachel had just stumbled out of a chapel married, ahead of Chandler and Monica. *Friends* was a cultural touchstone, a shorthand for the millennium, the number one show on the planet, everyone's favorite watch.

And that way of speaking! "Could this *be* any hotter?" had swept the nation, and now everyone was talking that way. Clinton was in the White House; the date September 11 meant nothing special, unless it was your birthday or your wedding anniversary. All the water in the world was flowing downhill into a sparkling lake, upon which the most beautiful, nameless birds endlessly floated.

Now, a messenger was at my door, interrupting my reverie. It was as if I was reenacting what had once happened to the Romantic poet Coleridge, who had been interrupted from his own buzz—he got his via opium—by the legendary "person from Porlock." At the time, Coleridge had the entirety of his poem "Kubla Kahn" memorized in his opiate-addled mind, but the messenger who had arrived at his door that day in 1797 had shattered that memory, leaving only fifty-four lines for posterity.

I was no Coleridge, but my buzz had been notable all the same—the view and the vodka tonic and the sweet Marlboro burn had rendered me into a safe place, where I was no longer unaccompanied, where somehow, back there in the house behind me, a beautiful wife and a gaggle of amazing kids were tumbling around in the playroom while Daddy had some quality time alone in his screening room. (You want to feel lonely? Watch a movie alone in a screening room.) It was at times like these, when the haze was deepest, that I could imagine my life was not filled with holes, that the minefield that was my past had been metal-detected by men in hazard suits into a benign and beautiful safety.

But now my doorbell was buzzing, killing my buzz, and because there was no wife, no kids, it was up to me to reluctantly answer it.

The "person from Porlock" handed me a package, inside of which was a script entitled *The Whole Nine Yards.* And my manager had written on it, "Could be pay dirt."

It was no "Kubla Khan," but I could see it was going to be huge.

I was always bad at reading scripts. Back then, I'd be offered millions of dollars to do movies and barely crack the first few pages. I'm embarrassed to admit that now, given that these days I'm writing scripts myself and it's like pulling teeth to get actors to respond. Maybe they feel how I used to feel: that in a life of fun and fame and money, reading a script, no matter the size of the number attached, feels all too much like school.

The universe will teach you, though. All those years I was too *this,* too *that,* to read a script, but last year I wrote a screenplay for myself and was trying get it made until I realized that I was too old to play the part. Most fifty-three-year-olds have worked their shit out already, so I needed to hire a thirty-year-old. The one I chose took weeks and weeks to respond, and I couldn't believe how rude his behavior was.

"Do I still have enough juice to even get an independent movie made?" I asked my manager, Doug, in frustration.

"Not really," Doug said.

But back then in 1999, my "person from Porlock" had brought me a script that even I could see had potential, and that potential was that none other than Bruce Willis was attached.

At the turn of the century, there was no bigger movie star than Bruce Willis. He'd already banked *Look Who's Talking* and its sequel, the *Die Hard* franchise, *Pulp Fiction. . . .* There was no one more successful back then. Not to mention that it would be a welcome relief from the seventy-two romantic comedies I'd just completed. Mitchell Kapner had written a funny script, filled with twists and turns, and it was easy to read: always a good sign. Best of all, Bruce Willis was in it, and I played the lead character. Show me an acclaimed and successful TV star and I will show you a frustrated wannabe movie star.

Pay dirt? You bet your ass. But first, I had to get through a dinner with the director and my costar's brother.

I showed up the next night at Citrus on Melrose. Back then, this was *the* Hollywood restaurant: expensive, exclusive, jacket required, a line of paparazzi at the door clicking away madly at everyone who came and went. That night, the comings and goings were me; the film's director, Jonathan Lynn, a short round British man who'd made *My Cousin Vinny* and who just so happened to be Oliver Sacks's cousin; and one of the film's producers, Bruce's brother, David (David got the hair, by the way, Bruce got the chin).

I had donned the requisite movie-star black suit for the dinner; I'd arrived a minute or two late, just because that's what movie stars do. The dinner went really well, even if no one touched their food, in the standard Hollywood way. Jonathan was very smart and funny—he had that dry, British approach to humor in which he'd say something that was seemingly serious, but there would be a twinkle in his eye, just enough to signal that he was busting balls. David was attentive and interesting and smart; as for me, well, I had already decided to do the movie. The original script had no physical comedy in it, so I said things like, "I think this would be a great opportunity for some physical comedy, and I'd be more than willing to fall down a flight of stairs and leap down some mountaintops to work with Bruce Willis."

Jonathan and David laughed and seemed relieved. Eventually, the "dinner" wrapped up. Jonathan said, "Well, you're our guy—we really want you to do this." Hands shaken, and paparazzi ignored, I jumped into my forest-green Porsche and squealed away.

I'm gonna be the lead in a Bruce Willis movie, I thought, as once again, all the lights on Sunset were green. Back at my house on Carla

Ridge, the moon had come up, lonely, mournful, casting a strange and awkward shadow across my view. I put on the TV, poured a vodka tonic, and waited.

The stars were lining up again; had the rise and rise of Matthew Perry just taken yet another giant leap forward? This is what I thought as the *actual* stars rose in a clear, dark sky. I started to count them, even though I knew the superstition that once you reach a hundred, you die.

I stopped at ninety-nine, just in case.

The following morning, I got a message on my answering machine.

"Matthew, this is Bruce Willis. Call me back, or I'll burn your house down and break both your knees and arms and you'll be left with just the stubs for hands and feet for the rest of your life."

Click, dial tone.

I figured this was a call I should probably return.

A few days later we met at Ago, yet another fancy Italian restaurant in Hollywood, in the private room in the back, the one that's reserved for people of Mr. Willis's status. Once again, I jetted up in my Porsche, barely putting it in park long enough to hand the valet my keys.

But this night, I was on time.

Bruce Willis did not disappoint—he *oozed* A-list. He didn't just take over a room, he *was* the room. In fact, I knew he was a real movie star when the first thing he did was teach the bartender how to make a perfect vodka tonic.

"Three-second pour," he said to the petrified man.

Bruce was forty-four years old, single (separated from Demi Moore at the time I met him), and he knew the exact recipe for the perfect drink. He was a party; to be near him was invigorating. After a while, we were visited in our private little room by Joe Pesci, whom Jonathan Lynn had directed in *My Cousin Vinny,* as well as several attendant attractive women. Bruce laughed at all my dumb jokes—he seemed to enjoy the spectacle of a younger, funny guy paying him his due respect and keeping up with his drinking (if he only knew). I was thrilled to be around him because he knew how to live life.

Dinner once again untouched, the two new best friends headed to his massive house off Mulholland—Bruce, too, seemed to like a view. The night ended with Bruce Willis and Matthew Perry, drinks in hand, hitting golf balls into the San Fernando Valley below.

Those balls are going to land somewhere, I thought, and before I could imagine the damage a shot from a well-addressed five iron could do, or even the metaphorical nature of what we were doing, I stopped thinking at all and had another drink.

"Welcome to the pros," Bruce said at one point, referring, I presumed, to the life of a movie star, not to my golf game. We had begun a friendship, one in which we drank together and made each other laugh and complimented each other's swings.

Eventually, as always happens, the sun came up, and we said our bleary goodbyes. As I drove home, I remember thinking, *Watch this guy—this is the way to be happy.* Nothing seemed to bother Bruce; no one said no to him. This was, indeed, the A-leagues.

Around lunchtime that same day, Bruce called to invite me back to his house for a screening of his next movie, but I was way too sick and hungover to even contemplate showing up. Making my excuses, I asked him what the movie was called so I could catch it later.

"*The Sixth Sense,*" he said.

So, I'd gotten *The Whole Nine Yards* and had embarked on a friendship with the most famous movie star on the planet, but even I knew I was drinking way too much to pull this movie off. Desperate measures would be needed. Some might be able to party perfectly well and still show up and do the work—but they were not addicts like I was.

If I was going to keep up with the partying, and with Bruce, and not go back to my hotel room and keep drinking, then I'd need something else to wind me down and make sure I could get to set the next day.

I called a friend—I use the term loosely—who I knew sold Xanax.

"How many would you like to purchase?" he skeeved at me.

"Give me a hundred," I said.

When they arrived, I sat on my bed, counting them. *This way I can drink with Bruce and the others but then when I'm finally alone I can just pop one of these and go to sleep.* I may have been a man with a plan, but I was also ignoring the fact that this was a completely lethal combination.

We flew on Bruce's plane (of course we did) to Montreal to make *The Whole Nine Yards,* arriving like conquering heroes ready to take the town by storm. I was the prodigal Canadian son, now returned, ready to party.

We set up shop at the Intercontinental Hotel. I had a regular room; Bruce had the whole top floor, which he immediately dubbed "Club Z," for no apparent reason. Within hours, he had also had a disco ball installed.

The Globe Restaurant became our other home away from home. The money and the drinks were flowing, and all the waitresses were hot.

Months earlier, I had started dating a woman called Renee. I'd met her at a restaurant in Los Angeles called Red. I was having dinner with the first assistant director of *Friends,* my pal Ben Weiss, and our waitress came and sat down next to me and started chatting to me. This was not normal waitress behavior, it seemed to me. When she had taken our order, I said to Ben, "Her name is going to be Samantha."

"Nah," he said, "she's definitely a Jennifer."

When she came back with our food, I said, "We're having a bet on your name. I have money on Sam, and my friend here thinks you're a Jen."

"Hi," she said, "I'm Renee." And somehow, a few drunken parties later, we were a couple.

Suffice to say, Renee had substituted for someone who'd broken my heart on an earlier movie, which put her already behind the eight ball . . . by the time I went to Montreal, we were mostly on the outs, but in any case—and I'm not proud to say this—I would have fucked mud at that stage in my life. Canadian mud at that.

The role itself was a snap. All I had to do was act scared of Bruce—which was easy—and act in love with Natasha Henstridge, which was even easier. The director, Jonathan, whom for some unknown reason I had taken to calling "Sammy," ran the kind of set I love—a very creative one. The best joke, no matter where it came from, would be picked, just like we did on *Friends*.

Amanda Peet was also in the cast. She was funny and smart and very attractive, and even though she had a boyfriend, she didn't mind flirting, which she did at the drop of a hat with both Bruce and me, to the point where one day Bruce shouted at her, *"Pick one!"*

At night, the parties raged under Bruce's disco ball in Club Z. Somehow, everyone still managed to show up at 6:00 A.M. for work. I say "somehow," but I know how I did: those hundred Xanax worked like a charm, though combined with my drinking they did tend to make my head resemble a Spalding basketball. Meanwhile Mr. A-list Willis over there looked like he could open an envelope with his chin.

Each day, with me nursing a killer hangover, but young enough to deal, we would gather and look at the sides (TV- and movie-speak for the work slated for the day). "We" was me, Jonathan Lynn, Bruce Willis, and the hilarious Kevin Pollak, who was playing Janni Gogolak, another mob boss. It was almost like a writers' room—we'd discuss what might be funny, what might go here in a scene, what might go there. A lot of the effort was to add physical comedy for me to do. I would run into windows, slam into doors. At one point I did a take in which I see a criminal, then turn, run into someone, get knocked back, clatter into a lamp, pick the lamp up and try to shield myself from the baddie with it. All my idea, all worked great.

At one point, Kevin had the line: "He shouldn't be able to breathe the air."

I suggested to him that he insert an unnaturally long pause before the words "the air." That was about the only time in my career where I could not keep it together—Kevin's performance of that line was so funny, and the pause kept getting longer and longer with each take we did, that in the end he had to do his coverage with me in a different room.

When the veil of Bruce Willis was removed, I just wanted to be his friend. I didn't want to be a suck-up to him like everybody else in the world. At one point when making *The Whole Nine Yards* we had a three-day weekend, and he flew me and Renee, and him and his girl-friend, to his house in the Turks and Caicos. It's a beautiful place with a stunning view of the ocean. They'd even thought to buy out all the surrounding properties so that paparazzi couldn't get their shots. All weekend we carried umbrellas with us to block us from the sun so that our faces wouldn't get too tanned and not match for the movie. A new movie star trick, one of many I learned from Mr. Willis.

But there was a big difference between Bruce and me. Bruce was a partier; I was an addict. Bruce has an on-off button. He can party like crazy, then get a script like *The Sixth Sense* and stop the partying and nail the movie sober. He doesn't have the gene—he's not an addict.

There are plenty of examples of people in Hollywood who can party and still function—I was not one of them. When I was in my drinking and using days, if a police officer were to come to the door and say, "If you drink tonight, you're going to jail tomorrow," I would start packing for jail, because once I start, I cannot stop. All I had control over was the first drink. After that, all bets were off. (See under: *The man takes the drink, the drink takes all the rest.*) Once I believe the lie that I can just have one drink, I am no longer responsible for my actions. I need people and treatment centers and hospitals and nurses to help me.

I can't stop. And if I didn't get ahold of this soon, it was going to kill me. I had a monster in my brain, a monster who wanted to get me alone, and convince me to have that first drink or pill, and then that monster would engulf me.

Despite the partying, we were all pros on that movie and managed to turn out a huge crowd pleaser. Early notices for it were positive—one, in *Variety* magazine, read:

> Bruce Willis will deliver the customers, but it's Matthew Perry who will attract the most attention in a pratfall-filled turn that bears comparison to what Tom Hanks was doing 12–15 years ago.

This was high praise indeed for someone who looked up to Tom. Bruce hadn't been sure the film would work at all, and I'd bet him it would—if he lost, he had to do a guest spot on *Friends* (he's in three episodes of season six).

The Whole Nine Yards became the number one movie in America for three weeks straight.

I had done it—the dream I'd had since the ninth grade had finally come true: *The Whole Nine Yards* was no *Back to the Future,* but

Michael J. Fox and I are the only two people who have had the number one movie and the number one TV show at the same time.

I should have been the toast of the town, but back in LA, it was clear, at least to me, that my addiction had progressed to dangerous levels. I was at the point where I was basically unable to leave the house—drugs and alcohol had completely taken over. I was so strung out on drugs and dealing with drug dealers that I couldn't actually leave my bedroom—instead of a grand moment of pure fame, dealing with dealers was all I was doing. I showed up to the premiere of the movie, of course, and put on *The Matthew Perry Show,* but I was bloated and driven by fear of something that I did not understand.

I've always had a dream of going on a talk show and being honest.

Jay Leno: *So, how you doing, Matthew?*
Me: *Man, I just don't know which way is up. I am totally screwed. I am so miserable. I can't get out of bed.*

This would have been the perfect time for that.

Four years after *The Whole Nine Yards* Bruce and I and Kevin shot a sequel (different director this time). If *The Whole Nine Yards* was the start of my movie stardom, it's fair to say that *The Whole Ten Yards* was the end.

We shot that second movie in Los Angeles—we were given all too much freedom and it sucked. You can seldom re-create a good thing, and it was true here; the jokes felt stale, the parties even staler. In fact, it was so bad that a while later, I called my agents and said, "I'm still allowed to *go* to movies though, right?"

When *The Whole Nine Yards* came out I had been so mired in addiction I could barely leave my room. I had been in a hellhole of despair and demoralization, and my fucked-up mind was slowly dragging my body down with it. Recently it struck me: this type of feeling should have been reserved for when *The Whole Ten Yards* came out. Anyone in their right mind would have been beyond depressed after that one.

Sometimes, at the end of the night, when the sun was just about to come up and everyone else had gone, and the party was over, Bruce and I would just sit and talk. That's when I saw the real Bruce Willis—a good-hearted man, a caring man, selfless. A wonderful parent. And a wonderful actor. And most important, a good guy. And if he wanted me to be, I would be his friend for life. But as is the way with so many of these things, our paths rarely crossed after that.

I, of course, pray for him every night now.

All Heaven Breaking Loose

Something happened, and I relapsed. As I've said, to relapse that's all it takes: something—anything at all—happening. Good or bad.

I was blowing yet another stretch of sobriety. I don't even remember why. I had been thriving. I'd had two years—I was helping other men get sober and I blew it all over something so minute I can't even remember what it was. What I do remember is there was lots of drinking, lots of drugs, lots of isolation. I always used alone—I was afraid that if anyone saw how much I was doing, they would be horrified and try to get me to stop. But I had already started, so stopping was not an option.

Something that has often saved my life is that I get scared. When I think things have gotten too out of control, I panic, pick up the phone, and ask for help. That time, a sober companion and my wonderful father came to the rescue. They moved in immediately; I started to detox off the drugs that very day.

I felt physically completely ruined . . . but the detox was going well. At least that's what my dad and the sober companion thought. What they didn't know was that I had hidden a bottle of Xanax in my bedroom. This is what it's like to be an addict: you do things you never dreamed you would do. My wonderful father had dropped everything to move in, to love and support me through one more self-created disaster, and I paid him back by hiding drugs in my nightstand.

One night I was desperate for sleep, any kind of escape from the brutal detox I was going through. That bottle of Xanax was calling to me, an evil beacon in the darkness. I thought of it like a lighthouse, only in this case, I turned my boat toward the wrecking rocks, not away from them. The childproof bottle cap was no obstacle for this child; in the other room, that child's father dozed, watching reruns of *Taxi,* while in my room by the metaphorical lethal cliffs, I dove into that bottle of Xanax and took four. (One was too many. But *four?*)

It didn't work. No escape came—those four Xanax proved no match for my racing thoughts. Sleep remained elusive. It was being held back by shame and fear and an intense self-loathing. So, what's the logical next move? Well for this drug addict, it was to take four more. (This wasn't just eight too many—this is a death-defying amount.) Somehow, these second four combined with the first four, and I finally managed to fall asleep. The sleep on Xanax isn't profound—the drug is notoriously shit at providing deep sleep—but I didn't care. I just wanted this brain of mine, this thing that stalked me, to quieten just for a few hours at least . . . and some relief from the incredibly painful detox I was going through.

I was fortunate enough to wake up, but the Xanax had done something worse than preventing deep sleep—it had fried my brain and made me insane. I was seeing things: strange visions and colors I'd never seen before, colors I didn't know could exist. The gray automated drapes in my bedroom had turned into a deep purple color. It was as if the rods and cones in my retina were sending new and unbidden messages through my optic nerve to my already barbecued brain stem. Regular blues were cerulean, now; reds were magentas; black was Vantablack or Black 3.0, the blackest of blacks.

Not only that, but I had run out of Xanax, and if something was not done quickly about that, I could die. (Remember: booze and Xanax are the only detoxes that can kill you—an opiate detox just makes you wish you were dead.) But I was coming off all of them. My only option was to somehow get more Xanax, but the setup in my house didn't allow for that. I would surely get caught. So, I would have to come clean about the fact that I had been taking it so I could get properly detoxed from it, too.

I left my bedroom and into a kaleidoscope of color of my living room. *Is this heaven?* I thought. *Did the Xanax kill me last night and this is what heaven is like?* I gently explained to my dad and the sober companion what I had done. They were both appropriately terrified. The sober companion leaped into action and called a doctor.

I was completely out of my mind. It was then that I decided to share with my father a fear I was having.

"Dad," I said, deadly serious, "I know this is going to sound crazy, but at any moment, a giant snake is going to come and take me away."

My father's reaction?

"Matty, if a giant snake comes and takes you away, I will shit my pants." To this day I am impressed by how my father rolled with my utter insanity.

At this point, the sober companion returned to the room, expressed his disappointment, but said he was still willing to help me out. But I needed to see a doctor right away. We headed off to see him. At the end of the consultation, I apologized to the doctor, shook his hand, and promised it would never happen again. And I meant it—I was done. The doctor ordered new detox meds, antiseizure medication (detoxing from Xanax can cause seizures). We headed home. My long-suffering assistant, Moira, was called to pick up said medication, and we waited. And waited. For some reason, it took her hours to complete this new mission.

The clock was ticking, though. If I didn't get this detox medication soon, some serious shit was going to go down. I could have a seizure; I could die. Neither option sounded good to me. Now, three grown men were staring at the front door, waiting for it to open, and two of those men were also staring at scared Matty.

After a while, I couldn't bear the scrutiny and removed myself to a small couch to the side of the kitchen. Reality, that acquired taste, was beginning to reassert itself, slowly, surely, like a lens focusing. And I felt absolutely horrible, both physically and emotionally. I was riddled with shame and guilt. I could not believe I had done this one more time. The men I was sponsoring had more sober time than I did. You can't give away what you don't have. And I had nothing.

I hated myself.

This was a new bottom; I didn't think you could get any lower than my previous bottom, but I had managed to do it. And all of this in front of my father, who was obviously terrified. The cunning, baffling, powerful nature of addiction had gotten me one more time.

The front door still wasn't opening. This was serious trouble. I was a desperate man. The drugs were in full flow, the drinking, too. Things were so bad I couldn't even cry. To cry might have signaled that there was at least a semblance of the normal somewhere abouts, but there was nothing natural about any of this.

So, a bottom—the lowest point of my life. This is a classic moment for an addict, a moment after which one seeks lasting help. . . . But hey, what's this now? As I sat there looking into the kitchen, I noticed a crinkle in the atmosphere. Perhaps someone not at their bottom might have waved it away as nothing, but to me it was so compelling that I couldn't look away. It resembled a kind of little wave in the air. I had never seen anything like it before in my life. It was real, true, tangible, concrete. Is this what you see at the end? Was I dying? And then . . .

I frantically began to pray—with the desperation of a drowning man. The last time I'd prayed, right before I'd gotten *Friends*, I'd man-aged only to strike a Faustian bargain with a God who had simply drawn a long breath and bided his damn time. Here I was, more than a decade later, chancing my praying arm once again.

"God, please help me," I whispered. "Show me that you are here. God, please help me."

As I prayed, the little wave in the air transformed into a small, golden light. As I kneeled, the light slowly began to get bigger, and big-ger, until it was so big that it encompassed the entire room. It was like I was standing on the sun. I had stepped on the surface of the sun. What was happening? And why was I starting to feel better? And why was I not terrified? The light engendered a feeling more perfect than the most perfect quantity of drugs I had ever taken. Feeling euphoric now, I did get scared and tried to shake it off. But there was no shaking this off. It was way way bigger than me. My only choice was to surrender to it, which was not hard, because it felt so good. The euphoria had begun at the top of my head and slowly seeped down throughout my entire body—I must have sat there for five, six, seven minutes, filled with it.

My blood hadn't been replaced with warm honey. I *was* warm honey. And for the first time in my life, I was in the presence of love and ac-ceptance and filled with an overwhelming feeling that everything was going to be OK. I knew now that my prayer had been answered. I was in the presence of God. Bill Wilson, who created AA, was saved by a lightning-bolt-through-the-window experience where he felt he was meeting God.

This was mine.

But, feeling this good was terrifying. I was once asked if I'd ever been happy, and I almost bit that fucker's head off. (At Promises once, during a rehab, I'd told my counselor that I was freaked-out by how happy everyone recovering seemed. "They're like a bunch of happy people living on a hill while I'm dying," I'd said, and he'd explained to me that a lot of those people weren't getting it and didn't understand what was going on and would eventually be back in rehab and things would be even worse for them next time around.)

After about seven minutes (insert "seven minutes in heaven" joke here) the light began to dim. The euphoria died down. God had done his work and was off helping someone else now.

I started to cry. I mean, I really started to cry—that shoulder-shaking kind of uncontrollable weeping. I wasn't crying because I was sad. I was crying because for the first time in my life, I felt OK. I felt safe, taken care of. Decades of struggling with God, and wresting with life, and sadness, all was being washed away, like a river of pain gone into oblivion.

I had been in the presence of God. I was certain of it. And this time I had prayed for the right thing: help.

Eventually the weeping subsided. But everything was different now. I could see color differently, angles were of a different magnitude, the walls were stronger, the ceiling higher, the trees tapping on the windows more perfect than ever, their roots connected via the soil to the planet and back into me—one great connection created by an ever-loving God—and beyond, a sky, which had before been theoretically infinite was now unknowably endless. I was connected to the universe in a way I had never been. Even the plants in my house, which I had never even noticed before, seemed in sharp focus, more lovely than it was possible to be, more perfect, more alive.

I stayed sober for two years based solely on that moment. God had shown me a sliver of what life could be. He had saved me that day, and for all days, no matter what. He had turned me into a seeker, not only of sobriety, and truth, but also of him. He had opened a window, and closed it, as if to say, "Now go earn this."

Nowadays, when a particular darkness hits me, I find myself wondering if it was just Xanax insanity, a continuation of the snake I had been sure was about to show up—the drug can cause what the National Institutes of Health describe as "reversible brief psychotic episodes." (I later had a gigantic seizure in front of my father, too, which wasn't the most fun I've ever had—nor was being rushed to UCLA Medical Center, which at the time I thought was an angel way station.) But quickly I return to the truth of the golden light. When I am sober, I can still see it, remember what it did for me. Some might write it off as a near-death experience, but I was there, and it was God. And when I am connected, God shows me that it was real, little hints like when the sunlight hits the ocean and turns it into that beautiful golden color. Or the reflection of sunlight on the green leaves of a tree, or when I see the light return to someone's eyes when they come out of the darkness into sobriety. And I feel it when I help someone get sober, the way it hits my heart when they say thank you. Because they don't know yet that I should really be thanking them.

A year later I met a woman I'd stay with for six years. God is everywhere—you just have to clear your channel, or you'll miss it.

7

The Benefit of Friends

Monica went first; she placed her key on the empty counter. Chandler went next. Then Joey—big laugh as he really shouldn't have even had a key—then Ross, then Rachel, and last of all Phoebe. Now, there were six keys on the countertop, and what do you say after that?

We all stood in one long line. Phoebe said, "I guess this is it," and Joey said, "Yeah," then almost broke the fourth wall by looking out at the audience briefly before saying, "I guess so. . . ."

But there was no fourth wall to break; there never had been, in fact. We had been in people's bedrooms and living rooms for a decade; in the end, we were an integral part of so many people's lives that what we'd missed was that there had never been a fourth wall to break in the first place. We'd just been six close friends in an apartment that was seemingly way too big, when in fact it was just the size of a TV set in a living room.

And then it was time to leave that apartment one last time. Now, though, there were eight of us—the six main characters, plus Monica and Chandler's twins in a stroller.

Before that final episode, I'd taken Marta Kauffman to one side.

"Nobody else will care about this except me," I said. "So, may I please have the last line?" That's why as we all troop out of the apartment, and Rachel has suggested one last coffee, I got to bring the curtain down on *Friends*.

"Sure," Chandler said, and then, with perfect timing, for the very last time, "*Where?*"

I love the look on Schwimmer's face as I deliver that line—it's the perfect mixture of affection and amusement, exactly what the show *Friends* had always given to the world.

And with that, it was over.

The truth was, we were all ready for *Friends* to be done. For a start, Jennifer Aniston had decided that she didn't want to do the show anymore, and as we all made decisions as a group, that meant we all had to stop. Jennifer wanted to do movies; I had been doing movies all that time and had *The Whole Ten Yards* about to come out, which was sure to be a hit (insert donkey's head now), but in any case, even though it had been the greatest job in the world, the stories of Monica, Chandler, Joey, Ross, Rachel, and Phoebe had all pretty much played out by 2004. It was not lost on me that Chandler had grown up way faster than I had. As a result, mostly by Jenny's design, ten was a shortened season. But all the characters were basically happy by this point, too, and no one wants to watch a bunch of happy people doing happy things—what's funny about that?

It was January 23, 2004. The keys on the counter, a guy who looked a lot like Chandler Bing said, "*Where?*" "Embryonic Journey" by Jefferson Airplane played, the camera panned to the back of the apartment door, then Ben, our first AD, and very close friend, shouted for the last time, "That's a wrap," and tears sprang from almost everyone's eyes like so many geysers. We had made 237 episodes, including this last one, called, appropriately enough, "The Last One." Aniston was *sobbing*—after a while, I was amazed she had any water left in her entire body. Even Matt LeBlanc was crying. But I felt nothing; I couldn't tell if that was because of the opioid buprenorphine I was taking, or if I was just generally dead inside. (Buprenorphine, for the record, is a detox med, and an excellent one, and is designed to help you stay off other "stronger" opiates—it does not *alter* you in any way. But, ironically, it's the hardest drug to come off in the entire world. Bupe, or Suboxone, should never be used for more than seven days. Fearing a nasty detox, I had been on it for eight months.)

So, instead of sobbing, I took a slow walk around the stage with my then-girlfriend—also appropriately called Rachel—stage 24 at Warner Bros. in Burbank (a stage that after the show ended would be renamed "The Friends Stage"). We said our various goodbyes, agreeing to see each other soon in the way that people do when they know it's not true, and then we headed out to my car.

I sat in the lot for a moment and thought about the previous ten years. I thought about *L.A.X. 2194* and the $22,500 and Craig Bierko; I thought about how I'd been the last one cast, and that trip to Vegas, where we could walk through a packed casino, and no one knew who we were. I thought about all the gags and the double takes, the Murray brothers, and some of my most famous/too-close-to-the-truth lines, like, "Hi, I'm Chandler, I make jokes when I'm uncomfortable," and "Until I was twenty-five, I thought that the only response to 'I love you' was 'Oh, crap!'" and "We swallow our feelings. Even if it means we're unhappy forever," and "Could she *be* more out of my league?"

I thought about the summer between seasons eight and nine, when I'd spent time in rehab, and *People* magazine had said on its cover that I was "Happy, Healthy, and HOT!" ("*Friends* funny guy talks about those dating rumors," the lede read, "the 'final' season, and his battle to get sober. 'It was scary,' he says. 'I didn't want to die.'") I had indeed spent that summer getting sober and playing a lot of tennis. I thought about the first day of season four, after the summer that I had very publicly gone to rehab. At the first table read obviously all eyes were on me. My pal Kevin Bright, one of the shows executive producers, had opened the proceedings by saying, "Anyone want to talk about their summer vacations?" and I took the opportunity to break the ice, saying rather loudly and soberly, "OK! I'll start!" thus releasing all the tension in the room. Everyone erupted in laughter and applause for me for turning my life around and showing up looking good and ready to work. Probably to this day, it was the smartest joke I have ever made.

I thought about how I'd had to beg the producers to let me no longer speak like Chandler for the final few seasons (not to mention getting rid of those sweater vests). That particular cadence—could it *be* more annoying?—had been so played out that if I had to put the emphasis in the wrong place one more time, I thought I'd explode, so I just went back to saying lines normally, for the most part in season six and then beyond.

I thought about me crying when I asked Monica to marry me.

And me being me, there were negative thoughts, too.

What will become of me now that I no longer have this insanely fun, creative job to go to every day?

Friends had been a safe place, a touchstone of calm for me; it had given me a reason to get out of bed every morning, and it had also given me a reason to take it just a little bit easier the night before. It was the time of our lives. It was like we got some new piece of amazing news every day. Even I knew only a madman (which in many moments I had been nonetheless) would screw up a job like that.

As we drove home that night, along Sunset I pointed out to Rachel a massive billboard promoting *The Whole Ten Yards*. There I was, fifty feet high, frowning in a dark suit and purple shirt and tie, standing next to Bruce Willis, he dressed in white T-shirt, pinafore, and bunny slippers. WILLIS . . . PERRY, it read, in six-foot letters, above the tagline: THEY MISSED EACH OTHER. THIS TIME, THEIR AIM IS BETTER. I was a movie star. (You remember what I said about the donkey's head, right?)

My future, even without *Friends,* looked rosy enough, though. I had a major movie coming out; I'd done two episodes of *Ally McBeal* and three of *The West Wing,* so I was developing serious acting chops as well as the comedy stuff (I'd gotten two Emmy nominations for my three *The West Wing* appearances). I'd also just finished wrapping a TNT movie called *The Ron Clark Story,* about a real-life small-town teacher who gets a job in one of the toughest schools in Harlem. There wasn't a single joke in the whole thing—it drove me crazy how serious it was—so off camera I created a character called "Ron Dark" who was drunk and who constantly swore in front of the children. Despite that, it was a big hit when it eventually aired in August 2006. I would garner nominations for a SAG award, a Golden Globe, and an Emmy. (I lost all three to Robert Duvall. I couldn't believe it—being beaten out by such a hack.)

But as I've said, *The Whole Ten Yards* would prove to be a disaster— I'm not sure even my closest family and friends went to see it. In fact, if you looked closely enough, you could see people averting their eyes from the screen at the premiere. I think it actually got a zero rating on Rotten Tomatoes.

And that was the moment Hollywood decided to no longer invite Mr. Perry to be in movies.

I had made arrangements to attend a 12-step meeting the day after the final taping of *Friends,* with the express intent of starting my new life on the right path. But facing the blank canvas of an empty day was very hard on me. That next morning, I woke up and thought, *What the fuck am I going to do now?*

What the fuck could I do? I was hooked on Bupe, with no new job in sight. Which was ridiculous, given that I'd just finished making the most beloved sitcom in TV history. On top of that, my relationship with Rachel was getting rocky—the physical distance was an issue, as was the emotional closeness. I was damned if I did, damned when I didn't.

And then I was single once again.

With no ridiculously high paying, dream-come-true kind of job to go to, and no special someone in my life, things slipped fast—in fact, it was like falling off a cliff. The insanity of using other, stronger drugs crept up into my diseased brain once again. It wasn't long before the seemingly impossible happened again. I started drinking and using.

Despite how it may appear, I was never suicidal, thank God—I never actually wanted to die. In fact, in the back of my mind I always had some semblance of hope. But, if dying was a consequence of getting to take the quantity of drugs I needed, then death was something I was going to have to accept. That's how skewed my thinking had become—I was able to hold those two things in my mind at the same time: I don't want to die, but if I have to in order to get sufficient drugs on board, then amen to oblivion. I can distinctively remember holding pills in my hand and thinking, *This could kill me,* and taking them anyway.

This is a very fine, and very scary, line. I had reached a point in my drinking and using where I was drinking and using to forget about how much I was drinking and using. And it took an almost lethal amount to accomplish that kind of amnesia.

I was also so lonely that it hurt; I could feel the loneliness in my bones. On the outside, I looked like the luckiest man alive, so there were only a few people I could complain to without being told to shut up, and even then . . . nothing could fill the hole inside me. At one point I bought yet another new car, the excitement of which lasted about five days. I moved regularly, too—the thrill of a new house with an even better view lasted a bit longer than the Porsche or the Bentley, but not by much. I was also so introspective that a proper give-and-take relationship with a woman was nigh on impossible; I was much better at friends with benefits, so that whoever I was seeing didn't discover that slow, creeping thought that I was irredeemably not enough.

I was lost. There was nowhere to turn. Everywhere I tried to hide, there I was. Alcoholics hate two things: the way things are and change. I knew something had to change—I wasn't suicidal, but I was dying—but I was too scared to do anything about it.

I was a man in need of a yellow light experience, so I was eternally grateful that it had happened that day in my house, because it gave me a new lease on life. I had been given the gift of sobriety one more time. The only question was: What was I going to do with it? Nothing had worked long-term before. I was going to have to approach everything differently, or I was a goner. And I didn't want to be a goner. Not before I had learned to live, to love. Not before the world made more sense to me.

Had my habit killed me, it would have killed the wrong person. I wasn't fully me yet; I was just parts of me (and not the best parts, either). My new approach to life would have to start with work, because that seemed to be the easiest place to start. Embracing effort was the only hope for me. I built up some sober time, was back on my feet once again. I also had a few friends-with-benefits things going on, but one was starting to slowly morph into something more. Maybe *much* more. I knew how to do friends with benefits—but this? This I was less clear about. I started to want her to stay *past the sex*: "Why don't you stick around and we can watch a movie?"

What was I doing? I was breaking all the rules.

She was twenty-three and I was thirty-six when we first met. In fact, I knew she was twenty-three because I'd crashed her twenty-third birthday party. Our subsequent initial make-out session was in the back of a really messy Toyota (to think I'd spent all that money on fancy cars and here I was in the backseat of a tan Corolla). When we were done, I said, "I'm getting out of the car now. Mostly because I'm thirty-six."

So began two years of probably record-breaking amounts of sexual intercourse, with no strings attached, both of us following the friends-with-benefits rules to a tee. We were on the same page. We never went to dinner, we never talked about each other's families. We never discussed what went on in each other's lives regarding other people. Instead, it was texting, and saying things like, "How about Thursday night at seven?"

She was tough at first. I remember an exchange early on where I told her I was wearing a suit and thought I looked pretty good.

"I hate suits," she said.

I broke her out of her toughness, but it took years.

Somewhere it is written in the actor's handbook—actually, it's probably in the book my dad gave me, the one he'd inscribed with "another generation shot to hell"—that you have to try to do new things and stretch yourself. If you have excelled at comedy, then it behooves you to make a direct right turn and become a dramatic actor. So that became the plan. I couldn't retire, and there was only so much time a grown man could spend playing video games. As my friends-with-benefits partner said to me one day, "You live the life of someone who drinks and uses, you just don't drink and use." (She was really smart, too—did I mention that?)

I was at a crossroads. What do you do when you are an actor, and you are rich and famous, but you are not interested in being rich and famous?

Well, you either retire (way too young for that), or you change it up.

I informed my manager and agents that I was now looking only for dramatic work.

I had dabbled in it with good results on *The West Wing* and *Ally McBeal* and *The Ron Clark Story,* so it didn't seem like a crazy move. I auditioned for some serious films, but I didn't get any of them. I shot a few indie movies that tried hard, but that didn't work out, either.

And then, a script came along that was white-hot.

I had never seen so much heat attached to a project—it was magnetic. *Studio 60 on the Sunset Strip,* written by Aaron Sorkin and directed by Thomas Schlamme, was the follow-up to their little show called *The West Wing.* Between them they had like fifteen Emmys, so their new project caused a frenzy in the fall of 2005 unlike anything else. I had never seen a project that had so much power behind it before it had even started. NBC and CBS went at it like gladiators to get that thing, with NBC ultimately winning out to the tune of something like $3 million per episode. All that fall, wherever I turned, someone was talking about *Studio 7 on the Sunset Strip* (its original name). I was in New York finishing up *The Ron Clark Story* and staying at my favorite hotel in the world, the Greenwich, in Tribeca. I really wanted to read this hot script. Because I was on the East Coast, the script would not get to my hotel until 10:00 P.M., so I waited up.

Aaron and Tommy had changed the way America looked at serialized TV with *The West Wing,* and I had changed how America spoke English via the cadences of Chandler Bing. Seemed like a potent combination.

By 11:30 P.M. I had read the script and decided to return to network television.

The lead characters were Matt Albie, the head writer of Studio 7 (and a role that apparently Aaron had written with me in mind), and Danny Tripp, his fellow showrunner, to be played by the kind and brilliant Bradley Whitford, both being brought back to save an *SNL*-like show called *Studio 60 on the Sunset Strip.*

Before a lick of it was filmed, it had "giant, Emmy-winning hit" written all over it. It had Sorkin, Schlamme, and me. What could possibly go wrong?

The first problem was the money. I'd been making a tremendous nut on *Friends* and realized I'd struggle to get that number again, but even so, the fact that everyone in this ensemble show about a comedy TV program was being asked to accept the same fee. . . . The conversation went something like this (think of this in Sorkin-speak):

Me: *I really want to do this.*
Manager: *Well, no one does this kind of thing better than Sorkin.*
Me: *This would be my return to television—it's the way to go.*
Manager: *The only problem is the offer.*
Me: *The offer? What is it?*
Manager: *The offer's what you get per episode. . . .*
Me: *I know that. Thank you. I meant, what's the number?*
Manager: *$50,000 per episode.*
Me: *I got more than a million per for* Friends. *Can't we get them up?*
Manager: *It doesn't look like it. They want this to be a true ensemble show and that is what they are offering everyone.*
Me: *I can't believe I have to turn down the best television script I have ever read.*

My manager, God bless him, didn't give up. He pointed out to the producers that even though *Studio 60 on the Sunset Strip* had indeed been conceived as an ensemble show, as soon as I stepped onstage it was going to be about my character, which is what ended up happening. With that argument in mind, after about six weeks of negotiations, we got them off their ensemble idea. I was to be billed as the star of the show, and we got them up to $175,000. Now, obviously that is an amazing amount of money to be paid a week, but three stages down, LeBlanc was being paid $600,000 a week to do *Joey*. But in the end, the writing prevailed (every actor is just looking for good material), and I accepted the lowball number (and they hired my good friend Amanda Peet to round out the cast).

We shot the pilot, and I would hold up that pilot up against any pilot I had ever seen—it was that good. There was an energy to it, a crackle that's rare in TV, and fans loved it, too. It opened huge. (All my shows after *Friends* opened huge and then suddenly they weren't anymore.) The second episode of *Studio 60* drew literally half the number of people that the first one did. No one cared about the show. It took me years to figure out why.

There was a fatal flaw to *Studio 60 on the Sunset Strip*, one that no amount of good writing or good direction or good acting could fix. On *The West Wing*, the stakes were as high as you could imagine: a nuclear bomb is pointing at Ohio and the president has to fix that shit? People in Ohio would tune in to a show like that just to find out exactly what might happen if they were invited to kiss their own asses goodbye by an incoming intercontinental ballistic missile.

A very small group of people—myself included—know that for a sector of show business, getting a joke right is a matter of life and death. These are bent, weird people. But people in Canton, Ohio, watching *Studio 60 on the Sunset Strip* probably thought, *It's just a joke, why doesn't everybody calm down. It's not that big a deal, what is wrong with all of you people?* This was not the Monty Python bit about Ernest Scribbler who wrote a joke so funny it killed Nazis. (The Brits are immune to its power because they don't speak German. And the actual German of the killer joke is gibberish, which is also funny.) There might have been a devoted set of viewers in Rock Center or working the door of the Comedy Store on Sunset, but outside of that, the basic premise of the show didn't reach the levels of edge-of-the-seat stakes. Trying to attach *The West Wing* stakes to a comedy show could never work.

On a granular level, I also found the *Studio 60 on the Sunset Strip* work environment to be frustratingly unlike that of *Friends,* or even *The Whole Nine Yards.* Aaron runs a very tight ship—that's just how he likes it—to the point where there was someone on set with a script making sure that if the original reads "he is angry" and I, or someone else, shortened it to "*he's* angry," we'd have to reshoot the entire scene—it had to be done *exactly as written.* (I nicknamed the production assistant whose job this was "the Hawk," and honestly, what a horrible gig she had, having to be a hall monitor to a bunch of creative types acting their balls off.) Unfortunately, sometimes a take with a slightly different rendering of the line had been the best take of all, but still, the one that got used was the word-perfect one, not the *best* one. The Aaron Sorkin as writer / Tommy Schlamme as director system was never really actor centered, therefore it was much more about getting the text right, as though it were Shakespeare—in fact, I heard someone say on set that this *was* Shakespeare. . . .

I also had a different view of the creative process generally—I was used to pitching ideas, but Aaron didn't take any of them. I had thoughts, too, about the arc of my character, but they weren't welcomed, either. Problem is, I'm not just a talking head. I have a brain, especially comedically. Aaron Sorkin is a much better writer than I am, but he's not a funnier man than me (he'd kindly once said that *Friends* was his favorite show). And in *Studio 60* I was playing a *comedy* writer. I thought I had some funny ideas, but Aaron said no to 100 percent of them. That's his right, and it's no knock on him that he likes to run his set this way. It just left me disappointed. (Tom Hanks told me that Aaron did the same thing to him.)

I guess I was lucky that I'd already learned that being on a successful TV show didn't fix anything. The show went out the gate gangbusters, the pilot pulling down a cool thirteen million viewers and a fourteen share, which was solid. The reviews were positive, too. *Variety* said, "It's hard not to root for *Studio 60 on the Sunset Strip,* a series that weds Aaron Sorkin's crackling dialogue and willingness to tackle big ideas with a beyond-stellar cast." The *Chicago Tribune* went even further, writing me a love letter and saying, "*Studio 60* is not just good, it has the potential to be a small-screen classic."

But the problem remained: it was trying to be a serious show about comedy and quality TV, as though those two things were as important as world politics. I recently read one really instructive critique about *Studio 60* on the *Onion*'s A.V. Club vertical. Its author, Nathan Rabin, writing a few years after the show aired, agrees that the pilot was a special piece of work.

> Along with much of the public, I watched the pilot in a state of feverish anticipation the night it premièred on September 18, 2006. When it was over, I couldn't wait to see what happened next. I re-watched it . . . a few months back [and] what I responded to most profoundly upon a repeat viewing was its infinite sense of possibility. *Studio 60* could go anywhere. It could do anything. And it could do it with one of the most remarkable casts in recent memory. The pilot for *Studio 60* still radiates potential the second time around, even if it was doomed to go fatally unrealized.

But Rabin also points out that the show probably took itself too seriously, given that it was supposed to be about gags, and that Sorkin's absolute control of the show left no room for anyone else to breathe.

> The show's arrogance extended to having Aaron Sorkin write every episode. Oh sure, staff writers got a "story by" credit here and there, but *Studio 60* was ultimately a one-man show. Sorkin's voice dominates. . . . [I]n its own strange way, *Studio 60* endures, albeit as an epic, intermittently fascinating folly rather than as a magnum opus.

Times had changed, too. We aired right as TV had morphed into a different animal. "Appointment TV," like *Friends* or *The West Wing*, was starting to crater. People were recording shows to watch later; this affected ratings, which in turn became the story of the show, rather than the show itself, which was otherwise really good.

By the end of the first—and only—season, viewers had tended to agree with Rabin's assessment, and we were down to four million viewers, and only 5 percent of TVs were tuned into the show.

We were doomed.

I wasn't devastated by the lack of success—as I said, I knew a hit TV show couldn't fill my soul. And in any case, something else was filling my soul.

The two years of "friends with benefits" had morphed into love. This was one of the most "normal" periods of my life. True, occasionally I'd have little slips, taking maybe two OxyContin, from which I'd then have to detox for six days. But the relationship had deepened to the point where there was now a question I urgently needed to ask her.

One day, I said, "I think we should stop kidding ourselves. We love each other," and she didn't disagree. I did love her, very much. That said, our intimacy issues were being sidestepped by the fact that we were both really into working. My fear of her leaving was still deeply in place, too, and who knows, perhaps she was scared of me leaving her.

Nevertheless, the moment came.

For Christmas, I'd paid a huge amount of money for an artist to paint the two of us. Our relationship had always been both sex- and text-driven—at least for the first four years—and I had found out from my business manager that we'd exchanged something like 1,780 texts. So, in the painting, on the bottom right corner, there she was, sitting down with a copy of *The New York Times* and some bottled water, as she always did, and on the bottom left there was me, wearing a long sleeve T-shirt with another T-shirt on top of it, which is what I'd always wear, holding a Red Bull and reading a *Sports Illustrated* . . . and all the while, we were texting each other. The artist had added 1,780 hearts, one for each text, and had smushed them all together to make one huge heart. I had never spent that kind of money on a gift before. I loved this woman, and I wanted her to know it.

My plan was to give her the painting and then ask the question. You know the one; I don't need to tell you how it goes, especially because . . . well, I never asked it. I gave her the present, and she was really moved by it, saying, "Matty, my little heart—what you're doing to my little heart."

And it was time. All I had to do was say, "Honey, I love you. Will you . . ." But I didn't say it. All my fears reared up like a snake, the snake I feared was coming to get me the year before I'd met her, the time when I'd seen God but managed to learn not enough from him.

I immediately went into Chandler fucking Bing mode.

"Hey, hey, hey!" I said, to her consternation, "look *at* this!" bringing that fucking Chandler cadence back one last time.

I had missed the moment. Maybe she'd been expecting it, who knows. I'd been seconds away; seconds, and a lifetime. I often think if I'd asked, now we'd have two kids and a house with no view, who knows—I wouldn't need the view, because I'd have her to look at; the kids, too. Instead, I'm some schmuck who's alone in his house at fifty-three, looking down at an unquiet ocean. . . .

So I didn't ask. I was too scared, or broken, or bent. I had remained completely faithful to her the whole time, including the last two years, two years in which for some reason I didn't want to have sex with her anymore, two years in which no amount of couples therapy could explain why I'd never asked the damn question, and why now I just looked on her as my best friend only. My buddy; my *best* buddy. And

I didn't want to lose my best buddy, so I tried to make it work for two years.

I didn't know then why the sex ended. I do now: the creeping, nagging, endless fear that if we got any closer, she would see the real me, and leave me. You see, I didn't very much like the real me at the time. Also, our age difference had become a problem. She always wanted to go out and do things, and I craved more of a settled life.

But there were other issues, too. Her single-mindedness about her career careened into my approach to life at the time, which was to do next to nothing. I was basically retired—I genuinely didn't think I'd ever work again. I was insanely rich, so I just played video games and hung out with myself.

But now, what was I going to do?

Embrace effort.

I created a TV show called *Mr. Sunshine.* I subscribe to the theory that life is about the journey, not the destination, and what I had not done yet was write, so this was my opening effort. Writing a network show about what you actually want to write about is almost impossible. There are so many cooks in the kitchen—executives and other writers who all insist on having a say—that the reality of your actual vision making it to the screen is something reserved only for people like Sorkin.

Mr. Sunshine is centered around my character, a guy called Ben Donovan, who runs a sports arena in San Diego; Allison Janney plays my boss. One of Ben's key foibles is his inability to be available to women. . . . And I even managed to put in an inside joke after the credits: my production company was called "Anhedonia Productions," and the ad card we crafted featured a cartoon of me sighing with boredom on a roller coaster. But despite putting my entire self into it, the show was a big success for about two weeks before everyone in the world decided they didn't want to watch it.

But it had been a very valuable experience, because I'd learned how to make a TV show from scratch. It's one of those things that maybe looks easy but is actually incredibly difficult—sort of like math, or having a real conversation with another human being. I had fun, but it was a marathon endeavor, and I'm a sprinter. And it quickly turned a sober, video game–playing rich man into an incredibly busy man, which was not a great idea. In fact, the show quickly became the priority over my sobriety, and as a result I relapsed, yet again.

I would *Go On* to make another show (no, no, that's what it was *called, Go On*) about a sports talk radio host trying to get over the death of his wife. NBC was pushing and pushing that one—they even aired it during the Olympics, and sixteen million people watched the premiere. But a comedy about grief therapy? The finale, in April 2013, pulled in a scant two and a half million. Yet again, a show I was leading opened huge and got canceled. With nothing to do, and no one to love, I relapsed one more time. I caught this one quickly, though, and checked into a rehab in Utah.

It was there that I met a counselor named Burton, a Yoda-like figure who told me that I liked the drama and the chaos of my addiction problem. "What are you talking about?" I said. "It's ruined my life. It's robbed me of every good thing I have ever had."

I was really pissed off.

But what if he was right?

Pockets

I was sitting in my room at the New York treatment center, and I was jonesing for opiates. The detox hadn't worked, and my body was screaming for drugs. I told the doctor, and I told the counselor, but I really didn't need to tell them anything—I was stirring and shaking, clearly withdrawing.

They did nothing. I was lost. I was sick. It was time to take matters into my own hands.

I picked up the phone and made some arrangements.

The rule was, if you left the premises, you had to do a pee test immediately upon returning. So I walked outside, met the vehicle, handed over some money, retrieved some pills, and they were off. Back in the treatment center I headed directly to the bathroom, did the pee test, then swallowed three pills.

Genius, right?

Not so fast.

Just as the pills kicked in, and my body was beginning to feel like warm honey again, it was almost as if the moment I stopped shaking, there was a knock on my door.

Oh fuck. Fuck fuck fuck.

The counselor and one of the nurses walked in.

"Somebody called to say there had been a drug deal outside the facility," the counselor announced. "I need to check your coat."

Fuck!

"Really?" I said, wide-eyed with fake wonder. "Well, you won't find any pills on me. I'm good," I said, already knowing they'd find pills on me, and I wasn't good, not even close.

Sure enough, there were pills in my pocket (I put them there). They took the pills away and told me that they'd deal with it in the morning. This meant I was still high for about four more hours, but there would be hell to pay the next day.

At 10:00 A.M. the following morning, all the powers that be in this awful place had gathered in a circle. Their message was simple: you're out.

"You're kicking me out?" I said. "I can't believe my fucking ears. This is a drug rehab, right? Why are you all so fucking surprised that someone did drugs here? I told two of you that I was sick and you did nothing—what the fuck was I supposed to do? And please, for the love of God, wipe those shocked looks off your faces. I'm a drug addict, I did some drugs, that's what we do!"

A few phone calls were made, and I was ushered off to some unknown rehab in Pennsylvania.

But there I was shuffled to another state like a ball in a pinball machine. The one upside? This place allowed smoking. Moments after arriving, I had my first cigarette in nine months, which felt awfully good.

Little problem though: I was addicted to six milligrams of Ativan at the time, and this new place didn't give out Ativan, something that maybe the New York place could have checked on but didn't. My own experiences and years of conversations with other addicts has led me to believe that most of these places are pieces of shit anyway. They're hell-bent on taking advantage of sick needy people and cashing paychecks. The whole system is corrupt and completely fucked-up.

Take it from me. I'm an expert. I've poured millions of dollars into this "system."

Did the money help me, or hurt me? There's no way I could run out of money doing drugs or alcohol. Does that make it harder?

I'm glad we'll never know.

8

Odyssey

After *Friends,* after the movies, after that six-year relationship, fall and rise and rise and fall—after everything—for the next six years I found myself bound upon an odyssey. Contrary to how it might appear, I was not a man with a lot of money with nothing much to do; in fact, I had more to do than ever. No, I was a man falling down a mountainside, lost in a raging river, hoping to find refuge on any safe and dry rock.

Between *Mr. Sunshine* and *Go On* I'd headed to Cirque Lodge, in Sun Valley, Utah—rehab number three, if you're scoring at home. The Lodge sits at the base of Mount Timpanogos, in the Utah Rockies. I am not a big nature guy—in terms of peaceful locations, I prefer the ocean, or at least a view of the ocean—but this place was stunning. The air was thin and true, razor-sharp, clarifying. There were turkeys all around, gobbling fit to bust (flying once in a while, too—who knew they flew?), and golden eagles, and some days, a moose would wander by, heavy and slow (no, really, there *were* moose there; I wasn't hallucinating).

Beyond its beauty, Cirque Lodge also boasted a crack staff—they knew what they were doing. My counselor Burton (who, if his face was green, I would have sworn was Yoda) wound up being deeply helpful to me—with both the real problems I brought with me, and the invented ones I carried with me at all times. (He happens to be one of the men I've ever said "I love you" to.) I arrived very scared (a prerequisite for entering rehab, but deeply uncomfortable nonetheless), and Burton's soothing voice made me feel a tiny bit better almost instantly.

"Discover, uncover, and discard" was one of the major mantras at Cirque, and I was excited to think I could at least do that last one—it was time to get rid of all this shit, once and for all. At this point I was such an expert on the 12 steps (and everything else they tend to focus on in rehab) . . . so much so that while at Cirque I spent a lot of my time helping out the newbies and trying to have a little fun. I had a Ping-Pong table brought in and even invented a game revolving around a red ball that we threw back and forth, all of which kept my fellow inmates enthused for hours on end and gave me a boost of purpose. I wanted to help so much; I was good at it.

I was under the impression that during this stay I was going to have to do deep trauma work, reaching back into my childhood, and pulling up all that old pain and loneliness, thereby beginning the very painful process of letting these things go. The idea was that if I got over these traumatic events, I would no longer feel the need to cover them up with drugs and alcohol.

Burton, however, saw things differently. He accused me of liking the drama of my addiction and asked how I could have so much fun while at Cirque Lodge yet be so troubled by almost everything that took place out there in the real world.

This question was instantly offensive to me. *I like this?* How could Burton look at my decades of addiction and terror, my lack of control, my obvious inner torture, and say I *liked* it?

During Family and Friends Week it was normal for participants to invite people to come and visit, but I resisted it hard. My father had visited me at Hazelden, my mother at Promises Malibu, and my

then-girlfriend had spent countless hours witnessing me rant while detoxing with a myriad of home nurses and sober companions. I didn't
want to put them through this yet again. It was too painful, too hard,
too unfair. I wanted them to catch a break; it was the least I could do.
I had gotten myself into this mess, I'd get myself out.

But one day around the time of Friends and Family Week, I found
myself sitting outside, alone, hoping a moose would show or a turkey
do its flappy thing up into the trees. The day was freezing cold, subzero,
but I still needed to smoke, so there was nothing to do but bundle up
and deal. . . . As I sat there puffing on a Marlboro, a light snow began
to fall, bringing on an intense hush, as though the universe was patiently listening to my head and heart.

I wonder what the universe heard.

I began to think about why I hadn't wanted any visitors during this
stay, and something profound hit me. . . . Why am I excusing my family and loved ones from having to go through this hell, and not *myself*?

With that thought, I realized that Burton's advice was right—I *did*
like the chaos. It was time to give myself a break. Drugs hadn't given
me what I needed in a long time, yet I kept going back to them and
risking my life in order to . . . what? *Escape?* Escape from *what*? The
worst thing I had to run away from was my alcoholism and addiction,
so using drink and drugs to do so . . . well, you can see the logical
impossibility. None of it made sense, not even in the slightest. I was
smart enough to see that; doing something about it, though . . . that
was another level of math that I hadn't yet discovered. Change is still
scary, even when your life is on the line.

But at least I was finally asking good questions, even if the answers
weren't entirely clear. I knew deep down that life is about the simple joys
of throwing a red ball back and forth, of watching a moose lope across a
clearing. I needed to let myself off the hook for all the things doing the
damage, like still being angry with my parents, being unaccompanied

all those years ago, of not being enough, of being terrified of commitment because I was terrified of the end of commitment.

I needed to remember that my dad left because he was afraid, and my mom was a kid who was just doing her best. It wasn't her fault that she'd had to commit so much time to the fucking Canadian prime minister—it was never going to be a nine-to-five job, even with a kid at home. But I couldn't see that back then, and here we are. . . .

I needed to move on, and up, and realize that there was a whole big world out there and it was not out to get me. In fact, it had no opinion about me. It just *was,* like the animals and the shiv-sharp air; the universe was neutral, and beautiful, and continued with or without me.

In fact, I was alive in a world where, despite its neutrality, I had managed to create for myself an important, meaningful place. I needed to realize that when I died, I wanted my *Friends* credit to be way down on the list of things I had accomplished. I needed to remind myself to be nice to people—to have them bumping into me be a happy experience, not one that necessarily had to fill me with dread, as though that was all that mattered. I needed to be kind, to love well, to listen better, to give unconditionally. It was time to stop being such a scared asshole and realize that as situations came up, I would be able to handle them. Because I was strong.

Eventually the snow slowed, and out of the coming gloom a moose silently bulked into the gardens. It was a female, that long face serene, as though it had seen everything at least once and wasn't fazed by anything. *There was a lesson in that,* I thought. Behind her, a couple of calves kept pace, filled with that energy only kids possess. They all looked at me, sitting there in the twilight, and then they turned and wandered away.

Perhaps this was the lesson the universe was sending. I didn't matter, not in any great cosmic sense. I was just one more human being spinning in infinite circles.

To learn that was enough. I stubbed out the Marlboro and headed back in to lead yet another game of Red Ball.

I came out of Cirque Lodge thin and happy and ready to take on the world, and ready to be with my girlfriend forever. But my then-girlfriend didn't like this new Matty very much—I got the sense that she didn't appreciate it that I needed her less than before. Perhaps my problems had created a sense of security for her. *This guy will never leave me, not while he is so wrapped up in his own problems.* She didn't like that I was better. And that unfortunate truth was our final downfall. After trying hard to make the various pieces fit, we admitted defeat and broke up. It was very sad all around. She was my favorite person on the face of the planet, but it was not meant to be. It was the right thing, but that didn't mean it wasn't sad.

Now what, yet again?

I filled the hole initially with activism, but in doing so I flew too close to the sun and managed to lose my last semblance of innocence.

Back in 2001 I'd spent time at a rehab called Promises, in Malibu (right after I'd first picked up AA's Big Book in Marina del Rey). There, I'd met a guy called Earl H. He had been hosting a class at Promises, and I had liked him immediately. He was funny and incredibly knowledgeable about AA. He had several other celebrity clients, too, who were doing well, so I thought he'd be my guy and I asked him to sponsor me. (He said he hadn't had a drink since 1980.) Over coffee I admitted that one of the concerns I had was that one day he'd pass me a script to read. He said, "Well, there *is* a script, but I wouldn't do that to you. . . ."

So began our relationship. I worked the steps with him—in fact, I would chase him down to do them. I was so desperate to get with the program and stay sober that I would call him daily and ask to work.

He claimed nobody had ever chased him harder, and over the course of the following ten years, he came to wear two hats—he was my sponsor, but he was also my best friend. I looked up to him and listened to him. We had the same sense of humor and sort of even *sounded* the same. I ignored the fact that he was sort of famous in the rehab world, a world in which everything should be anonymous.

But my biggest mistake was that I had sort of made him my higher power. If I had a relationship issue, if I had an issue with anything, I would call him, and he would be very smart about it. It got to the point where if he'd said "I'm sorry, Matthew, but you have to move to Alaska and stand on your head," I would have immediately booked a ticket to Anchorage. If he said, "You can eat nothing but green M&M's for the next three months," you can rest assured I would have been shitting khaki.

Deep down, though, I knew full well that making your sponsor your best friend was a bad idea, but Earl was everything to me. He'd become my father, my mentor. I would go watch him speak (he was a hilarious and very effective speaker); we would go to movies together. I would have my relapses and he would help, finding me treatment centers. It's no exaggeration to say that he probably saved my life several times.

And then, our friendship turned into a business. Yes, I went into business with my sponsor. Fatal fucking mistake.

Earl had started a company that was going to establish sober living houses around Los Angeles that he would then run. I invested $500,000 in the company and turned my house in Malibu into a sober living place called Perry House. Along the way, at the behest of a great guy called West Huddleston, head of the National Association of Drug Court Professionals, Earl and I headed several times to Washington, DC, to meet with lawmakers to push the efficacy of drug courts. Drug courts aim to decriminalize nonviolent addicts, offering them care and treatment instead of jail time. In May 2013, Gil Kerlikowske, then Obama's "drug czar," even managed to give me a prize, a "Champion of Recovery award" from the Obama administration's Office of National Drug Control Policy. I joked to *The Hollywood Reporter* at the time that "had I been arrested, I would be sitting in prison somewhere with a tattoo on my face."

I also guest hosted *Piers Morgan Live* that same month, talking to Lisa Kudrow and Lauren Graham, but also focusing on issues of addiction and recovery. I was trying to find out what I wanted to do moving forward, and I felt comfortable doing the show. I began by saying I was not Piers Morgan, and the way you could tell that for sure was that "I don't have a British accent, and I don't have a first name that sounds very pointy," which caused Lisa to giggle out loud. I thought, *Maybe this is my future?* I even got to joke that my forthcoming autobiography would be called *Still a Boy*.

Oops.

Either way, I was now a talk show host, and an award-winning addict. How the fuck did *that* happen?

Earl had originally been slated to appear on *Piers Morgan* with me but had bailed at the last minute. Still, we later headed to Europe to push the power of drug courts there, and I got to debate the issue on a late-night BBC news show called *Newsnight*. There was the moderator, a cranky guy called Jeremy Paxman who was famous for being rude to guests; Baroness Meacher, who was the then-chair of the UK All-Party Parliamentary Group on Drug Policy Reform and deeply on my side; and then a complete tool called Peter Hitchens.

I can't imagine what it's like to have a sibling whom everyone adores when you're the idiot brother everyone loathes, but I think Peter could well be able to weigh in on what that feels like. The loss of Peter's wonderful brother, the great Christopher Hitchens, still reverberates—an unmatched raconteur, writer, arguer, and bon vivant, and the world mourns Christopher still, more than a decade after his brutal death from cancer. Sadly, his younger brother, Peter, is still pontificating on things he has no idea about, mixing right-wing ideology with a kind of paternalism and moral tutting.

Hitchens showed up on *Newsnight* to expound his bizarre views that drug taking is just a case of weak morals ("There's an immense fashion at the moment," he sneered, "for dismissing the ability of people to take *control* over their own lives, and to make *excuses* for them," sounding like some insane great-aunt who'd had one too many glasses of sherry). Even more bizarrely, he later "argued" that addiction isn't even a real thing. I like to think that both the baroness and I ran rings around him—but frankly, that wasn't hard. Apart from pointing out that I thought he was going to show up wearing big-boy pants to the interview, but he clearly hadn't, I also managed to point out repeatedly that the American Medical Association had diagnosed addiction as a disease in 1976 and that he was about the only person on the planet who didn't agree with that assessment. He didn't like that much, and eventually the interview ended with Paxman and Baroness Meacher simply laughing out loud at how stupid and cruel Hitchens sounded:

Hitchens: *So how is it that people ever cease to be addicts if what you say is true?*
Me: *Well, Santa . . .*
Hitchens: *Yeah, that's* terribly *clever, but this is a very serious subject. And you treat it with immense levity . . .*

Proving, I suppose, that he knew nothing about either me, or the subject on which he pontificated.

Meanwhile, even though I'd made Peter Hitchens look like the fool he is and advocated for drug courts all over Europe, Stateside, Perry

House was floundering. Not enough people attended—it was simply too expensive, so I had to cut my losses and sell the property.

When I had lunch with Earl, I asked for my money back, and I'm still waiting. He was talking about crazy things, like maybe becoming an actor. Something was off, and I was so freaked out by the whole thing—well, I went home and used. This was no one's fault but my own, but two things were crucially lost forever: my innocence, and my trust in Earl H.

Eventually Earl moved to Arizona without even telling me, and our friendship was over. From sharing our lives and being best friends and agitating for drug courts and building a sober living home, I'd lost half a million dollars, my closest ally, and that innocence I'd cherished all those years. Heartbreak.

I had been writing television for years but always with a partner. The day after the Earl H. debacle, I was feeling especially uncomfortable and ill at ease, and I remembered that a wise man once told me that in times like these I should be creative. So, I opened up my laptop and started typing. I didn't know what I was typing. I just kept typing. It became apparent that what was coming out was a play.

I needed this; I'd recently let my standards down horribly, and I was determined to crawl my way back to something closer to being able to contemplate looking in a mirror.

I was angry at myself over what had happened on *The Odd Couple* on CBS. For a long time, I'd been a huge fan of the film of Neil Simon's play and had always wanted to do a new TV version of it. My dream came true in 2013 when CBS had finally green-lit the idea. *Go On,* the show I did before *The Odd Couple,* hadn't worked, but I felt more confident about this one. The source material was brilliant; the cast great; everything was set fair to have a hit. Yet, depression stalked me, and my addictions were back in full force. Accordingly, I'm completely embarrassed about my behavior on *The Odd Couple*. On top of the horrible depression, I showed up late all the time, and high, and ultimately lost all power on the show to a showrunner. But I take complete responsibility for what happened and would like to apologize not only to my fellow castmates but also to everyone involved.

With that disaster in the rearview, I had a play in hand at least. Feeling that dis-ease, that discomfort coming out of my skin, usually I would use drugs to replace it, to give myself ease. But I was sober now, so I knew I couldn't do that—I had to find something else. I wrote ten hours a day for ten days straight until I had completed the play—and it was actually good, according to the very few people I let read it. I'd called it *The End of Longing*, and though it had taken ten days to draft, I spent another year perfecting it.

I'd been inspired by—and when I say inspired, I mean I was trying to beat—*Sexual Perversity in Chicago*, and was happy with what I'd achieved. I'd put it up against that fine play any day. In describing what I was trying to do, I'd told *The Hollywood Reporter* that "there's a very popular notion that people don't change, but I see people change every day, and I wanted to put that message out there while making people laugh." Accordingly, the play finds four friends in a bar trying to discover love—my character, Jack, opens the play as an egomaniac who happens to be an alcoholic, and then it only gets worse.

Me being me, I was not content to have just written a play—I decided it needed to be staged and have me in it. Months later, *The End of Longing* premiered in London's hallowed West End theater district. I loved being the playwright as well as the lead—I could change things around when they weren't working. And though I knew I'd hate doing the big drunk scene every night—it was surely going to be intensely triggering—I knew, too, that I had to show just how low a person can go.

We opened in the Playhouse Theatre, an eight-hundred-seat venue, and quickly we were selling out. In fact, we were pulling down massive box-office records, but also, lousy reviews. For historical accuracy, there were seven major reviews and six of them were bad. London reviewers didn't like the idea of a Hollywood actor-boy going over there and doing a play. It was a huge success, though, and I was a playwright and I liked that idea.

There was also one person who wouldn't come to the play, even though I begged.

The woman I'd dated for six years was, by now, dating a British guy, and they were spending half the year in London, the rest in Los Angeles. We were still friendly enough that we'd had a couple of lunches and texted a few times. Knowing that she was in London, I'd invited her to see *The End of Longing,* but she'd texted back that she was way too busy. "I'll see you Stateside!" she wrote. I replied that I was a little hurt that she couldn't make it—the play was being performed in her town, for God's sake—and then a while later I got back an email telling me that she was getting married and that she had no room in her life for friends.

I never replied to that email, and we've never spoken since. It was an incredibly harsh way to reveal the news that she was getting married, and not something that I would ever do to a person, but there you have it. Even still, I will forever be planted in her corner. I'm glad she got married and that she's happy. I want nothing but the best for her, forever.

From London the play moved to New York. That was not fun. For a start, I had to tone the play down—the Brits didn't care about the salty language, but Broadway is Broadway, so I had to leaven it, and not just the language—I had to kill a bunch of the jokes, too. So, it was neither well received nor beloved in New York—*The New York Times* trashed it, calling it "synthetic," whatever that means, and I ended up making $600 for the whole New York run. That's not a typo. (I'd made one thousand times more—almost to the pound, shilling, and pence—during its run in London.) At least *The Hollywood Reporter* was nice about it: "Perry at least demonstrates that his extensive television comedy experience has rubbed off. The evening features many amusing one-liners (most of them, predictably, delivered by the author). . . . Perry displays his familiar expert comic timing and delivery." But the "at least" was pretty crushing, and I realized that *The End of Longing* wasn't going to be beloved enough to cement my future as a budding David Mamet. But there is still time!

Trauma Camp

There is such a thing as a Trauma Camp, and yes, I've attended, and yes, I made up that name.

It was in Florida—where else?—and I spent ninety days there, opening up the trauma of my life and reliving it, scene by scene. I did it in a group setting—others reciprocated their traumas until everyone was fainting and puking and shaking. At one point, I was asked to draw the stick figures of all my traumas, and then asked to show everyone what I'd drawn and describe it. As I tried to point to one of the drawings, my fingers started to shake, and subsequently my whole body joined in, and it wouldn't stop shaking for thirty-six days. I was like a goat who'd had a close encounter with a bear—the bear was gone, but the goat kept shaking.

At the end of trauma therapy, once you've gone back into the trauma and relived it, the therapists are supposed to "close" you back up—basically you're supposed to feel everything, and release it, and learn how to make it a story, not a living thing in your soul, so that it no longer has dominion over you in the way that it did.

Oh, and you're supposed to cry.

They didn't close me up right; and I didn't cry. I was afraid. I felt like I was back onstage. Being famous in rehab isn't perhaps what you imagine—everyone else there has a lot to deal with, so who cares if you're Matthew Perry? Later, in Pennsylvania, I attended a rehab with six other people who were all in their seventies, including Debbie, aka, the bane of my existence. Debbie was the only other smoker, so I had to see Debbie all the time outside. And Debbie had zero memory.

"Wait, have we met?" she'd say.

"No, Debbie, we have not. But I was on the show *Friends* once. That's probably how you know me."

"Oh! I like that show," Debbie would say.

Five minutes later, Debbie would pause, sucking on her cigarette, and turn to me.

"So, did we go to high school together?"

"No, Debbie," I'd say, as kindly as I could muster. "You are twenty-seven years older than me. You probably recognize me from the show *Friends. . . .*"

"Oh! I like that show," Debbie would repeat, and the whole cycle would begin again.

9

Three's Not Company, Three Ruins Everything

When a man or woman asks me to help them quit drinking, and I do so, watching as the light slowly comes back into their eyes, that's all God to me. And even though I have a relationship with God, and I'm so often grateful despite everything, I sometimes do want to tell God to go fuck himself for making my road so hard.

When I'm clean and sober, it is as if a light has been shown to me, one that I can share with a desperate man who needs help with stopping drinking. It's the same light that hits the ocean in a bright sunlight, the beautiful gold water glistening. That's what God is to me. (It also works at night when the moonlight hits the water—boom! It almost knocks me over. Because like that five-year-old boy flying across a continent alone seeing the city lights of Los Angeles and he knows he is about to be parented . . . well, it's all the same.)

Why is it so hard for me to stay sober when I see my fellows seemingly doing it easily? Why has my road been so racked with difficulty? Why have I wrestled so hard with life? Why has reality been an acquired taste, and why has it been so hard for me to acquire it? But when

I help that one man to get sober, or even helped thousands get sober in a weekend at a retreat or conference, all these questions get washed away. It's like I'm standing under a Hawaiian waterfall getting drenched by the beautiful warm water. That's where God is; you're just going to have to have to trust me on that.

I am no saint—none of us are—but once you have been at death's door and you don't die, you would think you would be bathed in relief and gratitude. But that isn't it at all—instead, you look at the difficult road ahead of you to get better and you are *pissed.* Something else happens, too. You are plagued by this nagging question: *Why have I been spared?* The other four people on the ECMO machine were still dead. There had to be a reason.

Part of the answer for me was my ten thousand hours of experience in AA and helping people get sober. That lights me up, loans me, in fact, a little bit of that golden light from my kitchen.

But there has to be more, God. Why did you spare *me?* I'm ready—give me the direction and I will follow it. When Woody Allen asks this very question to an alien in the movie *Stardust Memories,* the alien responds, "Tell funnier jokes." But that can't be it.

Either way, I'm ready. And I seek the answer every day. I am a seeker. I seek God.

My love life, however, is a different story. I have made more mistakes in my love life than Elizabeth Taylor. I am a romantic, passionate person. I have longed for love; it's a yearning in me that I cannot fully explain.

Once I reached my forties, the rules had changed. I had done all the sleeping with people I'd ever need to do—I was looking for a partner now, a teammate, someone to share my life with. Also, I have always loved kids. I think it's because I was ten years old when my sister Caitlin was born. Then came Emily, then Will, and then finally Madeline. I loved playing with them all, babysitting them, playing dumb games with them. There is no greater sound on the face of the planet than a child's laughter.

So, by the time my forties were in full swing, I truly wanted a girl-friend, someone I could count on, and who, in turn, could count on me. One night some friends and I were out celebrating that yet again I had achieved a year of sobriety. My still good friend David Press-man introduced me to his girlfriend's sister, Laura. We'd all gone to a Dodgers game together, but for me there was no game, no stadium, no hot dog vendors—instead, the world had receded to a beautiful face under a baseball cap. I tried to pull out the old Perry charm—anything to make her notice me—but she was too busy parading her glorious personality and wit to others. She was unimpressed that I had been Chandler, and though she was perfectly pleasant to me, I sensed there was no there-there for her.

As I drove home that night, I gave myself a speech.

"Yes, you're disappointed, but not every girl is not going to like you, Matty." I let it go, but I didn't forget her. Surely our paths would cross again.

And they did.

This time the group had decided to play Ping-Pong at the Standard Hotel in downtown LA. Now, I am no Forrest Gump, but I knew my way around a Ping-Pong table—in fact, if you've seen the finale of sea-son nine of *Friends,* you'll know that I'm at least good enough to beat Paul Rudd. I had heard that Laura might make an appearance, so I played Ping-Pong with one eye on the door.

And there she was, finally. It was as if she had been hurled into the club by a tornado—she was all energy and jokes.

"Everyone in here should kill themselves," Laura said, and BOOM! like a brick of interest slamming into my face. But this time I was ready. So began a night that resembled a knife fight, only with jokes. It turned out that the new object of my affection was a stand-up comedian and a successful writer in TV. It was clear from the get-go that we would never run out of things to say to each other.

Our first date was on New Year's Eve. A friend was holding a pajama party and I invited Laura to go with me. After that, our relationship developed slowly; she was careful, and I was willing to do whatever it took. But our affections deepened. It was all good . . . ah, but nothing is all good in my world, remember?

Enter Rome. I was two years sober and thriving in AA, healthy, sponsoring people, writing a TV show. I was happy, even pretty muscular, dare I say. (I *dare*: I'd been hitting the gym and everything!) I was asked to share my story at an AA meeting in West Hollywood, and you're not allowed to say no to an AA request. The room was packed, standing room only (I think word had gotten out that I was speaking). My story at the time had not reached the depths of the last few years, so as well as detailing everything I'd gone through, I was also able to get my share of laughs. At one point, I looked over to the kitchen area and noticed a woman pop her head through the window/hatch thingy, leaning on her elbows to prop herself up. She resembled a gorgeous, porcelain doll and was staggeringly beautiful. All of a sudden, there were only two people in the room. My AA share became directed only at Rome. It ended up being one of the greatest shares I had ever given, because this epic beauty was so captivating that I wanted her to know everything about me. I wanted her to know everything.

Afterward, as we all gathered outside for a cigarette, we started talking and flirting.

"So, what are you up to right now?" she said.

"I'm going to go home to write. All of a sudden, I've become a writer," I said.

"Well," Rome said, "I make an excellent muse."

"I'll bet you do," I said, then turned and walked away, completely bowled over by this mysterious person.

On the way home I gave myself a talking-to.

But what about Laura? Yes, of course, wonderful Laura, who I am falling for more and more each day. But now there is Rome. What is a fella to do? Forget about Rome and continue investigating this Laura thing that is going so well. Right? That's what a normal person does under these circumstances.

But Rome had cast a spell on me.

Despite my positive self-talk, this was when I made a crucial, killing mistake. I didn't know it was a mistake at the time—do any of us know that we are making mistakes while we are making them? If we did, perhaps we wouldn't make them?

The mistake was this, and it was a doozy: I began dating both women.

This is not a move I recommend under any circumstances, but especially if you are me.

I told myself that because I had not told either Laura or Rome that we were in a relationship, I was not being an asshole, but there was a little piece of me that knew I was doing something untoward because I cared about both of them, and despite outward appearances, I genuinely didn't want anyone to get hurt, including me. So, Laura and I would go to Kings games together, laugh and have a wonderful time, though somewhat chaste. The courtship with both women went slowly, but eventually both removed their sex embargoes, and I was now fully involved with two different women at the same time. It was amazing, and completely baffling and crazy making.

Did I mention that I had fallen madly in love with both of them? I didn't think it was even possible to do that. I even went online, read a few articles, and learned that this was something that did indeed happen. The feelings I had for both of these women were real, according to what

I read. Then, Laura and I pronounced ourselves boyfriend and girlfriend, Rome and I not so much—but I was still in trouble.

What was I going to do? I enjoyed my time with both of them equally. I loved them. This went on for about six months before I came to my senses and decided I had to pick one. I had to stop this nonsense and pick one. Rome was passionate, erotic, funny, smart, but she also seemed to have this fascination with death that confused me. Laura talked about movies and lighter things; there was a sense of being home with her that I had not felt with Rome.

I chose Laura.

I made the very difficult call to Rome. At first, she was chill about it, until she wasn't, subsequently screaming at me for two hours in the parking lot of Barney's Beanery on Santa Monica Boulevard when I tried to make amends. You would be hard-pressed to find an angrier person than she was with me that day.

But by now you know me; you know I can't do with getting closer and closer to someone, and that was what was happening with Laura. The fear was burrowing into me. To break up with Laura would be insane—she had it all. *We* had it all. We were each other's best friend. But the intimacy was scaring me. I knew once again that if she got to know me any better she would see what I already believed about myself: As ever, I wasn't enough. I didn't matter. Soon, she would see this for herself, and she would leave me. That would annihilate me, and I would never recover.

There was another option. I could remain in the relationship but turn back to drugs and try to maintain a low habit. This would protect me from the fear, allow me to drop my walls and become even more intimate with her.

Turning to drugs has led to nothing but chaos for me. And yet, inconceivably, I chose to do it one more time to deal with the Laura situation. I started taking one pill a day just in order to stay in the relationship. It worked out great at first, but as is the way with drugs, they always win. Six months later we had a shitstorm on our hands. I was a mess. Laura broke up with me, and I had to go on Suboxone once again and check into a sober living house. I was afraid I was going to die yet again. Rome was still yelling at me every chance she had, and Laura was hurt and worried, oh, and gone.

Oh, there was something else the magazines said about being in love with two people at the same time. It always has the same ending.

You lose them both.

So, there I was, living in a Malibu sober living house on 8 milligrams of Suboxone. Though it's a solid detox drug—the best—as I've said over and over, it is the hardest drug on the planet to get off. In fact, it made me suicidal to come off it. That's not quite accurate—I had suicidal feelings, but I also knew it was just the medicine, so I wasn't actually suicidal, if you follow. All I had to do was stave off the days when I felt suicidal, not do anything about it, and know that at some point I would feel better and not want to kill myself anymore.

To get off Suboxone, you have to drop a milligram a week until you get to zero. Doing so makes you feel insanely sick for two days, then you get used to the new level—in this case, 7 milligrams—and once you stabilize, then you drop again. The suicidal feelings don't start until you get down to 2 milligrams.

So, at 2 milligrams I did probably the most selfish thing I have ever done in my life. I was terrified about how I was about to feel, and I didn't want to go through it alone. Accordingly, I purchased three hundred dollars' worth of flowers, drove to Laura's house, and begged her to take me back. We sat on the couch in her living room and discussed the ins and outs of what this would mean. Driven completely by fear, I told her I wanted to marry her, possibly even have a child with her.

And then, something impossible happened. As we were sitting there, I heard a key slowly turning in her front door . . . and in walked Rome.

In walked *who* now?

How is it possible that these two women were standing in the same room? I would give anything to have a time machine, go back to that moment, and say, "How about a threesome?" But this was no time for jokes. My jaw was on the floor.

"I'm going to water the plants," Rome said, and she headed up the back stairwell and was gone.

"I think I need to take care of her," Laura said, and left me in the living room. When I realized she wasn't coming back, I took my 2-milligram addiction back to Malibu.

It turned out that Rome and Laura had met at an AA meeting, realized who they were, and become fast friends. The bulk of their conversations, as I'm sure you can imagine, were about what an asshole I was.

As for me, I couldn't stay in Los Angeles, so I hopped on a private plane to a Colorado recovery center where they said that they thought that they could get me off Suboxone without making me feel suicidal.

Well, so much for that idea. I felt suicidal for thirty-six days in a row and then flew to New York and appeared on Letterman, trying to hide that I was being held up with tape and paper.

Somehow, I pulled it off.

Seven years later, after I had learned a whole lot about myself, I made real amends to Rome and to Laura, and they both accepted my apology. Believe it or not, the three of us are friends, now. Laura is married to a lovely guy named Jordon, and Rome is living with an equally lovely guy named Eric.

Recently the five of us had dinner together at my place, and we all had a lovely time. Then, at around 10:00 P.M., the two couples left in their respective cars. I heard the engines recede down the canyon toward the city.

Out back, as I waited for something to come to me, anything that might make things better, instead I once again heard the sound of coyotes.

No, it's the sound of me, alone, fending off the demons for one more night. They'd won. And I knew I'd lost as I headed back up to my lonely bedroom to fend off those demons and negotiate sleep one more time.

Violence in Hollywood

I am not a violent man, but I have been both the victim and the perpetrator of violence one time each in my life.

Years ago, right after she quit seeing Justin Timberlake, I got set up on a date with Cameron Diaz.

At the time, I was working out a lot and had developed big arms. For the date I prepared accordingly, taking a long walk with my sleeves rolled to my shoulders so that my guns were appropriately tanned (pro tip: this helps them look even bigger). Yes, I literally tanned my arms for this date.

The date was at a dinner party with a bunch of other people, but upon seeing me, Cameron got almost instantly stoned—it was clear that she wasn't interested in me at all. But the party went on nevertheless, and at one point we were all playing a game—Pictionary, I think. As she was drawing, I said something witty to Cameron, to which she said, "Oh, come on!" and proceeded to punch me in the shoulder.

Or, at least, that's what she meant to do. But she missed and, instead, punched me smack in the side of my face.

"Are you fucking kidding me?" I said, realizing I'd just been punched in the face by Cameron Diaz and my big arms hadn't helped at all.

This was about fifteen years ago. But she'll probably call me. Don't you think?

Then there was this other time.

In 2004, I flew out to Chris Evert's tennis academy in Florida for a charity event, the Chris Evert / Bank of America Pro-Celebrity Tennis Classic. It was a veritable who's who in Hollywood. But I was most interested in Chevy Chase.

Chevy had long been a hero of mine. In fact, his performance in the movie *Fletch* had changed my life forever. One chilly night in LA, my best buddy Matt Ondre and I went to see a preview screening of *Fletch*, and at one point, we were literally rolling in the aisles with laughter. Chevy must have had three hundred jokes in that movie, and he landed each one perfectly. Later, as Matt and I sat at the bus stop awaiting our ride home, I vividly remember turning to him and very seriously saying, "Matt, I am going to talk that way for the rest of my life." And I have. Which makes this next story particularly painful for both Chevy and me.

Possibly more for Chevy.

Anyway, at the charity ball the night before the tennis event, Chevy walked up to me and said, "I just want you to know I'm a big fan." This was incredible.

I said, "Oh my God, all I do is steal from you," and we went on to have a mutually complimentary and quite lovely conversation.

Next day, it was time to play tennis.

Now, my skills were by this point admittedly rusty. I hadn't played in years, and my ground strokes needed a lot of work. What I did have, though, was an incredibly hard serve—in fact, they had a speed clock at the tournament, and I punched in at 111 miles per hour. The only problem was, I was not exactly sure where they were going. Which was fine at your everyday public court, not so fine in front of two thousand people. Even former president George H. W. Bush was there. . . .

The game begins. I am first up to serve. I have my partner in the ad court, and on the opposite side is Chevy, also in the ad court near the net, and his partner back at the baseline, to whom I would be serving directly. I toss up the ball, bring my racket around my back, hammer the tennis ball as hard as possible, and watch in horror as instead of it spearing across court to Chevy's partner, it goes directly straight, and it's heading for Chevy Chase. He is standing on the service line, which is exactly sixty feet from where I've hit the ball. This line is, coincidentally, the exact distance from the mound to home plate in baseball, so I can confidently tell you that if the ball was hit at about 100 miles per hour, this means it was traveling at about 146.7 feet per second, meaning Mr. Chase had 0.412 seconds to get out of the way.

Mr. Chase did not get out of the way.

More precisely, his testicles didn't get out of the way—I have just served something close to a professional-speed serve right into his Chevy Chases. If you know what I mean.

Here's what happened next: Chevy made a funny face—just like the one he makes in *Fletch* when a doctor gives him a prostate exam— and then dropped to the ground. (Remember, all this was going down in front of two thousand people.)

Event now over, it took four medics to dash onto the court, strap him to a gurney, and rush him to the nearest hospital.

If this is what I do to my heroes, Michael Keaton and Steve Martin better take cover.

And thus concludes the violent section of this book.

10

The Big Terrible Thing

Imagine this: you have to walk back onto a set where you have almost literally shat the bed for weeks before. You've been out of it, slurring lines, making bad decisions. You're in New York City, and even though you have not one but two sober companions, you call room service at the hotel, your voice shaking, detoxing, and say, "Please put a bottle of vodka in the bathtub of my room. Yes, the bathtub. Hide it in there."

And then, when the day is done, you head back to that fucking hotel room, and you drink the bottle of vodka, and you finally feel all right again for maybe three hours and then have to do it all over again the next day. You're shaking, pretending that you are not in very serious trouble whenever you talk to anyone. Using that same shaky voice, you call the hotel and tell them to do the vodka-bottle-in-the-bathtub thing again.

This is perhaps something that a "normy"—what we addicts call all you lucky nonalcoholics—might always struggle to understand. I'll take a stab at explaining it: when you drink an entire bottle of vodka, you are extremely sick the following day. Having a few drinks in the morning helps, but I was the lead in a giant studio movie, so I could not drink in the morning. You are sick and trembling, and it feels like every part of your insides is trying to squeeze out of your body. And that's all day—the entire fourteen-hour day.

The only way to fix how sick you are is to drink the exact same amount, or a little more, the following night. "So just don't drink," says the normy. We alcoholics feel like we will literally go insane if we don't drink—not to mention the alcoholic will be even sicker, and *look* sicker, if he doesn't drink the bottle.

"But what about the movie?"

Doesn't matter—I have to drink.

"How about taking a break for the night?"

Not possible.

Next question?

So, I'm in Dallas—I am on methadone, a quart of vodka a day, cocaine, and Xanax. Every day I would show up to set, pass out in my chair, wake up to do a scene, stumble to set, then just basically scream into a camera for two minutes. Then it was back to my chair for further nap time.

At this point in my life, I was one of the most famous people in the world—in fact, I was being burned by the white-hot flame of fame. Therefore, no one dared to say anything about this horrific behavior. The movie people wanted the film to be completed, slap my name on a poster, and make $60 million. And *Friends* . . . well *Friends* was even worse—no one wanted to mess with that moneymaking machine.

At one point during the filming of *Serving Sara* I thought maybe some Valium would help me somehow. A doctor arrived at my duplex hotel room to give me some. The night before he came to visit, I had drunk a party-size bottle of vodka, the one with the handle on it. When the doctor looked around the room, he saw the bottle and said, in a nervous voice, "Did you drink all of that?"

"Yes," I said, "may I have the Valium every four hours, not every six?"

With that, he turned tail and ran top speed down the spiral staircase and out the door, presumably so he wouldn't actually be in the room if Matthew Perry died.

But I went away to rehab after Jamie Tarses had told me I was disappearing, and eventually came back to finish the movie.

This was me during *Serving Sara*. I was a mess. I felt so guilty, and I apologized to everybody, and I like to think that I did a great job for the final thirteen days of shooting. Everyone tried to be kind about it, and they were doing their best, but they were pissed off; the director was pissed off—I'd ruined his movie; Elizabeth Hurley, my costar, was pissed off (she never got to do another movie, either).

I needed to make real amends—that's part of what AA teaches you. So, I rerecorded my slurred parts for the entire movie—which meant I looped the entire movie—days and days in a sound studio. Three beeps in a studio and I'd say my line to match my mouth. I happen to be good at that, and at the very least we got the slurring out of the movie. Then I committed to doing the most press possible in the history of press, bending over backward to make things right. I was on the cover of everything, on every talk show you can think of.

Of course, the movie tanked anyway. I was paid $3.5 million to do the movie and I got sued for the shutdown, even though it was a health issue. At the mediation table a team of insurance flacks faced me down, so I just wrote them a check for $650,000.

I remember thinking, *Man, no one taught me the rules of life.* I was a complete mess of a person—selfish and narcissistic. Everything had to be about me, and I matched that with a really handy inferiority complex, an almost fatal combo. I was all about myself from the time I was ten years old, from that moment when I looked around and said, *It's every man for himself.* I had to be so focused on me just to keep myself together.

But AA will teach you this is no way to live.

One of the things you do in the 12 steps of AA is create a personal moral inventory (it's the fourth step). In it, you write down all the people that you're mad at and why. (I had sixty-eight names—sixty-eight!) Then you write down how it has affected you, and then you read it to someone (this is step five).

What I learned from this process—and by the care and love of a great sponsor to whom I read my list—was that I wasn't the center of the universe. It's kind of a relief learning that. There were other people around who had needs and cares and were just as important as I was.

(If you're shaking your head now, go on, have at it. Let he who is without sin cast the first stone.)

Sobriety had now become the most important thing in my life. Because I learned that if you put anything in front of sobriety, you will lose that "anything" anyway if you drink.

I read my list to my sponsor one beautiful spring day at a wonderful meditation center in Los Angeles called the Self-Realization Fellowship Lake Shrine. Perched on a hill overlooking the Pacific, the place is truly peaceful—there's a lake and gardens and temples and even a pot of some of Mahatma Gandhi's ashes, the only such stash outside of India.

As I finished reading out my list, we realized a wedding was starting in the gardens. I watched as the couple beamed at each other, the families in their best attire, an officiant smiling, waiting to warble on about sickness and health till death do they part. I hadn't been there for anyone for so long, my addiction being my best friend and my evil friend and my punisher and my lover, all in one. My big terrible thing. But that day, up there with the view—there always has to be a view, of course—and with the soon-to-be newlyweds, and Gandhi somewhere nearby, I sensed an awakening, that I was here for more than this big terrible thing. That I could help people, love them, because of how far down the scale I had gone, I had a story to tell, a story that could really help people. And helping others had become the answer for me.

*   *   *

On July 19, 2019, the front page of *The New York Times* featured stories about Donald Trump, Stormy Daniels, a deadly arson at a Kyoto
animation studio, and Puerto Ricans who, according to the headline,
had "had enough."

I knew none of this. Nor would I know anything for the next two
weeks: not that El Chapo got life plus thirty years; not that some
nineteen-year-old shot three people dead (and himself) at a garlic festi-
val in Gilroy, California; not that Boris Johnson became the UK prime
minister.

When I awoke from my coma, I was screaming. My mother was
there. I asked her what had happened. She told me my colon had exploded.

"It's amazing that you're alive," she said. "Your resiliency is incredible. And with some life changes, you're gonna be OK. And they can
remove the colostomy bag in about nine months."

I thought, *I have a colostomy bag? That's great. Girls find that to be a
definite turn-on.*

I said, "Thank you very much."

After that I rolled over, and really didn't talk or move for two weeks.
I had been inches from death because of something that I had done. I
was attached to fifty machines, and I would have to learn to walk again.

I hated myself. I had almost killed myself. The shame, the loneliness, the regret, were too much to handle. I just lay there, trying to
deal with all of it, but there was no dealing with it. It had already been
done. I was afraid to die, which was in direct opposition to my actions.

But it was over. *The Matthew Perry Show,* canceled by opiates.

Sometimes I could sort of pay attention to what was going on in the
room, but that was about it. I certainly wasn't taking part in anything.
My best friends, Chris and Brian Murray, would come visit. About
three weeks into it, Maria, my sister on my father's side, came to see me.

"Are you ready to hear what happened?" she said.

I nodded (barely).

"After your colon exploded, they put you on a ventilator, which you vomited into. So, all of this bile and septic shit went into your lungs. They put you on an ECMO machine—somehow you survived that. And you were in a coma for fourteen days."

After that, I don't think I spoke for another week because I had realized that my greatest fear had come true, which is that I did this to myself. There was one upside, though. A fourteen-day coma makes it very simple to quit smoking.

I had been on opiates, and off opiates, and back on different opiates for so long that I suffered from a situation that only a subset of the population gets. Opiates cause constipation. It's kind of poetic. I was so full of shit it almost killed me.

Also, I now had a bowel situation.

The last thing I'd said to Erin before the coma, as I was spinning on the ground in Pain, right before I lost consciousness, was, "Don't leave me." I meant right then and there, but she, like the rest of my friends and family, took it literally. Erin pulled the night shift for five months in that hospital.

I often look back on that time and am so grateful that this happened before Covid, because then I would have been alone in that room for five months. As it was, I was never alone in that room once. That was God's love, in human form, made flesh.

Both my mom and I are experts in a crisis now. What I've always wanted to tell her is that the little show called *Friends,* and all the other shows, and movies? I essentially did it all for her attention. And yet that's the one person whose attention I did not really get from *Friends.* She mentioned it on occasion, but she was never boiling with pride about what her son had accomplished.

But I don't think there's possibly a way that she could have been proud enough for what I needed. And if you're going to blame your parents for the bad stuff, you also have to give them credit for the good stuff. *All* the good stuff. I could never have played Chandler if my mother weren't my mother. I would never have made $80 million if my mother weren't my mother. Because Chandler was just a hider of true pain. What better character for a sitcom! To just make a joke about everything, so we don't have to talk about anything real—that's how Chandler started. In the initial breakdown of the show, Chandler was supposed to be "an observer of other people's lives." So, he would be the guy who at the end of a scene would make some joke, comment on whatever has just happened—the Fool in *King Lear,* speaking truth where there had been none. But everyone ended up liking Chandler so much that he morphed into being his own major character. That he ended up superseding what I actually did in real life—getting married, having kids—well . . . some things I can't talk about all that well.

The bottom line is, I abandoned my mother, at fifteen, just as she'd been abandoned by my father. I was not an easy child to put up with, and she was just a child herself. She always did her best and was with me in my hospital room for five months after the coma.

When your colon explodes because of overuse of opiates, the prudent thing to do is to not ask for opiates to solve the situation . . . which is, of course, what I did.

And they gave them to me.

I was impossibly depressed and as always wanted to feel better. Also the hole in my stomach, the one that you could fit a bowling ball in, was ample excuse to get pain medication. Just so you are following along, I had come within inches of dying because of opiates and I asked the doctors to solve that problem with . . . opiates! So no, even after the catastrophic event, I was not done. I hadn't learned anything. I still wanted to use.

When I got out of the hospital after the explosion, I was actually looking really good. I'd lost a lot of weight, but I was so injured that they couldn't do surgery to replace the bag for at least another nine months. So, I went home to my apartment, lied to everyone about the severity of the pain to get pain medication. I was not actually in pain. It was more annoyance than pain. But doctors believed the lie and gave me tons of opiates, and obviously I started smoking again.

And that was kind of my life.

And let's not forget: that colostomy bag was constantly breaking, regularly—fifty times at least—leaving me with shit all over me.

Dear Colostomy Bag People: make a bag that doesn't break, you fucking morons. Did I make you laugh on *Friends*? If so, don't put shit all over my face.

When an addict takes a pill, they feel euphoric. But after a short while the pill doesn't make them euphoric anymore because a tolerance has built up. But the addict still really, really wants to feel euphoric again, so they take two instead to get the feeling that one originally gave them.

Then, two is not enough, and they go to three.

In the past, I had played that little game until the number got up to fifty-five pills a day. (Just watch the second half of season three of *Friends*. I was so frail and skinny and sick. It definitely showed, but no one said anything about it.)

The UCLA hospital was giving me opiates for my fake stomach pain, but I needed more, so I called a drug dealer. But I was on the fortieth floor of that building in Century City, and that meant that I had to figure out a way to go down forty floors, give the dealer the money in an empty cigarette packet, and get my pills. Then I had to get back to the fortieth floor unnoticed, take the pills, and I would get to feel good for a while.

Now, I had to do this with a sober companion, a nurse, and Erin all living in the apartment. Turns out I was terrible at it—I tried four times and got caught exactly four times. The UCLA doctors were not pleased with this and said I had to go to rehab.

I had no choice—I was addicted to everything they gave me. Had I just said, "No, fuck off," it might have been a glorious moment, but then the drugs would stop, and I would get crazy sick. I was put in the rather strange position of choosing where I'd be locked up for months—given the choice of New York or Houston. Maybe somebody more capable than me should be given that decision? I, being the least qualified to make any decisions, picked New York.

I was high as a kite and fakely clutching my stomach when we arrived at the recovery center in New York. Even though the place resembled a prison, the people in there were all smiles.

"What the fuck are you guys so *happy* about?" I said. (I had a tendency to be a bit grumpy.) I was on 14 milligrams of Ativan and 60 milligrams of OxyContin. I had a colostomy bag. I asked where I could smoke and was told there would be no smoking here.

"I can't stay here if I can't smoke," I said.

"Well, you can't smoke here."

"Yeah, I heard what you said. How in the world am I supposed to quit smoking on top of everything else?"

"We'll give you a patch."

"Don't blame me if I smoke the actual fucking patch," I said.

It was agreed that they would keep me on the Ativan, put me on Suboxone, and I could smoke during the detox, but not when I was on the main unit. This meant that I could smoke for four more days. When I wanted to smoke, the staff member would escort me outside and stand next to me while I puffed away.

That was relaxing.

Three nights went by, and then I met a very pretty, extremely smart nurse. She took very good care of me, and I flirted with her as much as you can flirt with someone who is changing your colostomy bag on the reg. The dreaded day where I would have to quit smoking was looming, so I was allowed to walk out with the wonderful nurse to get coffee. Accordingly, my mood lifted a bit. I made jokes, I flirted, in that "we're all in rehab so nothing-can-really-happen" way, and we returned.

Back at the center, the nurse said, "I need you to do something for me."

"Whatever you need," I said.

"I need you to stop trying to fuck the hot nurse."

She was referring to herself.

Jesus.

"I thought we were both flirting in a safe, never-going-to-happen way," I said.

I was there for four more months, and I never flirted with her again. Nor did she flirt back at my nonflirting, perhaps because she'd seen me covered in my own shit multiple times.

I moved up to the unit, met therapists—Bruce, Wendy, whatever—whom I wanted nothing to do with. All I wanted to do was smoke. Or talk about smoking. Or smoke while talking about smoking.

Everyone just looked like a giant cigarette.

I rarely left my room. The bag kept breaking. I called my mother and I asked her to come save me. She said that I would smoke if I left and that would be awful for the coming surgery. I called my therapist, begged her to get me out. She said the same thing my mom had.

I was fucked and stuck.

Panic set in. My bag was full. I was not high. There was nothing separating me from me. I felt like a little kid scared of monsters in the dark. But was *I* the monster?

I found that stairwell. The nurse? Nowhere to be found. Therapy? Fuck therapy. I hit those walls with my head just as hard as Jimmy Connors used to hit his forehands down the line. Lots of topspin. Right on the fucking line.

Stairwells.

I'm this close to dying every day.

I don't have another sobriety in me. If I went out, I would never be able to come back. And if I went out, I would go out hard. I would have to go out hard because my tolerance is so high.

It's not like the Amy Winehouse story, where she was sober for a while, and then the first drinks she had killed her. She said something in that documentary that is true for me, too. She had just won a Grammy and she said to a friend, "I can't enjoy this unless I'm drunk."

The idea of being famous, the idea of being rich, the idea of being me—I can't enjoy any of it unless I'm high. And I can't think of love without wanting to be high. I lack a spiritual connection that protects me from these feelings. That's why I'm a seeker.

The first time I reached fifty-five pills a day, like the character of Betsy Mallum in *Dopesick,* I didn't know what was going on. I didn't know that I was addicted. I'm one of the first famous people who went to rehab and people *knew* about it. In 1997, I was on the number one TV show in America and went to rehab and it was on the cover of the magazines. But I had no idea what was happening to me. Betsy Mallum in *Dopesick* graduates to heroin, and it's sayonara—you see her just kind of nod out, smile, and die. But that smile is the feeling that I want all the time. She must have felt so good, but it *killed* her. But that beatific moment is something I still seek, only without the death part. I want a connection. I want that connection to something bigger than me because I'm convinced it's the only thing that will truly save my life.

I don't want to die. I'm scared to die.

I'm not even any good at finding the drugs. Somebody at one point that I worked with introduced me to a crooked doctor. I would claim that I had migraine headaches—actually, I had maybe eight doctors going for my made-up migraines—and I would still sit through a forty-five-minute MRI to get drugs. Sometimes, when things were really bad, I'd go to drug dealer houses. The nurse of the doctor took over from him when he died. She had all the pills, and she lived in the Valley, and whenever I wanted to get pills, I would go see her. I'd be terrified the entire time.

She'd say, "Come in!"

"No!" I'd shout, "we're going to get arrested. Just take the money and let me get outta here."

Later she wanted me to sit and do coke with her. I'd get the pills, and because I was so terrified, I'd take three instantly and drive home and be high to take the edge off the fear, which just meant I was even more arrestable.

Much later, when I lived in Century City, I'd try to find excuses to go down forty stories to score. I was so sick and so injured at the time—my stomach hadn't closed yet, I was alone during Covid . . . I had a nurse on staff giving me drugs, but I wasn't getting high from them anymore. So I would call a drug dealer and get more Oxy. This way, I'd have additional drugs to the ones I'd been prescribed so that I could actually feel them. The street pills were something like $75 per pill, so I was giving the guy $3,000 at a time, many times a week.

But I got caught more times than I was able to pull it off. The UCLA doctor in charge of my case got fed up with me and told me he wouldn't help me anymore. I couldn't really blame him—everybody was terrified about fentanyl being in the pills and me dying from them. (When I got to the treatment center, sure enough, I tested positive for fentanyl.)

This disease . . . the big horrible thing. Addiction has ruined so much of my life it's not funny. It's ruined relationships. It's ruined the day-to-day process of being me. I have a friend who doesn't have any money, lives in a rent-controlled apartment. Never made it as an actor, has diabetes, is constantly worried about money, doesn't work. And I would trade places with him in a second. In fact, I would give up all the money, all the fame, all the stuff, to live in a rent-controlled apartment—I'd trade being worried about money all the time to not have this disease, this addiction.

And not only do I have the disease, but I also have it *bad*. I have it as bad as you can have it, in fact. It's backs-to-the-wall time all the time. It's going to kill me (I guess something has to). Robert Downey Jr., talking about his own addiction, once said, "It's like I have a gun in my mouth with my finger on the trigger, and I like the taste of the metal." I got it; I understand that. Even on good days, when I'm sober and I'm looking forward, it's still with me all the time. There's still a gun.

Fortunately, I guess, there's not enough opiates in the world to make me high anymore. I have a very, very, very low bottom. Things have to get truly awful—they have to get big, and terrible—before I quit anything. When I was doing the show *Mr. Sunshine,* I was basically running it—writing it, starring in it. Then, at home, I was working on notes for a writer on a script that he had written. I had a bottle of vodka next to me. I made myself thirteen, fourteen drinks—but homemade drinks, so *triples*. And after the fourteenth drink, I wasn't drunk anymore. So, I quit drinking.

I think now I'm at the point with opiates where it's the same situation. There are just not enough. I took 1,800 milligrams of opiates in Switzerland per day and wasn't high. So, what am I gonna do? Call a drug dealer and ask for *all* the drugs? Now when I think about Oxy-Contin, my mind flashes directly to having a colostomy bag for life. Which is something I could not handle. That's why I think it'll be pretty easy for me to continue being off opiates—they don't work any-more. And I could wake up from another surgery—there have already been fourteen since the first one—with an irreversible colostomy bag.

It's time to figure something else out. (As said, the next level is heroin, and I won't go there.) Me quitting drinking and opiates doesn't have anything to do with strength, by the way—it just doesn't work anymore. If somebody came into my house right now and said, "Here's a hundred milligrams of Oxy," I'd say, "It's not enough."

The problem remains, though: *I'm* there wherever I go. I bring along the problems and the darkness and the shit, so every time I leave a rehab, I do a geographic and buy a new fucking house. And then I live in it.

And the first thing I used to do when I looked at houses—which is a hobby of mine—was go through the homeowners' medicine cabinets to see if they had any pills I could purloin. You can't be a dick about it, though—you have to take the right amount. You can't take too many or they'll know for sure. So, you check the date on the pill bottle—you want something that's sort of out-of-date. If it's been a *long* time out-of-date, you could take a bunch of them. But if it's brand-new, you could take only a couple. I would hit five open houses on a Sunday—that'd be my whole day.

At one point, when I was taking fifty-five a day, I would wake up and somehow have to find those fifty-five pills. It was like a full-time job. My whole life was math. I need eight to get home; then I'll be there for three hours. So I need four more. And then I have to go to that din-ner party. So I need seven for that. . . . And all this to just maintain, to not be sick, to avoid the inevitable, which is the detox.

I imagine those homeowners arriving back after their open house and eventually, at some point, opening their medicine cabinet.

"Is it possible that Chandler . . . no, not *Chandler*. Surely not Chan-dler *Bing*!"

Now, instead of open houses, I'm having one built. I started the process because about eighteen months ago, I couldn't complete a sentence. Things got so flat, so awful for me. Doctors came in, my mother came in, everybody came in and took care of me because I couldn't talk. I was so out of it. I had to do something.

I had that $20 million penthouse apartment in Century City, where I was doing drugs and watching TV and having sex with my girlfriend of a few months.

One night I was passed out and she was passed out and when we woke up my mother and Keith Morrison were at the foot of my bed. I thought, *Am I in an episode of* Dateline? *And if I* am, *why is my* mother *also in it?*

My mother looked at my girlfriend and said, "I think it's time for you to leave."

This saved my life.

My dad has saved my life multiple times, too.

When he helped me get to Marina del Rey (after Jamie Tarses had told me I was disappearing before her very eyes), I was deathly afraid that I would never have fun again for the rest of my life. After about three weeks, I called Marta Kauffman and David Crane to tell them I was sober and could return to *Friends*.

"When are you coming back?" they said. "We need you to come back. It's going to be very work intensive. We have to start in two weeks, or we won't be able to do it."

But I was still very sick. My father had overheard the tenor of the conversation and called Marta and David back.

"I will pull him off your television show," Dad said, "if you continue to act this way around him."

I was so grateful for him for being my dad and doing the dad thing, but I also didn't want to be the problem. They were just doing their job; they had the number one hit TV show, and two of the main characters were about to get married. I couldn't just disappear. I just wanted everything to be OK. So, then I was moved from Marina del Rey to Promises, in Malibu, and was told I was going to need more than twenty-eight days—I would need *months* to get better from this.

Two weeks later, I was driven to the set of *Friends* by a technician from Malibu. When I arrived, Jen Aniston said, "I've been *mad* at you."

"Honey," I said, "if you knew what I'd been through, you would *not* be mad at me."

With that we hugged, and I got the work done. I married Monica and got driven back to the treatment center—at the height of my highest point in *Friends,* the highest point in my career, the iconic moment on the iconic show—in a pickup truck helmed by a sober technician.

Not all the lights were green on Sunset that night, let me tell ya.

I can't be useful in a relationship because I'm both trying to hang on and in so much fear that I'll be left. And that fear is not even real, because in my fifty-three years, and with all the wonderful girlfriends I've had, I've only been left once, many years back. You would think this would be outweighed by all the others I left . . . yet she was everything to me. The smart man in me sees it clearly, though: she was only twenty-five, just trying to have a good time; we dated for a few months, but I let all my walls down. I decided once and for all to just be myself.

And then she dumped me.

She had never promised me anything. I was drinking like a maniac, too, and I don't blame her.

I had to see her at a play reading a couple of years ago—she played my wife.

"How are you?" she said before the reading, and I pretended I was fine, but I was in hell. *Get out of there, do not engage,* I thought, *just pretend everything's OK.*

"I have a couple of kids with my partner now," she said, "and life is good. Are you with anybody?"

"No," I said, "I'm still looking."

I wish I hadn't said that because it made it sound like I was still looking ever since she dumped me. But it's true. I'm still looking.

Then the play reading ended, and she was no longer my wife, and I got the hell out of there, and she still looked exactly the same.

These days, I have faith in God, but too often that faith seems, well, *blocked.* But then, everything is blocked by the medication I'm on.

These days, too, I ask this question: Am I blocking my relationship with a higher power by taking Suboxone?

One of my big problems, and the reason that I've had so much trouble getting sober over the years, is I've never let myself feel uncomfortable long enough to have a spiritual connection. So, I fix it with pills and alcohol before God can jump in and fix *me.*

I did a breath work class recently. For half an hour you breathe in this very intense, very uncomfortable way. You cry, you see things, you kinda feel high. For me it's a freebie high, the best kind. But the Suboxone even blocks *that* feeling. . . . Half the doctors I speak to say I should be on Suboxone for at least a year, but probably the rest of my life. Other doctors tell me I'm not technically sober while I'm still on it. (It's very difficult to get all the way off it either way, which is ironic because it's a drug used to get you off *other* drugs. Recently, when I was hooked up to an IV of it, the dosage I was receiving was 0.5 lower than it was supposed to be, and it got me so sick and scared I had to bump it back up. You feel terrible when you stop taking it.)

When you take heroin, the drug hits your opiate receptors, and then you are high, and then it fades and you're not hitting the opiate receptors anymore, then you're sober for a while, and then maybe the next day you hit your opiate receptors again, and then you're high, and on and on. But Suboxone works differently, wrapping itself around the receptor, and it doesn't go away, which means it's basically damaging your receptors 24/7.

So, one of the theories that I have about my struggle with *happiness* is that I've damaged these receptors. My dopamine gets replaced by the Suboxone. The dopamine hit is what you get when you enjoy something, like looking at a sunset, or playing tennis and you make a good shot, or you hear a song you love. But I'm pretty sure my opiate receptors are very seriously damaged, possibly to the point of no return. That's why I'm always a little bummed.

Just like pancreatitis, maybe if I left my opioid receptors alone for an extended period they'd fix themselves and I'd be happy again.

I've seen God in my kitchen, of all places, so I know there's something bigger than me. (I know I can't make a plant, for a start.) I know it's an omnipresent love and acceptance that means that everything's going to be OK. I know something happens when you die. I know you move on to something wonderful.

Alcoholics and addicts like myself want to drink for the sole purpose of feeling better. Well, that's at least true for me: all I ever wanted was to feel better. I didn't feel good—I had a couple of drinks and I felt better. But as the disease progresses it takes more and more and more and more and more and more and more to feel better. If you puncture the membrane of sobriety, alcoholism kicks in and goes, "Hey, remember me? Nice to see you again. Now, give me just as much as you did last time or I'll kill you or make you crazy." And then the obsession of my mind kicks in, and I can't stop thinking about feeling better, matched with a phenomenon of craving, and what you're left with is a bruise that starts off one way and it never gets better. Nobody has a drinking problem and then stops and then drinks socially and it's fine. The disease just picks up.

The Big Book says that alcohol is cunning, baffling, and powerful . . . but I would also add that it's *patient.* As soon as you raise your hand and say, "I'm having a problem," it's as though addiction says, "Well, if you're going to be so *stupid* as to say something about it, I'll go away for a while. . . ." I'll be in a rehab for three months and think, *Well, I'm going to use when I get out of here, but I can wait for nine more to days to do it.* The disease is just drumming its fingers. In AA it's often said that when you're in a meeting, your disease is doing one-armed push-ups outside, just waiting for you to leave.

I've almost died several times, and the lower you get down the scale (death is as low as it goes, FYI), the more people you can help. So, when my life is firing on all cylinders, I have folks I sponsor, people calling me to help them with their lives. The two years from 2001 to 2003 were two of the happiest of my life—I was helping people, sober, strong.

There were other good side effects of sobriety. I was also single for some of it. So I'd go to clubs, but I didn't want to drink—the miracle had happened for me. And let me tell you, no one is more popular at 2:00 A.M. in a club than a sober guy who says, "Hi, how are you?" to a woman. I don't think I've ever gotten laid more than those two years.

But the disease is patient. You slowly stop going to all the meetings you're supposed to go to. *I don't really need to go to the one on a Friday* night . . . *!* And then, by the time you're deep into that kind of thinking, alcoholism is coming for you, baffling and powerful and patient. Suddenly, you're not going to any meetings anymore. And you've convinced yourself that you understand it all. *Now I don't need to do this anymore. I get it.*

Addicts are not bad people. We're just people who are trying to feel better, but we have this disease. When I feel bad, I think, *Give me something that makes me feel better.* It's as simple as that. I would still love to drink and take drugs, but because of the consequences, I don't, because I'm so late stage that it would kill me.

Recently my mother told me she was proud of me. I'd written a movie and she'd read it. I'd been wanting her to say that my whole life.

When I pointed this out, she said, "What about a little forgiveness?"

"I *do* forgive you," I said. "I *do*."

I wonder if she can forgive me for everything I've put her through. . . .

If a selfish, lazy fuck like myself can change, then anyone can. No secret gets worse just because it has been told. At this point in my life, the words of gratitude pour out of me because I should be dead, and yet somehow I am not. There must be a reason for that. It's simply too hard for me to understand if there isn't.

I don't believe in half-assing things anymore. The path of least resistance is boring, and scars are interesting—they tell an honest story, and they are proof that a battle was fought, and in my case, hard-won.

I have many scars now.

The first time I took my shirt off in my bathroom after returning from the hospital after my first surgery I burst into tears. I was so disturbed by it. I thought my life was over. After about half an hour I got my shit together enough to call my drug dealer, who proceeded to ask me what was wrong, like he was a social worker or a priest, not a drug dealer.

Three days ago, I had my fourteenth surgery—it's four years later. I cried again. I should learn to get used to it, though, because there will always be more surgeries—I will never be done. I will always have the bowels of a man in his nineties. In fact, I have never not cried after a surgery. Not once.

I've stopped calling the drug dealers, though.

There are so many scars on my stomach that all I need to do is look down to know that I've been through a war, a self-inflicted war. Once, at some Hollywood function—shirts allowed, nay, *insisted* on, in fact, thank God—Martin Sheen turned to me and said, "Do you know what Saint Peter says to everyone who tries to get into heaven?" When I looked blankly, the man who once was president said, "Peter says, 'Don't you have any scars?' And when most would respond proudly, 'Well no, no I don't,' Peter says, 'Why not? Was there nothing worth fighting for?'"

(Martin Sheen, like Pacino, Sean Penn, Ellen DeGeneres, Kevin Bacon, Chevy Chase, Robert De Niro—these are all fellow members of the "Famous Club" I've encountered, an informal little thing you join when you're in an airport or at a function and someone also famous comes up and says hi like we know each other.)

The scars, though, the scars . . . my stomach looks like a topographical map of China. And they fucking *hurt*. Sadly, these days my body just laughs at 30 milligrams of OxyContin. Oral meds don't work at all; the only thing that helps a little bit is IV medication, and I obviously can't take that at home, so off I go, back to the hospital.

In January 2022, I'd had a six-inch incision with metal staples. This is the life of someone who's been blessed with the big terrible thing. And they aren't letting me smoke. It'll be a good day if I get through it not smoking and nothing crazy happens. When I don't smoke, I gain weight, too—in fact, recently I'd gained so much weight that when I looked in a mirror, I thought someone was following me.

When you get sober, you gain weight. When you quit smoking, you gain weight. Those are the rules.

As for me, I would trade places with each and every one of my friends—Pressman, Bierko, any of them—because none of them had the big terrible thing to deal with. None of them had battled their entire lives with a brain that was built to kill them. I would give it all up to not have that. No one believes this, but it's true.

My life is no longer on fire, though. Dare I say it throughout all this turmoil. I have grown up. I am more real, more genuine. I don't need to leave the people in a room screaming in laughter. I just need to stand up straight and leave the room.

And hopefully not walk directly into the closet.

It's a calmer me now. A more genuine me. A more capable me. Sure, there is a chance that if I want a good role in a movie, I'd have to write it now. But I can do that, too. I am enough. I am more than enough. And I don't need to put on a show anymore. I have made my mark. Now it's time to sit back and enjoy it. And find true love. And a real life. Not one that is run on fear.

I am me. And that should be enough, it always has been enough. I was the one who didn't get that. And now I do. I'm an actor, I'm a writer. I'm a person. And a good one at that. I want good things for myself, and others, and I can continue to work for these things. There is a reason I'm still here. And figuring out why is the task that has been put in front of me.

And it will be revealed. There is no rush, no desperation. Just the fact that I am here, and I care about people, is the answer. Now when I wake up, I wake up curious, wondering what the world has in store for me, and I for it. And that's enough to go on.

I want to keep learning. I want to keep teaching. Those are the grand hopes I have for myself, but in the meantime, I want to laugh and have a good time with my friends. I want to make love to a woman I am madly in love with. I want to become a father and make my mother and my father proud.

I love art now, too, and have started collecting. I got my Banksy painting at an auction in New York. I bought it via the phone. I've never met him, but I want him to know that if there was ever a fire, my Banksy would be the thing I'd save. I wonder if he'd care. (Actually, he'd probably set fire to it himself.)

I have accomplished a lot in my life, but there is still so much left to do, which daily excites me. I was a kid from Canada who had all his dreams come true—they were just the *wrong* dreams. And instead of giving up, I changed and found new dreams.

I keep finding them all the time. They're right there in the view, in the Valley, on the edgings and flashes that bounce off the ocean when the sun hits . . . just so.

When someone does something nice for someone else, I see God. But you can't give away something you don't have. So, I try to improve myself daily. When those moments come and I am needed, I've worked out my shit, and do what we are all here for, which is simply to help other people.

The Smoking Section

One fine day, God and my therapist got together and decided to miraculously remove my desire to take drugs. A desire that has been plaguing me since 1996.

My therapist said to me, "The next time you think about OxyContin, I want you to think about living out the rest of your days with a colostomy bag."

God didn't say anything, but then, he doesn't have to because he's God. But he was there.

Having had a colostomy bag for nine long months, my therapist's words hit hard. And when this man's words hit hard, the prudent thing to do is to get into action immediately. What he said caused a very small window to open, and I crawled through it. And on the other side was a life without OxyContin.

The next move up from OxyContin is heroin. A word that has always frightened me. A fear that has undoubtedly saved my life. My fear, of course, is that I would like that drug so much, I would never stop doing it and it would kill me. I don't know how to do it, and I don't want to learn. Even in my darkest days that was never an option.

So, since heroin was a no-go and OxyContin had been the only drug I had ever wanted to take, it was safe to say that my desire to take drugs had vanished—couldn't find it if I tried, and I was not trying. I felt lighter on my feet. I felt a freedom. The monkey was off my back. The part of my brain that was out to kill me had vanished. Well, not so fast.

I had recently had my fourteenth stomach surgery, this one to remove a hernia that was protruding through my abdominal wall. It had been very painful, and I had been given OxyContin. We addicts are not martyrs—if we are in serious pain, we are allowed to have pain medication, it just has to be done carefully. This means the bottle of pills is never in my hand, and the medication is always administered by someone else, and as prescribed. It also meant I had a brand-new scar on my stomach, this time a six-inch incision. Really, guys? My colon burst, you opened me up to the point where you could get a bowling ball in there, but now I get the biggest scar?

After the surgery, the moment I took the drug my pain dissipated, but something else happened: I could feel my digestive tract freezing up once again. PTSD, anyone? And when that happened it was straight to the emergency room, where I knew they would either give me something to help me go to the bathroom or tell me that I needed surgery right away. And any time I had a surgery there was a chance I would wake up with a colostomy bag. It had happened twice already, it could so easily happen again.

You know what could ensure that I would never wake up from a surgery with an irreversible colostomy bag? Quitting doing OxyContin. Which I had already done. I was free. There are no words to describe how humongous this news was. I have not been interested in taking a drug since. So, I will steal Al Michaels's immortal words when a bunch of college kids beat the fucking Russians in ice hockey in 1980 in Lake Placid.

"Do you believe in miracles? Yes!!!!!!!"

I still can't watch that game without shivers running up my spine. Well, this was my time, my miracle.

I have always believed in the theory that God doesn't put in front of you that which you can't handle. In this case, God gave me three weeks. Three weeks of freedom. And then, he placed a new and gigantic challenge in front of me.

I had been ignoring it. Pretending that it wasn't really happening, or that it would suddenly disappear.

At that time, when I lay down to go to sleep, I started to hear a wheezing. Sometimes it was loud enough that I couldn't sleep, sometimes it was softer and lasted longer. But when I decided to look into it, because God thought I was ready, I was worried. My hope was that it was bronchitis or something that could be treated with an antibiotic, but I feared the worst.

My pulmonary doctor had a one-week waiting list, so I had seven days of lying down and hearing this awful sound during my most vulnerable and loneliest time of night. That week went by so slowly. Sometimes, I would sit up, and smoke a cigarette, and hope that would make the wheezing disappear. I am no rocket scientist.

Eventually, the morning of the appointment arrived, and along with the ever-present Erin, I showed up for a breathing test. I breathed as hard as I could into a tube for a couple of minutes and was then told to wait in the doctor's office for my results. I made Erin wait with me; I was afraid it was terrible news. Remember, folks, we are wanting to hear bronchial infection here. And because of the miracle three weeks earlier, I had no place to hide if it was bad news.

After a very long while, the doctor waltzed into his office, took a seat, and announced (rather nonchalantly, I thought, given the stakes) that my years of smoking had taken a great toll on my lungs and if I didn't quit smoking now—today—I was going to die when I was sixty. In other words, it didn't fucking matter if I had a bronchial infection.

"No, something much much worse," he said. "But we caught it early enough that if you did quit smoking, you could well live into your eighties."

Stunned, frozen in fear, grateful that we had caught it in time—these were the thoughts that swirled in my head as we left to get in the car. We just sat there for a while, me wishing the car was a DeLorean so we could go back to 1988 and I could never pick up one of these poisonous, life-engulfing things in the first place.

I somehow managed to be upbeat.

"Well," I said eventually, "we have a no-brainer on our hands here. I'm going to smoke for the rest of the day. And tomorrow morning at seven A.M. I'm going to quit smoking for the rest of my life."

I had quit smoking before, for nine months, but the process then had been disastrous. Erin—because she remains the single nicest person in the world—said she would quit with me.

I was initially allowed to vape, but eventually that would have to go, too.

And 7:00 A.M. the following day came around far too quickly. My home was cleared of all cigarettes, and I clung to the vape for dear life. I remembered from previous attempts to quit that days three and four were the worst, but if I could make it to day seven, I would be home free.

It was as awful as you might imagine. I basically stayed in my room and vaped and waited for the horrible feelings to go away. But I was brave. I could do this.

But day seven came and went, and I still felt terrible. I was craving a cigarette to such a degree that I didn't think possible. By day nine, I couldn't take it anymore—I walked out of my room at home and said, "I want a cigarette." The nursing staff was there to make sure I didn't do drugs, not to stop me smoking a cigarette, so they gave me one. When I tell you that I got high off it, I mean very high—the drive-home-in-the-red-Mustang-in-Vegas high.

The remaining eight cigarettes that I smoked that night did not feel that way. They just made me feel like shit while also scaring the shit out of me. ("Shit" used twice, although bad writing, is intentional.)

I was a fifty-two-year-old man, and unless this is the first page you've read in this book, you already know that my plan was to have the rest of my life be both the long, and the good, part. So, I tried! I lay in my bed not smoking for nine days.

I could quit every drug in the history of drugs, but cigarettes were going to be the toughest? Is everybody kidding?

It was decided that going from sixty cigarettes a day to zero had been too much for me to take and I would cut my smoking down until a better plan could be worked out. For the following few days, I managed to drop from sixty to ten. Though this was something, let's not forget: my life was on the line and I needed that number to go down to zero and fast. Any efforts to bring the number under ten were exercises in futility.

Enter Kerry Gaynor, hypnotist extraordinaire. I had tried quitting smoking with him before, but it hadn't worked. This time around proved to be a much different situation. Sitting in front of Kerry Gaynor that day was a desperate man who wanted to quit. I really wanted to quit—fuck, I needed to. I don't know real love, I've never looked into my children's baby blues. Plus, emphysema was a horrible way to go, its oxygen tanks and breathing tubes: "Hi, this is Matthew Perry, you've of course met my breathing tube."

But could a mind like mine be hypnotized? I had constant racing thoughts and auditory hallucinations. . . . So, if I can't control my mind, how is some hypnotist going to do it? I loved smoking—some days it was my only reason for living—in fact, I would stay up late just so I could keep smoking cigarettes. Plus, it was the last thing I had left. Without it there would be nothing separating me from me. I had quit drinking forever when God visited me in my kitchen. I had recently quit drugs for the rest of my life when a colostomy bag scared the shit out of me. Did I actually just say that? How could I possibly do it? What's the point of doing anything if you can't smoke?

Things did not start out well. I got to the place, rang the doorbell, a perfectly nice person opened the door, and I said, "Hi, is Kerry here, I'm supposed to meet with him?"

Kerry was not there, as it was the wrong house. I wondered how that person had felt having Chandler Bing ring his doorbell. . . .

Five houses down I saw Kerry standing in front of his house, waiting for my arrival. I was terrified—my last crutch, not to mention my life, hung in the balance.

Kerry's office wasn't quite what I was expecting from the highest priced hypnotist in the world—strewn with papers and pictures and antinicotine signs. We sat down and he started into his "smoking is terrible" thing—yeah yeah, I know that. Let's get to the good stuff.

I explained just how dire it was, and he told me we'd need three meetings—I am a special case, apparently. The chat over, I lay back, and for ten minutes he hypnotized me.

I felt nothing, of course.

You are supposed to keep smoking between meetings, which I was grateful for, but to make things easier on my lungs, and for Kerry, I stuck to just ten. (Anyone can smoke three packs a day, like I did, but you really need only about ten cigarettes to get the nicotine your body craves. The other fifty is just the habit.)

During the second session Kerry brought out every scare tactic he could muster. I was naive to think that the next cigarette wouldn't kill me. (I didn't.) I could have a cigarette right now, have a heart attack, and if no one was around to call 911, I was a goner. My next cigarette could make my lungs not function permanently, and I would have to live out the rest of my days carrying oxygen tanks and breathing only through my nose. (I thought, *That's worse than a colostomy bag,* but I didn't say it out loud.) Would I rather have a cigarette or breathe the next morning? (I knew the answer to this one.)

Before he hypnotized me this second time, I tried to explain my crazy racing mind to him.

"I'm not sure you're going to be able to hypnotize me," I said.

Kerry just smiled knowingly—he'd probably heard that line a thousand times I suppose—and told me once again to lie down.

I was on his side. I wanted this to work. But I still wasn't sure it was working. I left his office and went back to the ten per day, but something had changed: each one frightened me more than the last. If nothing else, Kerry had done a masterly job of instilling terror in each drag. Something really was different.

And then there we were, at our final meeting. This was it—after this, I was supposed to quit smoking forever. I had explained to him that I had had a horrible time every time I tried to do this—it was harder to quit than drugs. And I have done some pretty insane things (see under: head, wall) while quitting smoking. I'm terrified of the withdrawals.

Kerry listened patiently, then calmly pointed out that he had helped thousands and thousands of people quit smoking, and all his feedback said the same thing: there is a little discomfort on the first two days, and then nothing. But you can't touch nicotine—no vapes anymore.

But this had absolutely not been my previous experience, and I told him so.

"You've never wanted to quit before, and you have never done it the right way, with me," he said. He was right, I did want to quit. There was no doubting that.

With that, I lay down once again, and he hypnotized me. But this time it felt different—I was very relaxed and sleepy. I realized as Kerry talked directly to my subconscious that my mind was not racing.

Then, it was over.

I stood up, asked if I could give him a hug, and he obliged. Then I walked out of his office a nonsmoker. For good—no matter what. Back at home, the place had been cleared of all nicotine products and vapes (which can kill you just as fast as cigarettes can, according to Kerry).

By now it was about 6:00 P.M., and my job was to make it to 9:30 without having a cigarette.

But something had changed—I didn't want one.

Day one was slightly uncomfortable, as was day two. And then the bad feelings were gone, just as Kerry had told me they would be. I had zero withdrawal symptoms. Nothing. And I didn't want to smoke.

It worked. How he managed to remove my withdrawal symptoms and how that is even possible medically via hypnosis is a mystery to me. But I wasn't going to ask any more questions.

Sure, I reached for a cigarette at least fifty times a day, but that was just habit. I noticed something else, too—the wheezing was gone. Kerry Gaynor had saved my life. I was a nonsmoker.

It was another miracle. In fact, the miracles were flying around fast—duck or you might get hit with one. I don't want to do drugs, and I am a nonsmoker.

I had been off the smokes for fifteen days. I looked brighter, I felt better, I had to take fewer breaks during pickleball games. There was life in my eyes.

But then something happened. I took a bite into a piece of toast with peanut butter smeared on it, and all my top teeth fell out. Yes, all of them. A quick pop to the dentist was in short order—I am, after all, an actor, and should have all my teeth in my mouth, not in a Baggie in the pocket of my jeans. But disaster struck and major work was needed. The dentist had to remove every single one of my teeth—including the implants that were nailed into my jaw—and then replace them all with new ones. I was told this would hurt for one or two days and the pain could be handled with Advil and Tylenol. But these were just fucking throwbacks from the sadistic dentist played so well by Steve Martin in *Little Shop of Horrors*.

How long did it actually hurt?

Seventeen days.

Could this pain be blocked with Advil and Tylenol?

Absolutely not.

How far into this did I get overwhelmed and smoke a cigarette?

Three days.

I simply could not handle that degree of pain and not smoke at the same time. I felt like a miracle had been handed to me, and I gently tossed it back and said "No thanks, not for me."

I would like to take this opportunity to say a few words to the dental surgeon who was in charge of all of this: "Fuck off, you big piece of nothing fuck. Fuck asshole loser fucking fuck face."

Now I feel better.

After that, I basically began stalking Kerry Gaynor. I would meet with him any chance I could, and then buy a pack of cigarettes and have one, and then wet the rest of the pack under the faucet. I never lied to Kerry—I would tell him what went on, and thank goodness he would not shoot the wounded. I said all the mantras and developed a pretty severe fear of smoking—a little bit of fear with every puff.

But I was still smoking.

The not-wanting-a-cigarette did not return. I was going to have to come out swinging, which consisted of frozen grapes and twenty minutes on the treadmill every time I wanted a cigarette. I pictured a man who weighed a hundred pounds from all this treadmill walking saying in a very high-pitched tone, "God, I wish I had a cigarette!"

Vaping was not an option. The patch was not an option. Lying was not an option. (What good would that do?) I would get through four days and I would smoke and have to start all over again.

But I would not give up—I could not give up. *My life has been so difficult, I deserve to smoke. I wrote a screenplay, I deserve to smoke.* These thoughts had to be dispelled immediately because they gave the addict hope.

And then I had the wise idea to book Kerry two mornings in a row—surely, I couldn't smoke knowing I was going to see him the very next morning. It was a rough night, but I had had my share of those, and the next day I was able to saunter into his weird-looking office having made it and ready to have our brief conversation and get hypnotized again.

I could have played his role by now—we could have switched seats. I would be the one who would offer him a very weird-looking blue children's plastic cup of lukewarm water. But this was day two (it's the little wins). He hypnotized me, scared the shit out of me again, and sent me away with an appointment with him a week hence. Back at home I kept a very busy schedule because I could not let boredom in, it being the devil's playground and all.

Well, boredom, and that girl who broke my heart when I was thirty.

I used to take fifty-five Vicodin a day and I quit that, so I was not going to let this disgusting, smelly, absolutely calming and wonderful habit get me down. Would I rather smoke, or breathe? Breath—what a wonderful thing that we all take for granted.

Cigarettes had already made me very sick. Also, they are bad for you. It sounds like I'm joking, but these are the things you have to remember. I had my comeback as an actor to think of (I had not acted since my accident); I had a book to write and promote, and I couldn't very well promote it holding a cigarette in my hand. I also could not just eat my way out of this situation. "Quit drinking, doing drugs, smoking cigarettes! Here's how: just eat six chocolate cakes every night!" This wasn't exactly the message I wanted to convey.

I had a record I had to break: fifteen days. And with that would come the cooling comfort of not wanting to smoke. I've been there before, and I could do it again: the complete rebuilding of a man. I didn't know this man, but he seemed to be a nice guy, and it looked like he had stopped beating the shit out of himself with a baseball bat finally.

I was very eager to see who this man was!

11

Batman

I never imagined I'd be fifty-two and single and not playing fun, dumb games with very short, cute kids running around repeating nonsense words that I had taught them all just to make my beautiful wife laugh.

For years I thought I wasn't enough, but I don't feel that way anymore. I think I'm just the right amount. But still, each morning, when I wake up, there are a few brief moments when I am hazy, lost to dreams and sleep, and don't exactly know where I am, I remember my stomach and the scar tissue that comes with it. (I finally have rock-hard abs, but they aren't from sit-ups.) And then I swing my legs off the bed and tiptoe to the bathroom, so that I don't wake . . . um, no one. Yessiree, I am as single as can be. I look in the bathroom mirror, hoping to see something there that would explain everything. I try not to think too hard about the incredible women I had passed over because of a fear it took me too long to understand. I try not to dwell on this too much—if you spend too much time looking in the rearview mirror, you will crash your car. Still, I do find myself longing for a companion, a romantic one. I'm not picky—about five foot two, brunette, smart as a whip, funny, mostly sane will do. Loves kids. Tolerates hockey. Willing to learn pickleball.

That's all I ask.

A teammate.

Eventually, if I stare long enough, I watch as my face starts to disappear, and I know it's time to head out to my patio and my view.

Out there, below the bluffs and the freeways and the meditation center where I read my list to my sponsor, out there where the California gulls swirl and swoop, I watch the ocean ripple, slate gray with edgings of blue. I have always thought that the ocean mirrors the subconscious mind. There's beauty—coral reefs, brightly colored fish, spume, and refracted sunlight—but there's something darker, sharks and tiger fish and endless deeps just ready to swallow rickety fishing boats.

Its size is what most calms me; its size, and its power. Big enough to get lost in forever; strong enough to hold up great oil tankers. We are as naught compared to its vastness. And have you ever stood on the water's edge and tried to stop a wave? It goes on, regardless of what we do; regardless of how hard we try, the ocean reminds us that we are powerless in comparison.

Watching the ocean, I find myself most days filled with not just longing, but also peace and gratitude and a deeper understanding of just what I've been through, and where I am now.

For a start, I've surrendered, but to the winning side, not the losing. I'm no longer mired in an impossible battle with drugs and alcohol. I no longer feel the need to automatically light up a cigarette to go with my morning coffee. I notice that I feel cleaner. Fresher. My friends and family have all mentioned it—there is a brightness about me that none of them had seen before.

In the appendix, "The Spiritual Experience," at the end of AA's Big Book, I read this:

Quite often friends of the newcomer are aware of the difference long before he is himself.

This morning, and every morning out there on the patio, I am as the newcomer. I am filled with, energized by, the "differences"—no drink, no drugs, no cigarettes. . . . As I stand there, coffee in one hand and nothing in the other, and watch the distant waves in the ocean, I realize that I am feeling a wave of my own, inside me.

Gratitude.

As the light of the day deepened, and the ocean changed from silver to the palest aqua, the wave of gratitude grew until within the wave I saw faces and events and little bits of flotsam that had been moments in my eventful life.

I was so grateful to be alive, to have a loving family—this was not the least of it, and perhaps the best thing of all, in fact. There, in the water's thin spray, I saw my mother's face, and thought about her ineffable ability to step up in a crisis, to take charge and make things better. (Keith Morrison once said to me, "During all the four decades I have been with your mom, her incredible attachment to you has been the central part of her life. She thinks about you all the time. Way back in 1980, when things got serious between us, she said something I've never forgotten: 'No man will ever come between Matthew and me—he'll always be the most important person in my life. You'll have to accept that.'" And it's true—there was never a moment I didn't feel that love. Even in our darkest moments. If something is really wrong, she is still my first call.) I saw my father's ridiculously handsome face, too, and it seemed appropriate that I saw him both as my father, and as the Old Spice sailor guy, though that last image had long faded to a distant point on the horizon. I think about them withstanding being in the same room together when I was really sick, and what kind of love that betrays. They didn't belong together. I get that now. So, I'd like back all the coins I've dropped into wells, wishing that they were together. They both got lucky and married the people they were supposed to be married to.

My sisters' faces shadow my parents', as does my brother's, each of them beaming at me, not just at a hospital bedside, but also in Canada and Los Angeles as I tried to crack them up with my patter. They never dropped the ball once, any of them, never turned their backs on me, ever. Imagine such love if you can.

Less profound, but no less thrilling, images gurgled up from the roiling waters: the LA Kings winning the Stanley Cup in 2012, me in row seven screaming at the second line to keep up the pressure on the boards. And my rather selfish thought that God made them wind through the playoffs in a year when they only made the playoffs in the last days. I had just ended a very long relationship, and I'm quite sure the Kings went all the way because God said, "Hey, Matty, I know this is going to be a hard time for you, so here's something that will last three months and give you a tremendous amount of fun and distraction to make it better." Boom, it did—after charging through the playoffs like revenging angels of death, it was the Kings over the Devils in six in the finals, and that last game at the Staples Center, a blowout in a Stanley Cup game unlike any in two decades, LA up four–zip just a minute into the second period. I was at every game, even flying myself and some pals to the games on the road, too.

As the ice rink of my sports fandom slips back under the water, more faces appear: the Murray brothers, my dearest oldest friends, with whom I created a funny way of talking that eventually touched the hearts of millions. Craig Bierko, Hank Azaria, David Pressman . . . how their laughter was once the only drug I needed. But I would never have met them, or gotten anywhere, perhaps, without Greg Simpson casting me in my very first play. You never know where one thing will lead. . . . I guess the lesson is, take every opportunity, because something might come of it.

Something huge came of it for me. I closed my eyes, then, and inhaled deeply, and as I opened my eyes, I was surrounded by my *Friends* friends (without whom I would have starred in something called *No Friends*): Schwimmer, for making us stick together when he could have gone it alone and profited more than all the rest, and deciding we should be a team and getting us a million bucks a week. Lisa Kudrow—no woman has ever made me laugh that much. Courteney Cox, for making America think that someone so beautiful would marry a guy like me. Jenny, for letting me look at that face an extra two seconds every single day. Matt LeBlanc, who took the only sort of stock character and turned him into the funniest character on the show. Each of them was still just a phone call away. At the reunion, I was the one who cried more than anyone because I knew what I'd had, and the gratitude I felt then matches the gratitude I feel today. Beyond those principles there was all the crew, the producers, the writers, the actors, the audience members, so many faces churning into one face of joy. Marta Kauffman, David Crane, and Kevin Bright, without whom *Friends* would have been a silent movie. ("Could this *be* more of a silent movie?") The fans, so many fans who stuck with it and still watch—their faces peer back at me now, mute as God, as though I'm still on stage 24 in Burbank. Their laughter, which for so long gave me purpose, echoes still up these canyon sides, almost reaching me all these years later. . . .

I think about all the sponsors, and sober companions, and doctors who had helped me to not screw up the greatest job in the world.

I look out at the water, and I say, very quietly, "Maybe I'm not so bad after all." And then I head back in for more coffee.

*   *   *

In the house, I find Erin—she's always there when I need her. I don't tell her what I've been thinking about out there, but I can see in her eyes she has an idea, maybe. She doesn't say anything because that's what best friends do. Erin, Erin, Erin . . . She saved my life at the rehab when my insides exploded, and she saves it every day still. Who knows what I'd do without her; I intend to never find out. I can tell she's itching for a cigarette, but she doesn't break. Find a friend who'll quit something with you—you'll be amazed what that does for a friendship.

Now, the sun is higher, the perfect Southern California day almost at its prime. Way off in the distance I can see boats, and if I squint, I swear I see surfers lounging in the calm waters. Still this gratitude swirls about me, even stronger now as more faces appear: characters from the Woody Allen movies I love, the TV show *Lost,* Peter Gabriel, Michael Keaton, John Grisham, Steve Martin, Sting, Dave Letterman for having me on for the first time, Barack Obama, the smartest man I have ever spoken to. On the breeze I hear the piano version of "New York, New York," by Ryan Adams, recorded at Carnegie Hall on November 17, 2014. I realize all over again that I'm so lucky to have been in this business, to have had not just access to extraordinary people, but to have also been able to affect people the same way something like "Don't Give Up" by Peter Gabriel affects me (let's not discuss the video with him hugging Kate Bush; it's almost too much to bear). When I think about all the actors who take chances I get a flash, then, of Earl H.'s face, the good version, not the bad, and quickly it's replaced by the face of my current sponsor, Clay, who has talked me down so often. I think about all the doctors and nurses at the UCLA Medical Center for saving my life. I am no longer welcome in that hospital for getting caught smoking in there one last time. To Kerry Gaynor for making sure there was never going to be a one last time. And behind them all, the specter of Bill Wilson, whose establishment of AA has saved millions upon millions of lives one day at a time, and whose organization still refuses to shoot the wounded and always let the light in for me.

I was grateful for dentists. . . . No wait—I hate dentists.

Somewhere behind me, farther up the hill, I catch the hint of the sound of children laughing, my favorite sound of all. I pick the pickleball paddle up off the patio table and do a few practice swings. Until recently I'd never heard of pickleball, never thought I'd be well enough to play any kind of sport again. I'd long since stopped swinging a tennis racket, but this new Matty now actually looks forward to afternoons at the Riviera, hitting the bright yellow plastic pickleball.

My reverie is interrupted by Erin.

"Hey, Matty," she says from the kitchen door, "it's Doug on the phone." Doug Chapin has been my manager since 1992, and like many people in the business, he has often waited patiently as I dug myself out of whichever hole I was in. To finally be able to work again? To be able to write? Who knew such things were possible.

My eyes filled with tears now, the sea seemed farther away, like a dream. So, I close my eyes and feel such gratitude for all that I have learned in this lifetime; for the scars on my stomach, which just proved I'd lived a life worth fighting for. I was grateful that I was able to help my fellow man in times of strife and struggle, and what a gift that was.

The beautiful faces of women flash across my retina, the wonderful women who have been in my life, and I am thankful again for them animating me and pushing me to be the best man I can be. My first girlfriend, Gabrielle Bober, was the one who pointed out that something was wrong with me and sent me to rehab for the first time. The beautiful, magical Jamie Tarses, for not letting me disappear.

Tricia Fisher, for starting it all; for Rachel's face; for the nurse in New York who was a bright shining light during one of my darkest times. I am even grateful to the woman who dumped me after I'd opened myself up. And I am so grateful for all the wonderful women whom I had broken up with simply because I was afraid—I am grateful, and sorry.

Oh, and available.

I would not bring fear-based mistakes into my next relationship, whenever that may be. . . . I know that much.

The sun at its highest, it's time to head back inside to the shade. I hate leaving that view; I'm not sure anyone could quite ever know what a view like that means to me, an unaccompanied minor no more when I float above the world like that, about to be parented once again.

Life keeps moving; each day is an opportunity, now, a chance for wonder and hope and work and forward motion. I wonder if the A-list actress who has expressed strong interest in my new screenplay has said yes yet. . . .

As I step inside, I pause on the threshold. My life has been a series of these portals, between Canada and LA, Mom and Dad, *L.A.X. 2194* and *Friends,* between sobriety and addiction, despair and gratitude, love and losing love. But I'm learning patience, slowly acquiring the taste for reality. Sitting back down at the kitchen table, I dig into my phone to see who has called. Not the A-list actress, but there's time.

This is how life is now, and it's good.

I look over at Erin, and she smiles at me.

Being in a kitchen always brings to mind God. He showed up to me in a kitchen, of course, and in doing so, saved my life. God is always there for me now, whenever I clear my channel to feel his awesomeness. It's hard to believe, given everything, that he still shows up for us mortals, but he does, and that's the point: love always wins.

Love and courage, man—the two most important things. I don't move forward with fear anymore—I move forward with curiosity. I have an incredible support group around me, and they save me every day, because I have known hell. Hell has definable features, and I want no part of it. But I have the courage to face it, at least.

Who am I going to be? Whoever it is I will take it on as a man who has finally acquired the taste for life. I fought that taste, man, I fought it hard. But in the end admitting defeat was winning. Addiction, the big terrible thing, is far too powerful for anyone to defeat alone. But together, one day at a time, we can beat it down.

The one thing I got right was that I never gave up, I never raised my hands and said, "That's enough, I can't take it anymore, you win." And because of that, I stand tall now, ready for whatever comes next.

Someday you, too, might be called upon to do something important, so be ready for it.

And when whatever happens, just think, *What would Batman do?* and do that.

Acknowledgments

Thank you to William Richert, David Crane, Marta Kauffman, Kevin Bright, Megan Lynch, Cait Hoyt, Doug Chapin, Lisa Kasteler, Lisa Ferguson, Peter Levine, Lisa Kudrow, Ally Shuster, Gabrielle Allen, and especially the brilliant Dr. Mark Morrow. And Jamie, sweet, magical Jamie, whom I will miss and think about until the day I die.

About the Author

Matthew Perry is a Canadian American actor, executive producer, and comedian.